The Complete Angler

Also by James Prosek:

Trout: An Illustrated History

Joe and Me: An Education in Fishing and Friendship

The Complete Angler

A Connecticut Yankee
Follows in the Footsteps of Walton

JAMES PROSEK

HarperCollinsPublishers

HarperCollins books may be purchased for educational, business, or sales promotional use. For information please write: Special Markets Department, HarperCollins Publishers, Inc., 10 East 53rd Street, New York, NY 10022.

FIRST EDITION

Designed by Robin Arzt

Library of Congress Cataloging-in-Publication Data

Prosek, James, 1975–
    The complete angler : a Connecticut Yankee follows in the footsteps of Walton / James Prosek. — 1st ed.
      p. cm.
    Includes bibliographical references
    ISBN 0-06-019189-9
    1. Fishing—England. 2. Walton, Izaak, 1593–1683—Homes and haunts. 3. Prosek, James, 1975– —Journeys—England. 4. England—Description and travel. I. Title.
SH606.P76 1999
799.1'1'0942—dc21
        98-55756

99 00 01 02 03 ❖/RRD 10 9 8 7 6 5 4 3 2 1

TABLE OF CONTENTS

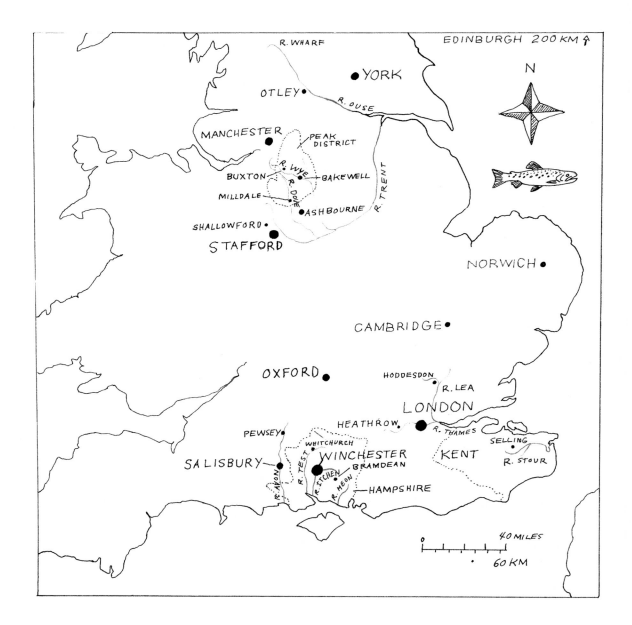

EDINBURGH 200 KM

N

R. WHARF

YORK

OTLEY

R. OUSE

MANCHESTER

PEAK DISTRICT

R. WYE

BUXTON

BAKEWELL

R. DOVE

MILLDALE

R. TRENT

ASHBOURNE

SHALLOWFORD

STAFFORD

NORWICH

CAMBRIDGE

OXFORD

HODDESDON

R. LEA

LONDON

HEATHROW

R. THAMES

PEWSEY

WHITCHURCH

SELLING

SALISBURY

WINCHESTER

BRAMDEAN

KENT

R. STOUR

R. AVON

R. TEST

R. ITCHEN

R. MEON

HAMPSHIRE

0   40 MILES

60 KM

PROLOGUE

Izaak Walton was my excuse to go to England. I had been thinking through ideas to get money from Yale in the form of a traveling fellowship for two years, and several attempts had failed. The most notable of these was my proposal to fish the headwaters of the Tigris River in Eastern Turkey, the site of Eden in Milton's *Paradise Lost*. I'd told the judges on the committee that I thought I would glean some great wisdom from catching trout that were descendants of those which had witnessed man's fall from Paradise. They didn't bite.

My more realistic approach, which was still a hard sell, was that I was going to fish in the footsteps of a legitimate seventeenth-century author, Izaak Walton. You know, he's the guy who wrote *The Compleat Angler*, the book that everyone's heard of but not everyone has read. "It's the third most frequently reprinted book in the English language after the Bible and the works of Shakespeare," I told the committee, "it went through over four hundred editions in three hundred years." I told them during my interview that Walton's words spoke to me, that fishing was my passion, and that his book represented and defended every facet of the art of angling more lucidly than I ever could. I lied; at that point I hadn't even read it.

Shortly after I won the fellowship, I read the *Compleat Angler* cover to cover and began to believe my lie, or at least my lie had become a prophesy that was being fulfilled. The book settled my mind and pulled me into both its pastoral fantasy and its philosophies concerning the timelessness and immortality achieved through fishing. I began to draw out my route, to imagine where I would go, and the places I wanted to touch that perhaps Walton had. I wanted to see his ghost, the ghost of this great and humble man who during the English Civil War, one of Britain's most turbulent times, wrote this seemingly simple and wonderful book that would become the most widely acclaimed piece of angling literature, moving beyond the cultish circle of fisherman and into the mainstream.

Walton was sixty when *The Compleat Angler* was published, a sage man whom everyone liked, a man who was a simple tailor but because of his genial nature had won the company of kings. I began to identify with Walton; I was simple too, a Connecticut Yankee whose intention now was to enter the highest classes of English society, to fish in the backyards of lords and princes and to make them my friends. Fishing was a common bond that would break all boundaries. And when some American gentleman at one of my talks suggested that my winning the fellowship to go fishing in England was a boondoggle I got defensive. I wanted to strike him down with my defense of angling armed with Walton's words.

Fishing is my religion and the trout stream is my temple. Izaak Walton was the anglers' Messiah, and I was prepared to go on this pilgrimage to England and meet the people who were connected with Walton's ideals. I didn't exactly know what I would find, but I *was* going, and had sent letters to key people who owned private water to ask if I may fish. If I didn't get permission I figured I'd trespass; as far as I knew they'd stopped beheading people for poaching. But even after I got permission to fish in what I would come to realize were some of the best trout waters in the world, I felt like a spy, as if I were stealing the king's game, that I was invading a foreign society. I felt like Alice must have felt in Wonderland or like the Connecticut Yankee in King Arthur's court; I was in this strange and beautiful world where everyone was mad, completely batty, except me. It felt like I had mistakenly walked into an asylum.

"Don't let the similar language thing fool you," my British friend warned me when he picked me up from the airport, "England is very different from America." He was right, they drove on the wrong side of the street.

And where did Walton fit into all this? He was the reason I was there. I had a plan, I was going to visit the fishing temple his friend Charles Cotton built on the river Dove, the place where they used to hang out and discuss angling after a day of fishing. I heard it still existed and I wanted to touch it. The temple became the object of my pilgrimage.

And I had to trespass to get to it: the American way! In fact, the American way worked the whole time I was there. While I was dressed in a T-shirt and jeans, anglers I came across were in their Burberry tweeds and ties, but I caught more fish than they did. I taught them a new cast(e) system, these strange people in England; an Englishman couldn't have done what I did. They didn't admit it but they admired Americans.

This book is about the people I've met and some places I've been; it is about my budding love affair and exploration with the English language and how fishing provided our introduction. As Walton's was, this book is a defense of angling, and in being a defense of angling it is a justification of the life I have lived until this point. In an effort to show that the trials that Walton endured and the things he said about life are still relevant, through the course of this story I will draw parallels between his life and mine. This text, therefore, inevitably leans toward the autobiographical. Books on Walton have been written, many biographies of his little-known life as well as his times, and writing another, without displaying my own feelings, even if I had some startling new evidence about his sexuality or something, in my opinion would be worthless. I'm exploring why Walton and his book have survived for almost three hundred and fifty years, and in doing so hope to revive the popularity his works have at times enjoyed. Walton's originality as an author is striking, and we wonder as we read him, as well as about him, how a man born so humble, a tradesman, could have evolved into one of the most gifted literary innovators of his time. When one begins to read Walton it becomes apparent immediately that he had an extraordinary gift for friendship, and what makes him so appealing is that he extends this friendship to his readers and invites us to follow through this pastoral fantasy world to the trout stream:

> You are well overtaken, Gentlemen, a good morning to you both; I have stretched my legs up Tottenham-hill to overtake you, hoping your business may occasion you towards Ware, whither I am going this fine fresh May morning.

Brook trout we caught for Bloom

1
Casting Lines

Many of the discoveries and advances that have surfaced along the river of my life have been serendipitous consequences of my passion for fishing. My essay for college entrance was on ice fishing, and the man who interviewed me at the Yale admissions office was a fisherman. I matriculated at Yale and on the second day of school in New Haven, I joined the crew team because they rowed on the Housatonic River where I grew up fishing. Sophomore year I entered a contest for book-collecting sponsored by the rare-book library at school and won with my collection of trout books, introducing me to the community of Yale bibliophiles. Junior year my own book on trout was published, and suddenly it was no longer taboo to talk about fishing during dates. My senior-year roommate and I put our affinities for singing and acoustic guitar playing together in our band called Trout, playing our original tunes at local coffeehouses, which did even more for my dating life. So you see, when it came time to write my senior essay for the English major, it was only natural that I choose for my subject Izaak Walton and his book *The Compleat Angler*. The library on campus had ninety or so editions, and when I would flip through one of them, first carefully dusting it off, a quiet world was revealed through silent etchings of Walton making a toast in an English pub (to a good day of fishing, no doubt) or conversing with milk-maids who sang him songs by the stream. And as I sat on the cold stone library floor, I could hear the stream pushing from its spring and the trout sipping flies; could see swallows dipping to take those flies, their shadows cast on the stream bottom by the sun behind them.

I'd always had a desire to see new places, so during my undergrad years I made several attempts at traveling fellowships offered through various endowments given to Yale. There was one called the Bates Fellowship that would give several thousand dollars to students who wanted to study or had worthy and studious projects to do over the summer. The first year I tried to get it I proposed a trip to Colorado to attempt to rediscover the yellowfin cutthroat trout, a fish that was thought to have been extinct. The project was deemed of no "merit." Who cared about the yellowfin cutthroat? Clearly not the selection committee who interviewed me. *Merit* came to be a word that eluded me. In fact, I had a long history of proposing projects for fellowships that just didn't quite seem to make the cut. An extensive study on trout and their habitat for a ten-thousand-dollar scholarship in high school was runner-up to a girl and her computer program that taught elementary school kids geography. When they announced the winner in front of three hundred people, my argument that kids could learn more geography from walking a trout stream than from a computer program seemed to lazily dissolve like so many inhibitions washed away by the din of clinks and rings of congratulatory drinks. Some people think fishing is sitting on a log with your line in the water, and I'll admit, sometimes it is. I've already mentioned that I proposed to the Bates committee that I wanted to travel to Eastern Turkey and catch trout in the headwaters of the Tigris River, sage descendants of those which had witnessed man's fall from Paradise. At the interview I declared: "In his *Paradise Lost*, Milton stated, 'There was a place, where Tigris at the foot of Paradise, Into a gulf shot underground, till part Rose up a fountain by the Tree of Life,' in the Garden of Eden." That idea didn't fly either. A combination of the danger of fishing where Kurdish guerrillas were fighting the Turkish army and what they imagined would be my problematic attempts to interview trout about man's fall contributed to their decision.

But I knew that if I persisted, as all good fishermen do, eventually I'd get something. When, as a sophomore, I'd won the Adrian Van Sinderen book-collecting prize, and was awarded $350 with which to enhance my collection of trout-fishing books, I became friends with the chairman of the selection committee, Stephen Parks, curator of the Osborne Collection at the Beinecke Rare Book and Manuscript Library at Yale. Parks made it his imperative to introduce me to every bastion of Yale society, and though he was an erudite powerhouse—Yale B.A. 1961, Cambridge doctorate, Edinburgh University postdoctoral fellow—I did not find him intimidating. He is a gentle man and took a keen interest in the book about trout that I was writing at the time, as well as our mutual love of books and art. He wore his tweeds and British cap, rain or shine, and spent Thanksgiving in England. "Thanksgiving?" he would say in jest. "Is that the one with turkey and cranberry sauce, or is that the Fourth of July?" Though born in Columbus, Ohio, he was educated in the United Kingdom for at least seven years, and I considered him more of an expatriate Englishman than an American by the way he talked and carried himself. He was one of many Anglophiles I'd met in America before realizing that I was one myself.

Dinners at his house, which he affectionately called "Liberty Hall," on Bradley street in New Haven, became a twice-a-month affair. One night, drinking red wine and eating his soufflé, he suggested that instead of proposing projects for fellowships that I would never win with, I should propose something that would appeal to the committee. Steve Parks had never cast a line in his life, though he was sensitive to my fishing passion because he had done scholarly work on Charles Cotton, the good friend of Izaak Walton, and knowing of my affinity for *The Compleat Angler,* he suggested that I propose to go to England and fish in the footsteps of this father of angling while stopping along the way, of course, to see some old books in some old libraries.

He was right. It made sense and was perhaps my best and only chance of winning a fellowship for a fishing-related project. It was the right mix of the scholarly and the playful, and Walton, besides Hemingway, is probably the only figure who has been taken seriously in literature for writing on fishing.

They just might bite. It was a brilliant idea because I would, of course, be doing research over the summer for the senior essay that I would write in the fall.

The next day, on the way to see my Shakespeare professor, I stopped at the post office to get my mail, and a package was waiting for me. I knew what it was, addressed from the publishers, the first copy of my book, *Trout*. I stowed it in my green backpack and skipped cheerily through the late March day to the Humanities Center on Whitney Avenue. It was the first time I had ever gone to see a professor about a paper. I wanted to do well on it but was slightly nervous about approaching the man who, in class, had said he had the greatest memory of anyone in the twentieth century and could recite Milton's *Paradise Lost* first word to last and all of Shakespeare's thirty-eight plays from memory. The first time I had gone to see Professor Harold Bloom at his office hours he had a note on his door that said he'd been feeling ill. Today, carrying my newly received confidence on my back, I found the door of his second-floor office was open and he, the Dr. Samuel Johnson of our time, was sitting in his chair, sheltered by the encroaching fortress of the books on his shelves.

"Come in, my dear," he said, his great locks of white hair flowing behind and all around him, "come, come, do sit." He opened the window a bit to the damp and dark March air. "It's frightful out there isn't it, my dear; shouldn't you be wearing a coat? But I should think we'd want some fresh air as I find it dreadfully stuffy in here." As in class, he articulated every syllable. I was enamored of the way he recited passages. "Please tell me, dear, what is it you've come to see me about?" At the end of every question his voice would rise to a pleasing crescendo and his pursed grin would ironically fill the room. He leaned back, his black-sweatered mass reclining in his chair, his slightly shaking, interlocked hands resting on his belly, his intent eyes on me.

"I came to ask you about the Shakespeare term paper," I said. "I mean, my topic for the paper."

"Yes, yes, yes, please continue, my dear."

"Well, you'd mentioned in class the importance of lines in Shakespeare's plays composed of only monosyllabic words, like 'There would have been a time for such a word,' 'Keep up your bright swords, for the dew will rust them,'or 'I'll fight, till from my bones my flesh be hacked.'"

"Yes of course, my dear, those are indeed some of the most compelling and some of my favorite lines in all of Shakespeare," he said as he looked out the window, "and as far as I can recall, no one has ever done a paper on this topic for me, or for that matter, has anyone ever published a paper on monosyllabic lines in Shakespeare. You might also want to look at the way Mr. Stevens uses the mono-line in his poems," and he recited a Wallace Stevens poem. "Or Marlowe," he added. "Indeed, my dear, I think it would make a wonderful essay."

"O.K.," I said.

"Very well."

"Well." I was thinking I had something else to say before I left.

"Yes?"

"I wanted, I mean, I thought I'd ask you, too; I've been thinking of writing my senior essay on Izaak Walton, his *Compleat Angler*, and was wondering if you knew anyone on campus who might know anything about him, who could be my advisor for the senior essay."

"Well," he said with his hand poised on his chin, "I should think that no one on the Yale campus knows more about Walton than I do. I will be your advisor." I was surprised by his straightforwardness. "What a pleasant idea, I can't think of anyone who has yet done a thesis on Walton, a much neglected author lately. You will want to consult no doubt a book entitled *The Making of Walton's Lives* by David Novarr, and another book on Walton by Margaret Bottrall. And, my dear child, have the necessary forms provided for me to sign, as I assume you will be writing your essay this fall and the English Department will be demanding their forms soon. Let me give Uncle Hollander a call at home to see if he has any thoughts." And with that he picked up his phone and dialed another professor, John Hollander, but he was not home. "I will talk with John about it. You are an angler yourself, no doubt?" he asked, bright-eyed and smiling, continuing to articulate the words, measured and slowly. And I remembered the trout book I had in my backpack and I pulled it out to show him.

"I got this in the mail today, it's the first copy of my first book." He thumbed through it.

"Prosek," he said looking at my name on the cover, "Eastern European? Czech?" almost rhetorically.

"Yes, my father's from Brazil, but his father was from Prague."

"What a lovely book," he continued, and he turned to the back page and read the last line, "it makes one almost want to cry."

"You can have it," I said, "I can sign it for you." I wanted to give it to him.

"No, absolutely not, my dear," he said almost sternly, "you must never give away the first copy of any book. When you receive more copies from your publisher then I should be honored to have one and will cherish it," ever so slowly articulating his last two syllables.

I came out of his office with one of the best feelings I'd ever had. I had an advisor and someone who would support my Walton project, someone respected on campus to help in my defense of angling. I felt as if I'd made a friend.

Though *The Compleat Angler* was my connection between fishing and academia, I still had not read it. After talking to several fishing friends and asking them if they'd even heard of *The Compleat Angler*, I concluded that it was the least-read best-known book—on angling at least. When I say I hadn't read it, I mean that I had not given it the attention that it deserved. I had looked through it and read some passages, but in no way approached the intimacy with its words that I would later foster. I now consider it the *first* book that I ever truly read.

It was almost my turn to visit with the committee for the Branford College Class of 1960 Traveling Fellowship. I found myself waiting nervously under an arch outside the fellows' lounge in Branford College, in the dark and rain, wondering how the guy who had proposed to teach English in China was faring. Anxiety had a way with me in that late winter cold, in my jacket and tie shivering with a folder full of arguments, maps, and books prepared to make my defense of angling. *Well,* I said to myself stepping in, *this fellowship is the only thing that will save you from having to get a summer job.*

I nodded at my competition as he left the room, and took his place in the chair before the committee.

"Izaak Walton?" I said. "You know, he's the guy who wrote *The Compleat Angler,* the book that everyone's heard of but not everyone has read."

"It's *complete* spelled 'e-a-t' right?" one committee member put in.

"Yes. It's also the third most frequently reprinted book in the English language after the Bible and the works of Shakespeare, over four hundred editions in three hundred years." I showed them my trout book and maps of England and where I wished to travel to convince them that it wasn't just a "fishing trip" but a pilgrimage to the source of my passion.

After the interview, I walked below towers and trees, cut stone and leaded windows, some lit solemnly, some dark. My folder was soaked under my arm and in it was my last best idea. My neck was wet with rain, the sky purple with the city reflected in it. I walked through tunnels of stone and stairs to my room and sat in a stone chair in a stone world and fell asleep there while the committee decided on my life. The college Master woke me several hours later, speaking through the telephone and the rain from a dry room and a warm chair. He told me that I was going to England.

It was through Steve Parks that I made my first connection with a piscatorially challenged Englishman. David Scott, a slim and physically frail man of about thirty, who looked much younger, had won a fellowship to come to America and pursue his postdoctoral studies on the English Civil War at the Beinecke Library. I met David at dinner at Liberty Hall. Steve Parks had to endure the angling conversation which continued on past dinner. Being that all his home waters were private, David couldn't believe that most of the waters in Connecticut were open to the public for fishing. He also couldn't believe that I'd won a fellowship from Yale to go fishing. We made arrangements to fish the next afternoon, and I took him to my favorite trout stream near campus called the Farm River.

Almost in view of the New Haven skyline, the Farm River rambles through the largest working dairy farm I knew of in Connecticut. It was the closest a local stream came to resembling the mental images I'd been cultivating of Walton's waters. Cows munched the just-greening mid-April grass, and yellow warblers darted through the mazes of multiflora rose. It was also one of the few streams around that had a population of wild brown trout, whose ancestors came from Europe. David said cordially, while casting the rod I'd lent him, "We must fish together when you come to England." He added that he could pick me up at Heathrow Airport in London when I arrived. He would reserve day tickets for us to fish a stream that Walton had fished, the River Wye in Derbyshire.

About this time, when the trout book had come out and my notoriety as "trout boy" spread across the campus, I was asked by the *Yale Alumni* magazine to pose in full fly-fishing gear in my college courtyard for a photo. The photo appeared on the cover of the April issue and was circulated to eighty thousand *blues*, young and old, many of whom I happily found out were anglers. By no coincidence, some of Yale's greatest monetary contributors and dignitaries, Perry Bass, a Texas oil man; Joe Cullman, chairman emeritus of Philip Morris Company; and George Bush fished quite often, and I received handwritten accolades from them. The article mentioned that I had won a fellowship to go to England, and I received calls from several alumni eager to help me get fishing on some of Walton's waters.

One late April day I got a call from a man in Southport, Connecticut, named Reece Howard.

"This is Reece Howard. I just picked up your trout book on a trip to San Francisco, and I hear you are going to England. Well, I'm calling because I may be able to help you. I'm friends with a lovely woman in the south named Victoria Wakefield." He went on to explain that all he needed do was call her, and that she would probably put me up for a few days at her country estate. He said that Victoria had friends all over the Winchester area and that she would be able to arrange some fishing on many of the private waters, including the Rivers Test and Itchen. Because I knew that Walton was buried in the cathedral at Winchester, this offer was especially appealing. A copy of my trout book, he said, along with a copy of the article from the alumni magazine, was already en route to England.

Reece Howard, a man of about seventy years, continued to help me with possible leads for places I might go. We arranged to fish on a day in May when school was out, and by that time he said he should have news for me from Victoria.

The Complete Angler

* * *

Reece Howard was a small old man framed in the vestibule of his Connecticut home. A vodka tonic in his hand, he showed me around, offered me a "scoop," and told me the names of the various artists who painted the English equestrian scenes on his walls. His home was packed with sketches and paintings of foxhunts, the walls decorated with the mounted snarling heads and bushy tails of foxes. Other than dry fly-fishing for trout, he explained, horses and foxhounds were his passion. Two Jack Russell terriers continuously assaulted me on his couch as he told me that he'd been reading the complete works and letters of Virginia Woolf. After another drink, we headed upstate, to his private trout club in the northwest corner of Connecticut, and fished the evening rise on the stream for trout.

"Dammit, my legs aren't what they used to be, and that old heart just doesn't tick right all the time," Mr. Howard said as we walked through a cornfield to the stream. He ended phone conversations with "cheers" or "right, old boy" and used several other anglicisms in his speech. Sure, he did some foxhunting in northern New Jersey, and he could satiate his passion for horses as head of the Saratoga Race Club; he was a member of The Brook Club of New York, affectionately named for Tennyson's poem "Song of the Brook"; he had graduated from Yale, America's Oxford Disneyland, but in the end these American translations of English society were not quite the same; he, too, was an Anglophile. "I feel at home in England," he would tell me. As we walked the stream he reminisced, in his own rough and raspy tone, about his annual trips to England. And, oh yes, he'd received word from England; Victoria would be delighted to have me at her home.

"You must always bring black tie when you go to England," he said, casting in the failing light, "you never know when you'll be asked to a party." And then he spent the next ten minutes trying to decide if I should bring tails.

Reece Howard only fished a dry fly upstream, as was the proper way of fishing in England, though not during Walton's time. Since then, some of these often practical idiosyncrasies have grown into rules on some club waters.

That evening there was a great hatch of mayflies, and trout were rising in every corner and eddy of the stream. It was a bonanza, and we shared this great fishing treasure until the sky turned dark and we returned to the club's house for dinner. The house had a dining hall, lounge, library, and sleeping quarters, and we intended to stay the night and leave in the morning instead of trying to make the hour-and-a-half drive home. After dinner and a couple drinks over fishing conversation we went to bed.

The Compleat Angler is written in dialogue. It begins with a conversation between a fisherman, the character *Piscator* (Latin for fisherman), and a hunter, *Venator* (Latin for hunter). The two meet casually as strangers on holiday from London and fall into a world very much like a dream, transcending the day and all incidents of time and decay, while walking along the road to a trout stream—glimpsing, as it were, immortality. In this sense, the narrative proceeds structurally in the "there and back again" manner of Carroll's *Alice's*

Adventures in Wonderland, Tolkien's *The Hobbit*, or C. S. Lewis's *The Lion, the Witch and the Wardrobe* in that the characters leave their everyday world, enter a dream state, and ultimately return to the world from which they'd come. The fisherman is on his way from London to fish the River Lea (pronounced, and sometimes spelled, *Lee*) for trout, and the hunter on his way to hunt otter. Since otter prey on trout and are considered a menace to anglers, the fisherman and hunter get along immediately. Each of them give discourses defending their pastimes, and the fisherman eventually convinces the hunter that angling is the recreation most worthy of pursuit. Piscator proceeds to teach Venator, philosophically and practically, the art of angling. In this sense the relationship that the fisherman has to the hunter is similar to the master-scholar relationship of Socrates to his pupils in Plato's dialogues (the *Symposium* in particular). Much of the technical and practical matter in *The Compleat Angler,* published in 1653—that is, the parts on how to catch fish and directions to tie flies—are cribbed from other books, Thomas Barker's book on fishing of 1651 called *The Arte of Angling* or *Barker's Delight*, and Dame Juliana Berners' *Treatise of Fishing with an Angle* of 1496 among them. Apparently back in the seventeenth century, plagiarizing was more a form of *borrowing*. But, while the matter on how to cook fish, raise ring worms, and tie flies is well done and charming, the magic of Walton's text lies in his philosophies, told through the generous and sociable character Piscator, who is Walton himself. The conversations between Piscator and Venator are the essence of many of our own on the stream and remind us that friendships developed through the common thread of angling can form immediately. The five days spent with Piscator and Venator in *The Compleat Angler* are filled with lessons by the master on fishing and life; days which end with good food, a cup of ale, and good company.

Throughout the text of the first edition were illustrations—copperplate engravings of various fish—and actual sheets of music from which the reader was intended to sing. Jonquil Bevan, foremost living Walton scholar, who teaches at Edinburgh University, Scotland, has said of *The Compleat Angler*, "With his songs and poems, the engraved illustrations of fish, and the little inset dramatic scenes, Walton has provided us with a multimedia entertainment of a highly original and experimental kind." The book's dialogue format was apparently not uncommon for books of instruction during this period (e.g., Erasmus's *Colloquies*). Though Walton would not likely have been aware of it, there was a book published in France in 1588, written by Thoinot Arbeau, called *Orchéosographie*—a treatise in the form of dialogue whereby all manner of persons could easily acquire and practice the "honorable exercise of dancing." There was even a book called *the Arte of Angling*, published in 1577, which used the same characters, Piscator and Viator, as Walton used in his first edition of *The Compleat Angler* (in subsequent editions Walton changed Viator, Latin for "traveler," to Venator), though it is not so much a "philosophical discourse," as Walton refers to his own book. (Though attributed to William Samuel, the author of *the Arte of Angling* is uncertain. The book was discovered in the attic of an English country house in 1954, then purchased from a London bookseller by the well-known collector of angling books, Carl Otto von Kienbusch. It is the only known copy and is now in the collection of the Princeton University Library.) Jonquil Bevan notes that by the mid–1600s when *The Compleat Angler* was written, the Puritans had largely succeeded in closing public theaters and people were forced to read plays. Therefore, dialogue would have been a comfortable medium in which to read a story that would otherwise have been performed. If Walton had read any Shakespeare, then I am certain he would have identified with the banished Duke Senior of *As You Like It,* who praises life in the forest of Arden, "exempt from public haunt," finding "books in the running brooks,/sermons in the stones, and good in everything." I know of only one scripted version of *The Compleat Angler* that was performed as a play, and it exists as a small pamphlet in the stacks of the Yale Library (*The Compleat Angler, a Play*, by Arthur Scott Craven, performed by Charles Hawtrey). Jonquil Bevan also expresses, in an Oxford edition of *The Compleat Angler* which she edited, that the book has not enjoyed a great deal of critical praise lately because it fails to fall into a particular or fashionable category. One would do *The Compleat Angler* an injustice to brand it simply as "fishing literature," just as it would to categorize Audubon's paintings of birds or Homer's Adirondack or Bahamian paintings as simply "wildlife art." Part of the exploration in this book involves attempts to ask ourselves, what exactly *is The Compleat Angler*? Idyll, pastoral drama, piscatory eclogue, coded political and religious allegory, georgic—or simply a little book on fishing.

So I prepared to go to England in May, and to have my forms in order so that I could work on my senior essay for its December deadline. When the papers were ready to be signed I brought them to Professor Bloom. I expressed to Bloom that I was interested in exploring in my thesis Walton's influences for his use of dialogue in *The Compleat Angler*. He suggested that I write my own dialogue with Walton as one of the characters, and I liked that idea. "I would like you to read," he said, "'The Artist as Critic' and 'The Decay of Lying,' by Oscar Wilde and you will see that, indeed, you can succeed in writing a dialogue that is both creative and critical, despite what the Director of the Undergraduate Studies in the English Department may say. I should think you can include your journal from England as well.

"Yes, my child," he continued, "before you leave for England I would be delighted if you would come to dinner at my house. My wife can cook the trout that you will catch and bring to us, and we will feast and you will share with us your travel plans in the wake of Izaak Walton."

One spring afternoon when the orchards hung with apple blossoms, I asked my friend, Joe Haines, if he'd go with me and help catch trout for a dinner with my professor. I caught one and Haines caught two, one of which was a very good-sized brook trout. They looked very handsome, cleaned and colorful on a stone near a bed of violets. When I arrived at Bloom's home in New Haven, I found him in his chair, writing on his pad of yellow lined paper in a dimly lit corner of his living room, which was stacked to the ceiling with books. He put down his pad, stood up, and followed his wife and me into the kitchen to see the trout that I had brought. "Ooh, these are the most magnificent trout I'm sure I have ever seen," he said.

Mrs. Bloom set a wonderful dinner and Mr. Bloom opened a bottle of wine. We sat down to eat and I told them what I planned to do in England. When I expressed uncertainty as to whether I might be favorably received by the upper classes of Englishmen who owned the water where I would be fishing, Bloom remarked, "Nonsense my dear, you are a writer and a painter. You are class-less."

I took that to mean that my position transcended class structure, not that I lacked social grace.

With this blessing, I was prepared to leave on this pilgrimage to England and meet the people there who might still hold connections to Walton's humble ideals. I didn't exactly know what I would find, but I *was* going, and I had sent letters to key people who owned private water to ask if I may fish. Steve Parks's friend, David Scott, had sent me a letter that said he was doing his best to arrange some fishing for us on or near Walton's waters—the River Dove in particular, in Dovedale, which I considered to be central to my spiritual journey.

"For mere mortals," he wrote, "it is almost impossible to fish in Dovedale. Apparently the waiting list for membership to these clubs is longer than those for hip-replacement operations on the National Health Service. Your name has to be put on when you're nothing but a twinkle in your grandfather's eye if you want to be fishing before you're liable to need a hip replacement yourself. However, with suitable amounts of cash it should be possible to swing something."

I had taken a somewhat fluvial approach toward my itinerary, marking several pools I'd visit along the way, but mostly planning to allow one contact to flow into the next, figuring that method the most appropriate given the subject matter. My trip was to be three weeks long, starting about May 12 somewhere in the north with David, moving south to visit a Jesuit friend of Steve Parks at Oxford. Then east and south to London to stay with my friend Margaret, from Yale, who was taking classes at the London School of Economics, and finally on to Hampshire to see Victoria and the various other people she wanted me to meet.

I allowed the admission that I did not know what I would learn in England, but was content in knowing that the fishing would be enough. Along with the paperbacks of Walton's works that I stashed in my bags went clothes, no tails but a blazer and tie, my fly rod and flies, waders, my journal, high-quality watercolor paper and paints, some copies of *Trout* to sign as gifts and tools of favor—and several small expectations which I selected carefully, ones not too grand or heavy, as I always endeavor to travel lightly and simply.

Haddon Hall on the River Wye

2

A Connecticut Yankee in England

on't let the fact that the language is similar fool you—England is different." David, who had apparently been reserving his *true* sentiments on England and life in England for my arrival, began his oral manifesto when he picked me up at Heathrow. The quiet, congenial, and always cordial nature he'd supported in my presence while studying at Yale gave way to David Scott, iconoclast, as he was in his element now. We went to pick up the Volkswagen I would be renting for the next three weeks at the car "hire" place, and since I'd never driven on the left side of the street we signed up for insurance on a second driver, and I trusted David, the native, to drive me safely out of London. But it took until we had a near scrape coming out of the car rental lot for him to tell me that he had only received his driver's license the day before. To make it worse, this car was a stick shift, and he had earned his license driving an automatic.

"Why didn't you tell me?" I said as the car lunged forward, "I would have driven."

"Yes, but I've been driving on the left side longer than you have."

"But only by several hours," I returned. All I could do was sit back and adjust to the idea of the glove box being where there was customarily a wheel. Things *were* different here.

"What," I asked, "you didn't need a license before?"

"No, I lived in London and York and rode the train."

"So why did you get one now?"

"Because my bloody girlfriend made me get one, so she could be driven around town," he said in his acrid but humorous tone.

He managed to drive out of the maze of airport roads to the highway and eventually to the place where he lived in Golders Green in order to pick up his fishing gear and bags for our fishing trip. He lived and studied in the type of academic's quarters I was used to: small rooms, austere and minimalist, several books and a bed. When he'd finished pulling his fishing gear out of his closet and stuffing it into the trunk of the car, we set out on the road for Manchester.

Just outside of London there were great fields filled with yellow flowers, and I was happy to be in England. "Wow," I said, "those fields are beautiful, what is that?"

"What! All that yellow stuff—haven't you got any of that in America? It's rape, they make oil from the seeds—rapeseed oil. Horrible for people with allergies."

We drove on. He looked like a caricature of himself hunched over the wheel, and I began to resent him for spoiling my pearly images of England.

"I read the introduction to your trout book," he said, as we drove toward the highway. "A bit romantic isn't it? I mean it's a little overdone."

"You think so?" I said smiling.

"Yeah, but it's great that you can say it," he said *yeah* very nasally and slowly. "So, James—what is it for you with fishing; why do you like it?"

"Well I like to be outside, you know, walk the trout stream and catch a few fish here and there, thinking about life. I don't even need to catch fish to have a good day of fishing. Just walking a trout steam and watching fish feed is enjoyable."

"Walking a trout stream and not fishing it," he said, "is like half a *Sherman*."

"Half a what?"

"Half a Sherman, you know, half a wank. Sherman tank—WANK."

"What?" I could figure out at least what half a wank was, and you can too.

"It's a Cockney rhyme, you know *Cockney* 'born within the sound of the Bow bells,' [St. Mary-le-Bow Church] low-class London. Cockney people rhyme the second word of a phrase, 'Sherman *tank*' with the word they want to say, *wank*, and then just say *Sherman* and no one knows what they're talking about except Cockney. Let's see," he said driving. "Get me an oily; oily rag—*fag*. And a fag is a cigarette. Pick up the dog; dog and bone—*phone*." It was hard enough with his accent for me to make out the words he was saying, never mind this roundabout communication.

"Wait, let me try," I said. "Don't brown."

"Don't *brown?*"

"Brown trout-*pout*; don't pout."

"Great James. Right." I laughed.

David was not a Cockney but he was not upper class either. He spent the next couple minutes trying to demonstrate how the upper class talk.

"The first problem with England is that everyone's class can be identified by their accent. But frankly, I find the upper class speech to be much less rich than say the Cockney. My boss is a chin-in-the-air, everything is bloody this, bloody that, or ab-so-lu-tely, or marvelous, or he's dotty. Pretty much those four words. But they mix them around too, or stick them together, you know, 'he's *absolutely dotty* about cricket and *bloody marvelous* at it too.'"

Now I realized why David had held back on his opinions while in America, because Steve Parks, his sponsor at the library, was an admirer of the English and English Gothic and had fond memories of his years at Cambridge and was curator of an English literature collection and made trips to England every summer to buy books. Parks had been good for England's economy, and England had been good to him. England apparently had not been kind to David.

"My Pakistani girlfriend Yas (short for Jasmine) is enamored of upper-cruster ideals," continued David. "Because the Pakistani community is so far removed from English high society, she's intensely fascinated by the trappings of the establishment, although she has very funny views about just what these trappings consist of. Apparently because I sometimes rub shoulders with penurious peers such as the Earl Russell, she thinks I have a hotline to the palace or something."

We continued driving down the nondescript highway as David's monologue rolled.

"Sometimes the English don't realize they're different than Americans, but look around you, look! That guy in his car, that lady there. They are all thin. All English people are thin and all Americans are fat."

"I'm not fat am I?"

"You're just as fat as the next American."

"I give up."

"Sure, we eat a lot of butter and cream here, but there's not a fat Englishman among us." David himself was quite thin, almost sick looking, no doubt from long days in dim libraries. I looked around and finally saw a guy through the window riding in a car alongside us on the highway who was indeed fat in face and chest and his fat fingers were on the wheel, and I said to David, pointing:

"What about that guy?"

"He's thin too, you know, he's not *fat* like Americans are *fat*."

I suppose David had meant that Americans were metaphorically fat, economically fat, geographically fat—generally healthy looking—and that Englishmen were white and pale and fading away.

"We English are so thin, and getting thinner, that soon all you'll see of us is our teeth, and that's nothing to brag about."

We arrived from the nondescript highway in the humble residential town of Stockton and came to the door of John Tysac's home. Stockton is just south of Manchester, and the big news when we arrived was that a bomb had gone off in the center of town that day killing four people. It was suspected to have been the IRA. David's lifelong fishing friend greeted us at the door.

"You're early," he said, "we've just got to rid ourselves of a little company; I'll meet you guys at the pub in about an hour."

David and I ambled down the road, savoring our feelings of hunger. David told me that John had reserved day tickets on the River Wye at Monsal Dale for two people. I wasn't sure who the odd man out would be, but figured it would be David. From only a brief glimpse of their interaction, I could tell that David was the subservient end of the friendship.

We walked into the dimness of the pub, which continuously echoed the sounds of a Manchester band called Oasis that had recently made it big. We sat in the booth and I began the process of forgetting who I was and being absorbed by this England. The chatter around the dark tables, the low-hung ceiling and heads and warped floors, pints of lager and ale of various shades of brown and amber, the laughs, the language, all contributed to my assimilation with this place—very old and loud but at the same time quiet and solemn, with an atmosphere I was not used to and had trouble articulating.

When John arrived we all got acquainted. My theories concerning their friendship showed credence when John kept knocking David about his fishing ability. But it was all in good fun, and after David and I finished the shepherd's pies we'd ordered, the three of us shared several pints of Guinness until the table grew tacky beneath them. With travel and alcohol conspiring to erode consciousness, my head was drawn into the half-dream of exhaustion. It was there I imagined, while digging elbows into an impervious table, what the Wye might be like and trout "lingering by shingly bars," and "loitering by cresses" as Tennyson had written of his streams in Lincolnshire.

After the pub we retired to the round table in John's kitchen to tie flies, and it became apparent that John was serious about his fly-fishing.

I felt that before anything could happen, I needed to catch a trout in England, one that I felt may have been the descendant of one that Walton had caught. The next morning, the three of us rode in John's car to the River Wye through the tidy hamlet of Buxton to Monsal Dale. The Peak district countryside through which we drove was a maze of rock walls that traced the crests of rolling hills like teeth on the ridge of a shark's jaw. Trees stood as individuals or in small clusters, very reserved in stature, but exploding in blossom within their self-defined spheres; windswept oaks and the occasional elm also punctuated the countryside. I was told that the white-blossomed trees were hawthorns. Cows seemed to occupy defined territories in the landscape as trees did, as if they had been instructed where to stand to best economize the living space. It even seemed as though the positions of the giant black and white blotches of their hides had been considered, as in a Motherwell painting. This was a wide-open countryside—sprawling but staid, wild but tame—and in the distance there was always this peculiar, inexplicable atmosphere, some kind of quaint and illusionary cloud that made every object a fairy tale and every home a cottage. Suddenly, the landscape paintings I'd seen in the British Museum back at Yale—Turners and Constables—that I had never really believed, became realist renditions. I felt like I was in the seventeenth century and that it wasn't the first time; strangely familiar is the best way that I can describe the scenes I saw.

John drove the narrow country roads—no median line, not really roads that seemed suited for two-way traffic—and grasses that leaned in from the endless pastures beat their flowering heads on my window as we passed. I began to recall lines of English poetry, the romantic poetry that I'd been studying the last three years in university, and discovered that these poems were a product of their country and that one must see the country firsthand in order to really understand them.

The first lines that came to me were Wordsworth's, which he'd composed, incidentally, on a trout stream. There is a quality of green in this English land-scape that he describes well in "Tintern Abbey," a poem he wrote in 1800 on revisiting, after a five-year absence, the banks of the river with which he had once had an intimate friendship—the River Wye. Not the one we were head-ing for, but another river of the same name in Wales.

The day is come when I again repose, and view
These plots of cottage-ground, these orchard-tufts,
Which at this season, with their unripe fruits,
Are clad in one green hue, and lose themselves
Mid groves and copses. Once again I see
These hedge-rows, hardly hedge-rows, little lines
Of sportive wood run wild: these pastoral farms,
Green to the very door; and wreaths of smoke
Sent up, in silence, from the trees!

But it's true, everything is green, "green to the very door." What the English had succeeded in doing was creating a fiction with the landscape through cultivation, through all its trimmed hedgerows and bleating lambs keeping the grass in check and English gardens cleverly manicured to look as though they've assumed their opulent designs themselves. I had not expected such expanses of pasture and openness. My prearrival impression of England, being that it was an island, was that it had surely overpopulated itself and filled every livable nook by now. Instead I found *this*, and sunshine too, and began to imagine how the landscape shaped its writing, or perhaps how the writing shaped the landscape. And then another line about green came to me from Marvell's poem "The Garden"—

> *Annihilating all that's made*
> *To a green thought in a green Shade.*

Now I could identify with Marvell. I was having green thoughts in this great English garden. And curiously, it was not a New England green, the green of my Connecticut home. It was a gentler green. This was an enduring and endearing green, a mild green, a damp green. The New England green was an opportunistic green, a green that came only after a long and snow-covered winter and only when it could, not an English green, caressed by warm Atlantic currents that keep it so despite its near arctic latitude. Well, I'd never lived an English winter; I knew it was darker, but I heard it was milder.

I became used to seeing stone cottages and stone towns with little windows and window boxes gushing flowers, and when we came around a corner, as we wound up a hill several miles outside of Buxton, we had a view of the River Wye and the hawthorn-studded Monsal Dale it wound through.

Charles Cotton, Walton's good friend, a consummate fly fisherman, and considered the father of modern fly-fishing, described the Derbyshire Wye in 1676: "The river Wye is a most delicate, clear river, and breeds admirable trout and grayling, reputed by those who, by living upon its banks, are partial to it, the best of any." Cotton knew the land of the Peak intimately and wrote many lines of poetry that use the region's rivers and peculiar rock forms as a vehicle through which to express his disgust with the political climate of his times.

There is a distinction to be made between New England streams and the English chalk streams that Izaak Walton fished. New England streams are primarily freestone streams, streams whose bottoms are paved with glacial deposit rocks. The streams of my home are somewhat faster flowing because of a steeper gradient; there is white water where the stream is pushed through a narrow gorge, there are riffles, and waterfalls crash, and the movement of the water makes various sounds and musics. Sure, there are waterfalls and fast-flowing rivers in England, but Walton mostly fished the flat, gentle rivers that move very quietly and stealthily through the farmland valleys. When I first walked the River Wye, I noticed that the stream somehow matched what I'd divined of Walton's temperament. Walton was a humble, quiet, pious, and contemplative man, and the River Wye, typical of the type of water that Walton fished, is not at all ostentatious; its gifts are well concealed by lowliness and quietness—if you'd come up on it blindfolded you would not know it was there unless you were familiar with that cool refreshedness that greets the angler when arriving at its banks.

The Wye starts near the town of Buxton, and here the water as described by Cotton is dark or even "black." But along its course before reaching Buxton it is supplemented, and seemingly supplanted, by water from great clear springs, hundreds of gallons per minute rushing out from limestone caverns underground. These are the river's abrupt birthplaces from their sources into the light, and throughout its journey to the sea it loses relatively little elevation; the land gives it little opportunity to speak up again. It is the collective effort of the clear springs pushing its flow that promotes the river's perpetuity, and only if it tumbles over a small weir or finds its course interrupted by a rock that breaks its glassy surface will you hear it mumble. You can stand in it and feel the push of the water against your legs—deceptively strong and forceful pressure—but not hear it at all. And seldom to never do these streams flood, because the land around is very porous. Because they never flood some homes are built over the rivers, often mills converted to homes, with the water running under their kitchens and dining rooms. The water that springs from the ground runs a constant temperature year round, usually a cool and trouty 52–56°F. I had fished streams very similar in disposition to this pleasant Wye in America, the pastoral, spring-fed creeks of central Pennsylvania, but still it was nothing I was used to or wanted to be eternally seduced by—finding such a gentle stream and white lambs and greenness after long periods of exposure, dangerously melting to any strong conscience or will. In America these streams are called spring creeks. The English call them chalk streams because most are saturated with dissolved limestone from the cavernous chalk reservoirs of their sources. Unlike the infertile streams of my home, made acidic by the tannins contributed by the roots of oaks and hemlocks lining the banks, these streams with their lime-saturated waters are very fertile, the alkalinity promoting plant life, which in turn promotes insect life, which in turn makes the trout that feed on the insects big and healthy. The nature of the stream also affects the personality of the trout. Whereas the small streams of Connecticut, given their acidity and infertility, create opportunistic trout that will feed eagerly on any fly stealthily presented, the fish of the English chalk streams, because there is such a profusion of food, can afford to be selective and are, by most accounts, more difficult to catch.

There were several stone houses nestled in the fertile crook of Monsal Dale and her winding Wye. The green was up to our knees as I followed John and David from where we'd parked the car to the door of a small cottage where I imagined the riverkeeper lived. Starting toward it with the enthusiasm that two sweets-hunting children would on discovering a home of gingerbread and frosting in a forest of spinach, we the anglers through his well-kept garden walk made our way.

When we knocked, an old man came to the great arched wooden door nestled in the stone house's vestibule. We told him our names, that we'd reserved "day tickets" for two rods, and then paid him the twenty pounds for each ticket. He walked us down the path, with the aid of a cane, from the door of his old home to the Wye.

It was warm and the man limped his way through the pleasant air to a small stone bridge over the river. We followed him, our rods still in the car, and leaned over the bridge as he did, bracing ourselves against the cool stone with our bellies, our hearts beating against the air, anticipating the possibilities such a gorgeous stream might offer.

"Those are me babes down there," he said looking into the water and then at us, and squinting one eye. "Can't fish off the bridge."

Where the shadow of the bridge cut the glare from the clear water you could see about a dozen great big trout finning. The old man lifted his head and walked up the gentle slope of the arc of the bridge to its peak, with one hand still on the stone and in that hand his cane, not giving indication that we should follow. He spied a single yellow buttercup that had flowered in a crack in the stone and, bending carefully with his head looking straight and not down, he picked the head of the buttercup and resumed his place beside us. Inspecting the petals against the May sunlight, he chose one, and plucking it, dropped it off the bridge. There was very little wind and the shining yellow petal drifted unencumbered and swooped and rolled until it gently skated on the water resting on the outside of its concavity like a small yellow boat made for an ant. The petal was caught in the current and drifted over the nose of the largest trout holding in the water below us. The trout moved slowly for the petal, and had us all at the edge of the stone in anticipation. It came up nearly to the petal, as if it were going to ingest it in its giant maw, touched it with its nose with the gentleness of a fairy's kiss in refusal, and fell back to resume its position.

"They are good fish, these," he said and looked at us. He told us that we could only fish the water upstream from the bridge and asked why there were three of us for two day tickets. John explained that David was just tagging along and would not be fishing. The old man walked back into his home.

John and I took our fly rods from our tubes, strung the line through the rod guides, and pulled out our boxes to compare flies. I showed him what I usually fished with in America, a small brown nymph, very plain looking, and told him how I fished it, that I cast it up and across the stream and let it drift down as naturally as possible, watching for any hesitation in the line that might indicate that a fish had taken my fly. "Sure that will work," he said, "what have you got for dries?" I showed him all my buggy little insect patterns for when the trout were feeding on the surface. I regretted not having a fly that imitated a buttercup petal. "Those will work too," he said picking through my box of dries. John dug into his vest pocket for a box of flies and picked out a half dozen or so to give me, one in particular, a dry fly called a "gray duster," which he swore by. This duster was blue-gray in the body and had grizzly hackle wound around the front of the hook without a tail. I returned the favor and gave him a few flies from my box.

We were off down the stream, eyeing resting cows in the shade of the blooming hawthorn. John stayed to fish the water nearer the bridge and David and I walked upstream. The path was packed hard by anglers and cows. David and I spotted a good trout in the stream, down a steep hill, and I offered David my rod to go fish for it, taking into account the discomfort he'd told me he experiences when walking a trout stream without fishing.

"Naw you go for it—go for it," he looked at me. "Yeah, yeah, go ahead." But I could see there was a lot of good water ahead, and I decided the way the sun had been coming up over behind us in the morning that if I walked down the hill to the pool now my shadow would spook the fish.

"We'll wait till afternoon," I said.

We came to an open meadow along the Wye where sheep were grazing. Among the white puffballs we spotted one particularly big one that seemed to be stuck on its back and dying, its eyes white, glazed, and teary. It reminded me of Kafka's *Metamorphosis* character, who woke up on his back one morning to find that he had turned into a gigantic insect, watching his pitifully thin little legs wave helplessly before his eyes. Two little lambs stood beside it bleating, encouraging it to get up. We stared at it a little longer and then passed by thinking it doomed, but I stopped and suggested to David that we turn around and try to tip it back over. I put my rod down, and, burying our hands in wool, we pushed and nudged and rolled it until our knees were in wool too. It jumped to its feet and ran off at a considerable speed, the two lambs following close behind. I picked up my rod and we moved on.

I stopped at the bottom of a riffle, David behind me, and took a few casts. After a bit, David walked upstream to see if he could "spot some fish," and I promptly had a strike and lost a rainbow trout that jumped several times. The rainbow trout, incidentally, was introduced to England around the turn of the century from America, and this river is one of the only two in the country where they reproduce successfully. None of the trout in this section, or "beat," as pieces of river are called, were stocked; they were all wild, including the brown trout, which is the native trout to England. The second fish I hooked I landed, a beautiful wild rainbow trout, and I called David over to see it.

"Why don't you take a cast," I said to David.

"No, no you keep going, I get to fish here all the time; well, really, that's not true but . . ." I handed him my rod; that's what Walton would have done.

After sitting and watching one or two of his casts, I began to get impatient because I wanted to show him how to do it, and I knew there were several fish in the riffles. He hooked the hawthorns behind him and then a rock and broke off the fly in a rage. "What's that Walton said about fishing being a 'contemplative man's quiet recreation?' It's the most bloody frustrating thing I've ever done." He relinquished the rod. "I'll watch you," he said.

Along the banks were scattered little seepholes and springs pushing trickles of cold water into the Wye. I found it a very comfortably sized stream, not more than thirty-five feet across in most places, with lush green waterweed—ranunculus, water celery and starwort—and watercress growing from the bottom and spilling off the banks.

David and I fished upstream, catching several wild brown trout on my little brown nymph. In one turn of the Wye, part of the water seemed to go underground, because there was only a tiny riffle and a deep undercut bank. I drifted the nymph under the bank and felt a tug and pulled a little brown trout out, splashing onto a bed of watercress. Its back was olive, covered with black spots with light-colored halos. On the sides were scattered red spots with cream-colored halos, the belly a lemon yellow blending into an intense egg-yolk color. The fish was no bigger than my hand, and in that clear water with his fins flared, gliding over waving beds of waterweed, it swam magnificently away.

It was not Walton's custom to let trout go, as many anglers do today; he admired them both for their physical and culinary beauties.

> Honest Scholar, come let's to supper. Come my friend Corydon, this Trout looks lovely, it was twenty-two inches when it was taken, and the

belly of it looked some part of it as yellow as a Marigold, and part of it white as a lily, and yet methinks it looks better in this good sauce.

A farmer no doubt had built the small weir that formed the large pool we came to next. The pool was dark with overhanging limbs dense with early greens, and it was at the head of the pool that David spotted several fish rising to small insects. I tied on the "gray duster" that John had given to me and walked across the stream at the bottom of the pool to get a better cast. David's coaching was unwanted; in fact, at times he was more annoying than I might let on, but I supposed that I'd be doing the same if he were in the river. He wasn't supposed to be the helpful gillie in tweeds that escorted old Sirs on these venerable streams.

I took two trout from under the trees on the near side of the river, beautiful brown trout that rose nearly imperceptibly for the fly, making the most dainty ripples that disappeared before they saw the bank. Both trout jumped too, making large wakes when they landed, showing another side of themselves.

The three of us rendezvoused to eat the lunch we'd packed. John offered that we could get some fishing that afternoon on the Duke of Rutland's water, where the Wye flowed by Haddon Hall, a great castlelike estate where the duke spent the summer. This water to my eye was not as lovely as Monsal Dale, but the idea of fishing the duke's private water was a treat. As it happens, John is a very good fly fisherman and though he does not rub shoulders with the duke, he does with the duke's bailiff. After I had caught my tenth trout of the afternoon I was quite content to lay down my rod and sit in the grass by a little bridge to write in my journal. David came by to ridicule me for not fishing. He was satisfied because he had caught some fish himself. "That's the Dorothy bridge you're sitting on," he said. The narrow bridge crossed the river and led up a path to the castle. "It was the very same footbridge that Dorothy, heiress to one of the Elizabethan earls of Rutland, crossed when she eloped with that dastardly stable boy, John Manners, who of course lent his name to the present dukes of Rutland." This bridge, then, symbolized the rupture of class tissue for David.

The pints in the pub at Stockton tasted especially good that night. John's friend Mark met us in the pub and we got talking about Walton.

"The basic idea of the book," I said, "is that Walton is leaving London, walking out of the city to fish the river Lea and encounters a hunter who becomes his scholar. But metaphorically Walton is escaping the turbulence of civil war to this pastoral fantasy world where cuckoos call and milkmaids sing songs. The calm, quiet pursuit of angling offers his tonic, a rest to his soul and a calming of his spirits. And my project, which I'd like to make into a book, is my journey in the wake of Walton—reading Walton through the medium of someone who is still alive—myself— in order to show that what he said then is still relevant today."

"Well James," said John leaning into his beer, "I have a question. Walton was escaping civil war when he went fishing, David is escaping the office, Mark is escaping his boss and wife, I'm escaping the clients I have to deal with every day. What is it that you are escaping? I think you owe us an answer by morning."

"That is the subject for a whole other book," I said.

And really, though I never answered John, I suppose what I wished to tell him was "it is more what I am seeking than what I am escaping." Though this may not entirely have been true.

We ordered Indian food and ate it on our laps in John's living room with a healthy supply of wine at hand. I alluded to a guitar I'd seen in a corner of a room on the second floor of his house and his wife suggested we take it out and play. Anglers very often have guitars in their houses somewhere. I picked it up and tuned it the best I could and played the song Walton wrote for *The Compleat Angler*.

The Angler's Song
(The Catch)
Man's life is but vain; for 'tis subject to
pain, and sorrow, and short as a bubble; 'tis a
hodge podge of business and money, and care, and
care, and money and trouble. But we'll take no
care when the weather proves fair, nor will we
vex now, though it rain; we'll banish all sorrow
and sing till tomorrow, and Angle and angle again.

This was met with considerable laughter and good humor.

We know from the diaries of a contemporary of Walton's in London, Samuel Pepys, that music was a central part of daily life in the seventeenth century. Says Richard le Gallienne (who also wrote a biography of Walton) in the introduction to my copy of *Passages from the Diary of Samuel Pepys*:

> Music and drinking made a great part of the merriment. Of both the diary is full, and it will be noticed that, when gentlemen got together in a tavern, they were never long without a song—and good singing, too.

The day seldom began, however early, or ended, however late, without a song—in which the pretty "mayde," or the "rascal" boy, were usually able to take part—or without some brief melody on lute or violin.

If you live within convenient distance of New York City you can go to the Metropolitan Museum and see and listen to the instruments that Walton and his seventeenth-century kinsmen would have heard: dulcimers, lutes, virginals, harpsichords, shawms, serpents, trumpets, bassoons, and oboes. Some of these sounds may have accompanied their voices in the low-ceilinged taverns of London or at festivals outside the Temple Bar on Fleet Street. Bevan notes that of the three dozen verse quotations in *The Compleat Angler*, eight sets of verses are meant to be sung rather than spoken. "Most of the songs are sung to well-known tunes, some of which have survived, but the music for 'The Catch' was composed specially for Walton by Henry Lawes, Milton's friend, and Walton saw to it that the music was printed in the editions published during his own lifetime."

I told David and John and the rest of the company that singing purges the soul as angling does and was something Walton greatly enjoyed. "'The Angler's Song' is Walton's hymn for the fisherman—you know that fishing was his religion."

"I think you speak for all of us," said John taking the guitar. He played an old Irish tune, mimicking an Irish accent, and then I played "Barbara Ellen," a sad old folk song. John and I played and harmonized and played some more until everyone else had cleared the room and gone to bed. We hadn't even noticed.

David took me to the River Wharf the next day, northeast of the Wye, out of Derbyshire and into Yorkshire. I had become intrigued with David's situation and his attitude toward England. We bought our day tickets for fishing in the nearby town of Ottley. It was called the Bolton Abbey beat because from most of the fishable water the great ruin of this gothic abbey loomed high. Personally, after having seen many of these abbeys and their cathedrals ruined by time and wars, with their high stone walls and no longer functional buttresses and little left but mazes of sewer systems, I came to find them somehow more charming than those that were still intact—their floors green lawns and their roofs the sky, cows grazing where monks once prayed. Still, because of its immensity it was somewhat fearful, and darkened great swaths of greenity in shade. We walked to the Wharf—a great wide moorland river with tea-colored water, quite different from the character of the gentle little Wye—and I could not keep my eyes from Bolton Abbey and the quiet, pastoral atmosphere she held in her looming gravity.

"What a beautiful backdrop to our fishing," I said to David pointing with my fly rod toward the abbey.

"That thing? It's a bloody eyesore, they should raze all of them and build skyscrapers. You only like it because you've got nothing older than seventeenth century in your own damn country." I asked David if he knew how old the abbey was. He said it was "twelfth century or something." Anything established or hiding under the auspices of tradition he wished to summarily crush, or at least he said he did, fearing that if he didn't the weight of it would crush him.

"If there was a revolution," he said when we began casting, "I'd be manning the guns." When he expressed to me that no one could say anything in his "bloody country" I said, "well, don't you have a democracy?"

"A democracy. *Bullocks!*"

There were many grayling in the Wharf which took dry flies with seeming rapture and frivolity, gorgeous fish with great, colorful dorsal fins, flamboyant yet understated as they surfaced only fleetingly. They took daintily from underneath, sometimes teasing, and occasionally one would jump entirely out of the water and capture my fly on its way down. If only we could take matters of survival with such humor and elegance as the grayling.

Upstream from Bolton Abbey the river narrowed and gurgled and plunged through dark forests. Dark English forests are somehow different from New England ones—there are more gnarls and less undergrowth; it is concealment without concealment, which is more fearful. These were forests of Stubbs's paintings, where lions are waiting by dark ledges to take stray horses by the neck and drag them screaming to the soil. The water in the forest was not fishable, it sunk through rock and swirled and was very deep. I passed out of the forest to open moorland again.

I had caught eighteen trout and grayling on the Wharf and was very satisfied, not to mention hungry, when we left the river for the town of York. David had grown up in London and later moved to York with his father and brother, where he attended University. We were heading for his father's home there to spend the night.

We drove to the outskirts of York and into a little community with small and newly built two-story apartments. I met David's father, a tall, thin and white-haired man with an air of broken melancholy but simple joy, and David took a back seat to his father's story.

"Hungry?" David's father asked. "I bet you are, having been out fishing all day." He looked at David, "Shall I give James a tour of the house?" he asked.

"There's not much to see, Dad," David said.

It was a very modest and very clean home. I followed David's dad up a narrow stairs to the second floor. "When David and his brother lived here too, it was a bit crowded; they slept in this room. Now I've made it into a studio." When Mr. Scott's wife died he'd quit his job as a businessman in London to teach art to schoolchildren in York so that he'd have hours conducive to raising two boys. It was kind of a sad story, the old man painting copies of Paul Klee and Juan Gris in a bedroom studio in north England. But he seemed very contented and free with his story, a freedom which David had not yet found.

When we returned to the first floor Mr. Scott showed me that he slept in a cavity under the stairwell. He pulled back a curtain that revealed a space which neatly held a little bed. He explained that as a boy during World War II when the Germans were bombing London, he would hide with his family in the stairwell of their home because it was the most secure place in the house. He shrugged, to show that he agreed that this was strange, but he was not embarrassed by it. "I've slept in stairwells since then." One day as a boy, while walking in the streets of London, he was caught under the spitting of ammunition rounds from German aircraft. He told me the plane was so close he could see the goggled pilot in the cockpit.

David, in the meantime, had been reading the *Times*, adamantly pretending he had not heard his father's story. "Scots moving up on the English, eh," he said remarking on the *football*. "Soccer," his dad said to me, pulling from the oven the cooked egg-and-potato casserole he'd made for dinner. "Isn't that what you call it?"

The dinner was very good, peppers, egg, onions, and potato in a baking dish, and a glass of milk. I ate more than my share.

In the morning, David's girlfriend Yas drove in from London. I was warned about Yas by David's father. "She's simply autocratic," he'd said. I found her pleasant. She was manicured and makeupped. We left in our two vehicles, myself and David in my rental car and Yas behind, and headed south via Bakewell to Ashbourne. I planned to stay for several days in the vicinity of Ashbourne, as it was near Walton's birthplace and other Waltonian landmarks. David suggested I practice driving to Bakewell under his supervision. Being accustomed to the opposite, the hardest thing about driving with the wheel on the right was judging how far away the edge of the road was on the left. I hugged the median as best I could. I came especially close to collision on narrow two-way town streets where cars were parked and others were coming the other way and someone had to pull over. I found roundabouts particularly infuriating. But we made it to Bakewell alright, with frequent complaints about my driving from David. "I nearly wet my pants driving with James," he told Yas.

Bakewell was a beautiful stone town through which a lovely stretch of the river Wye flowed. David had suggested we stop there because of the monster trout you could see off the bridges in town. I was surprised to see the Wye so clear both in and below town—not just clear, but with trout in it. David told me that Bakewell was known for its tarts—I assumed he meant the pastry—and that I must have a Bakewell tart before we left town. So we walked to a small bakery and each got one and ate them, and then David suggested we get some bread to feed the trout. I went back in the bakery and bought two rolls for thirty pence. We could not fish for them, but it was fun to watch the trout take the hunks of bread we tore off and threw to them. Some trout took the bread demurely in their lips, others assaulted the sodden pieces of loaf with explosive crashes. I tried to see how large a piece of bread the trout would take, starting small and working up from there. Occasionally a trout would come into contact with an aggressive duck vying for the same piece of bread. The trout had barely slowed down their feeding by the time we had run out of food. We walked along the Wye through a park. Yas took off the heels she'd been wearing and walked barefoot on the grass.

My first solo flight driving on the wrong side was following David and Yas out of Bakewell. They were going to help me find a bed and breakfast near the town of Ashbourne, which would be my headquarters for the next few days.

Having received my introduction to England in my first three days through David's eyes, it was no surprise that my views on class structure were skewed toward his. That is not to say that my impressions were warped, because although David was born into the lower middle class and a good deal of the resentment for higher classes that goes with it, he was quite rational, objective, and intelligent in his commentary. He was one of the most articulate and opinionated people I'd ever met, a combination I've discovered is quite rare.

If America was as stratified socially as David's England was, I hadn't noticed. But after meeting David, I observed fellow Americans with a more critical eye. I began to think about what it meant to be an American and how we had been born from England—the rebels and dissenters who'd left because of their distaste for the monarchy or the wish to practice their religions. Surely if David had lived during Walton's time and was possessed by his current hatred for the increasingly impotent royalty, he would either have started a revolution or crossed the Atlantic to America.

I followed David and Yas with little incident southward to Ashbourne and then deep into the Derbyshire countryside on narrow streets lined with very tall grass and hedgerows behind. I was led to a small bed and breakfast in the small town of Alkmondton where they had once stayed. David and Yas bid me good luck on my pilgrimage and headed for London.

These "farmhouse accommodations" were a staple of the English countryside—farmhouses whose owners made extra money by fixing up a room or two in their homes for paying guests. When I checked in, the lady inside explained to me that her family ran the dairy, but that the revenue from the B and B had encouraged and enabled them to convert several more rooms to accommodate boarders and even consider quitting the farming business. She had landscaped the front lawn beautifully and planted flowers around the iron furniture. The home was of modest size, built with bricks of a rich vermilion color. I'd noticed all the buildings in this small town were constructed of this same red brick.

I told my hostess that her front garden was beautiful, and she asked what I had come to England for. "I'm fishing and studying, in the footsteps of Izaak Walton," I said, and since she indicated to me that she knew who Walton was, I continued by telling her that Walton was born in Stafford, not too far from Ashbourne, and that he fished at different times during his life in this area.

"Izaak Walton's footsteps are good ones to be following," she said as she showed me to my room.

I drove into Ashbourne, about fifteen minutes away, for a dinner of fish and chips and, returning to the dairy house, took out my watercolors and painted a picture of the barn for the lady. She was very gracious when I gave it to her the next day, and she packed me a lunch. I tied flies that night for the fishing I hoped to do in the coming weeks, overwhelmed by the comfort of my planned loneliness, and fell asleep to the sound of bleating lambs when the golden sun had gone below the fields. The more immersed I became in this solitary pilgrimage, the more I realized how essential it actually was to my life. I felt as though many static events, static on a shelf, static in ink, were soon to become animated, that desires would be heightened by hardships and somehow dance before me and allow me to observe them and live among them, that I was no longer an individual learning on a plane in an institution but was partaking in a three-dimensional continuum by painting a solitary garden or writing in my journal from a small farm in a minute town on a small island in a cold ocean.

Leaping trout and mayfly

3
Fishing and Friendship

I had a lead before I'd left Connecticut from Reece Howard's wife's daughter, who lived in London, that there was a certain Izaak Walton museum outside of Stafford. Mr. Howard had provided the phone number, which I called from the B and B to ask its location. The man who answered, James Walcock, told me that the museum was in the town of Great Bridgeford just outside of Stafford. While I had the man on the phone I asked him if there was anyone who might be able to take me fishing on the River Dove, knowing that Walton had very likely fished there and that the fishing was not open to the public. I explained to him that I was a student from an American university and that I planned to do my thesis on Walton. "Well," he said, "as a matter of fact, there is a gentleman named Tony Bridgett, who takes foreign anglers who are interested in Walton out fishing on the Dove. He sort of *collects* them. I believe he just took a young German fellow out last week who was studying *The Compleat Angler*. Just mention my name when you ask him. Tell him 'James Wolcock said to call you about fishing on the Dove.' Alright?" And he gave me Tony Bridgett's telephone number, which I promptly called. I was surprised to get ahold of Mr. Bridgett on the first try.

I introduced myself and my cause. "So you're interested in Walton," he said, "and you want to go fishing on the Dove," which he pronounced *Doov*, "Well, let's see; Monday is good for me." Monday was the next day and I said "Of course, that would be great," and he told me to meet him by the Esso gas station in his town of Leek, 10 A.M. the next day. I told him I planned to go to the Walton Museum today. "Very good," he said, "we'll see you 10 A.M."

After a big English breakfast of eggs, English bacon (not like our crispy kind but more like sliced ham), and a grilled tomato, I drove out of the dairy house B and B greatly excited about my fishing date, headed for Stafford and the museum with renewed hope that the marriage of fishing and friendship transcended oceans and continents.

It took about an hour to get to Stafford—the town of Izaak Walton's birth—under the warm sun and white sky. As I saw it, Stafford was typical of these small English towns, narrow winding streets and stone buildings built on a human scale. I had trouble finding my way through and out of English towns, I imagined, because these towns were not planned for motorist convenience, but evolved mostly for foot and horse traffic. Lost in the maze I parked on the street to walk around town. I peered into a brook that flowed through a narrow slot between two stone buildings, a tributary of the River Sow, which abuts the town of Stafford on its west and south sides, and in the slightly discolored water saw a large pike about six or eight pounds finning just up the bridge from me. Says Walton in his chapter on pike:

> Sir Francis Bacon in his History of Life and Death, observes the Pike to be the longest lived of any fresh-water-fish, and yet he computes it to be not usually above forty years; and others think it to be not above ten years; and yet Genser mentions a Pike taken in Swedenland in the Year 1449 with a Ring about his neck, declaring he was put in to that Pond by Frederick the second, more than two hundred years before he was last taken, as by the Inscription in that Ring (being Greek) was interpreted by the Bishop of Worms.

I couldn't believe it, was almost stunned by its immediacy, and was tempted to fish for it, but resisted, imagining I'd enter some bout with the Stafford police, contenting myself with the thought that Walton may have at one point fished this stream or watched an ancestor of this ancient pike finning here, maybe even the same one. I stood looking into the water at my reflection, wondering if Walton had visited the water's surface here as a child. How many rivers had he stood over and fished, and how many of his aging faces throughout his charmed and turbulent life stared back at him in the river's reflection.

Not far from this spot in this sleepy, narrow-streeted town, Walton was baptized in St. Mary's Church on September 21, 1593. His date of birth would have most likely been in the month of September, as children were baptized on the same day or shortly after their birth. Walton's parents Gervase and Anne would have witnessed their son's immersion in a basin of water by the parish priest, as was customary for the times, pulled out dripping like a fish. The font in which Walton was purportedly baptized is still in St. Mary's.

The home of Walton's birth was thought to have been either a cottage in the countryside outside of Stafford, a dwelling on Eastgate Street or the ancient High House on Greengate Street. The least likely of these is the High House because it was one of the finest mansions in Stafford and not the type of place that Walton's father, a humble tippler (alehouse keeper), would have been able to afford. A more romantic view held the country cottage outside of town as Walton's birthplace, a small timber-frame house near to the "Shallowford brook" he writes about in *The Compleat Angler*. It is most likely that he was born in a humble place on Eastgate Street, since torn down, which was said to have resembled a coachhouse or stable with rooms off to one side. The site of Walton's birth is now occupied by the Stafford Police Station. The following description of the home is from Marston's book of 1908, *Thomas Ken and Izaak Walton*.

> It is situated in East Gate Street, Stafford, in St. Mary's Parish, and is of considerable age. There is no exact knowledge that this was the birthplace of Walton, but a lady, a relation of the late Mr. Ralph Wright of Stafford, who resided in a house opposite to this, perhaps a century ago, stated that she had always been given to understand that this house was the one Walton was born in.

Izaak was the youngest in a family of three children, and shared this dwelling with his parents and brother Ambrose and sister Anne. Gervase Walton's father, George, Izaak's grandfather, was a bailiff, a middle-class rural Elizabethan. As an alehouse keeper Gervase would have been of the lower or lower middle class. Needless to say, young Izaak was not of the ilk who, at college age, would have been sent for study at Oxford or Cambridge or on a grand tour of Italy with a private tutor. Growing up in the boot-making town of Stafford, not even on the main road from Chester to Coventry, Walton was destined for a humble life as his father and grandfather lived. The plague was said to have been prevalent at the time of Walton's birth and could have been the cause of Gervase's death. Walton's father was buried in February 1597 when Walton was four years old. His brother Ambrose had died the year before.

Three months after Gervase Walton died, Walton's mother Anne moved with her children to a place by the North Gate of Stafford. The dwelling or "burgage" was said to have been between the wall and the "Towne Dyche." Izaak and his sister would have spent at least some of their youth there, perhaps developing a love for fishing in the small watery ditches off the River Sow.

A year and a half after the tragedy of Gervase's death, Izaak's mother was remarried to a Humphrey Burne of Stafford, an innholder and baker. And so, young Izaak acquired a stepfather as well as a stepbrother, Humphrey Burne Jr. We don't really know what occupied young Izaak's time or what he looked like as a child. The only portraits that survive are of Walton the aged and venerable author. Arthur Munson Coon in his "Life of Walton" imagines of Walton's childhood appearance:

He must have had blue eyes, and the strong chin, high forehead, prominent nose, and delicate fingers that those portraits show. His height is a matter of conjecture; the portraits suggest a person of average height or less.

Coon continues by saying that it is difficult to imagine Walton having been anything but an old man, "staid, subdued and mature."

At some point in his youth, Izaak Walton learned to read and write and sing. We see from *The Compleat Angler,* in which he prints the words and music for the "Angler's Song" and gives an account of milkmaids in song, that he was quite fond of singing.

Around the time of Walton's youth there was reported to have been a free school for grammar in Stafford, and it is distinctly possible that he attended. Coon tells us that the school was originally known as St. Bertelin's, housed in St. Bertelin's Church, and later as Edward IV Grammar School. Elementary grammar and other subjects would presumably have been taught by a clerk in holy orders. This same cleric would have employed the boys in services for the founders of the chapel and taught them to sing. James Russell Lowell says of Walton that he "contrived to pick up somewhere and somehow, a competent mastery of his mother tongue." Walton could also have learned to write at home. We know at least that his father was literate, because he wrote and signed his own will, but he died before he could have ever taught his son. We could conjure images of this cleric taking Walton under his wing and teaching him the Bible as well as other important things like how to braid a horsehair line for fishing. But really, such images should not be left to propagate because

Walton tells us himself that he did not begin fishing until he was thirty-nine.

From Walton, on the nature of his own education we have the following statement from the preface to his collected biographies, *The Lives*.

> When I sometimes look back upon my education and mean abilities, 'tis not without some little wonder at myself, that I am come to be publicly in print.

Such modest tone you will increasingly come to discover is Walton's trademark. But it is something to wonder at, remarkable really, how Walton grew to be one of the most respected literary men of his time. Such ascent from tradesman to the stratum of literati was not unheard of; Ben Jonson was the stepson of a bricklayer, and, though later, William Blake was the son of a hosier. These days, in America in particular, men and women are more often commended than shunned if their flowers of success bloomed from a low-opportunity background, but during Walton's time such success was not common, nor was it fashionable. Walton showed England that there was indeed room for a brilliant mind and gentle spirit to move up in the ranks of society. As pro-England and promonarchy as Walton was, his success story is distinctly and ironically "American."

There is no evidence that Walton ever received a classical education, that is, was taught even rudimentary Latin. Coon says "his Latin, and consequently his schooling in general, could not have been extensive." The only Latin books in his personal collection, such as his copy of Ovid's *Metamorphoses*, now in Salisbury Cathedral Library, were English translations, and he rarely if ever quoted or mentioned the standard authors read by beginners of Latin: Cicero, Terence, Virgil, Ovid, Sallust, and Horace.

Walton's sister Anne had married the London seamster Thomas Grinsell about 1608. It is possible that Izaak Walton gained his education, however basic, somewhere between 1608 and 1613 when he moved to London to live with his sister. At this time Walton would have been between the ages of fifteen and twenty. Walton came to London to be apprenticed into a trade. He may have been apprenticed under his sister's new husband. In 1851, a John Nicholl, historian of the Ironmonger's Company, one of the London Guilds, discovered in the books of the company an entry regarding Walton.

> November 12, 1618. Isaack Walton, late apprentice to Thomas Grinsell, was now admitted and sworne a free brother of this the Ironmonger's Companie, and payd for his admittance.

Walton would have served the customary term for apprenticeship of seven years before being sworn into the "companie" which would have put him in London at least by 1611, or at eighteen years of age.

That Walton was part of the Ironmonger's Company does not mean that he was indisputably an *ironmonger*, one who deals in iron articles and hardware. The Ironmonger's Company was simply a trade guild that incorporated varied trades, including that of seamster. In the biographies I've read, Walton was said to have been a milliner (vender of bonnets, ribbons, and gloves), seamster, linen draper, ironmonger, haberdasher, vender of fish hooks, hosier, and shirt maker. We know for certain that he could not have been all of these at once.

We can state with reasonable certainty that Walton had something to do with the sale or working of cloth. It is thought that he may have apprenticed for a man named Henry Walton, but more likely, even if only peripherally, as is stated in the records of the Ironmonger's Company, was his apprenticeship to his sister Anne's husband, Thomas Grinsell. Izaak most likely lived with them too, and not too poorly. It is apparent from properties listed in Grinsell's will that he was of the middle class and fairly well-to-do. Handsome fortunes could most certainly have been made in the drapery business, as one way for men to gain attention was through ostentatious dress. Coon says that during Izaak Walton's early years in London he was insulated by "industrious, conservative, God-fearing people of the rising middle class." Eventually Walton moved to the north side of Fleet Street in London, two doors west of the end of Chancery Lane, where he started his own business as a linen draper or cloth dealer. The parish books of St. Dunstan's-in-the-West Church, near to Walton's home, and where Walton attended services, indicate that Walton lived on Fleet Street between the years 1628 and 1644.

Apparently Walton's shop was near or part of the Royal Exchange, a place set up by Sir Thomas Gresham, financial advisor to the crown, for the purpose of bringing merchants together to meet and trade. Walton never talks or writes about these early working years. His life as a tradesman, before his incarnation as a writer, went unspoken, and probably intentionally so. It is unclear when or how Walton's cryptic metamorphosis from seamster to literary great began. Most likely it was some time around 1624, at thirty-one years of age, that Walton put down his sewing needle for a quill pen.

Walton, a practicing Anglican, developed friendships with like-minded contemporaries through his religious affiliations. The clerics John and Henry King may have introduced Walton to a literary circle that met at a place called the Mermaid Tavern. Through this association Walton may have encountered prominent literary figures such as Michael Drayton, Samuel Page, Ben Jonson, Browne, Wither, Brooke, Davies, and Chapman. Walton may have met John Donne through this same circle as well, and would have known that Donne's father was an ironmonger. If not at this time, Izaak certainly met Donne later when this former dean of St. Paul's became priest or vicar of Walton's church, St. Dunstan's-in-the-West, in 1624. James Boswell, in his life of Samuel Johnson, quotes the Dr. Johnson as having said: "It was wonderful that Walton, who was in a very low situation in life, should have been familiarly received by so many great men, and that at a time when the ranks of society were kept more separate than they are now." Jonquil Bevan tells us that Walton was associated with a particular intellectual group called the Great Tew Circle, who "evolved a tolerant belief that all things necessary to salvation are, by definition non-controversial." The absence of acrimony and dispute are the qualities, Walton tells us, to which brothers of the angle should aspire.

At thirty-two years of age, Walton married Rachel Floud, who was nineteen. They probably met at St. Dunstan's, which had many Flouds in its parish. That Walton came to marry Rachel, descendant of Archbishop Cranmer, one of the principal clergymen under Henry VIII, and generally from a very good family replete with Cambridge graduates, suggests that by this time he had achieved considerably more wealth than he had started with. Being married to a prominent and prosperous member of the parish could only have contributed to the seeming facility with which he ascended in society and became circulated among so many prominent people. We know little about the relationship between Izaak and Rachel, save their misfortunes in childbearing. Rachel bore seven children, none of whom survived their fourth year. Although infant mortality was quite common at the time, these deaths were no doubt extremely tragic in their lives. Rachel died young, in May 1642. The date of her death was recorded by Walton in his prayer book.

Two years after the death of John Donne in 1633 the quarto volume *Poems by John Donne* was published by Walton's friend on Fleet Street, John Marriott. It was thought by Sir Harris Nicolas that Walton was its editor, though it is certain that he wrote "An Elegie upon Dr. Donne," which appeared at the end of this volume and was one of Walton's first published literary efforts, or at least the first we can be absolutely certain was his. It is evident from these verses that Walton had an intimate friendship with and great admiration for Donne. Coon describes these verses as "unremarkable," but they display the modest, almost self-deprecating style that becomes characteristic of Walton. Walton writes with the same tone on the death of his friend William Cartwright when he says, "my aims are like myself, humble and low." In the end, even though such modest displays were commonly expressed, Walton was probably as humble and pious as he and his friends portrayed. But at this point, I can at least offer an alternative explanation for his hesitation in talking about himself.

It is possible that Walton did not talk of his life because he was trying to hide what he had come from. We hear nothing from him about his years as a draper, nor do we hear any reference to that occupation by his friends. Walton may have developed this modesty and vagueness about his own life in order to bury his years as a tradesman and continued to wear this front later as a matter of convenience. Given the choice, Walton would rather have been considered an author of the gentlemanly class and not a draper. And it seems that over the years some of his biographers and editors, in the words of Richard le Gallienne, "have been uncomfortable because Walton was a tradesman." Dr. Thomas Zouch, who wrote Walton's biography as preface to a 1796 edition of *The Lives*, and seemed to have been aware of a disheartened anxiety because of Walton's low social position at his genesis, can be quoted as having said impassionedly on this issue, "Let no one, however elevated in rank or station, however accomplished with learning, or exalted in genius, esteem him the less for that." And I cannot tell you how many times I have seen wrongly printed in widely circulated publications the error of calling the author of *The Compleat Angler Sir* Izaak Walton, as if they want to elevate him to some unnecessary knightly status. Walton moved up in the ranks of the Ironmonger's Company, being chosen junior warden of the yeomanry in 1637 and then senior warden a year later. We know this from the company records, not because Walton tells us. I only raise this issue of concealment because I find it strange he left little record or mention in any of his writings of what he'd done during the first part of his life.

In 1638 Walton's commendatory verses to a book called *The Merchant's Map of Commerce* by Lewes Roberts were published. His next literary work was "The Life of Donne," which prefaced a collection of Donne's sermons published in 1640. As Walton explains in the first paragraph of his "Life of Donne," upon Donne's death Sir Henry Wotton had begun to write his biography, and knowing Walton's acquaintance with Donne asked if he might help collect information concerning this poet and eminent clergyman. Walton likely made visits to Sir Henry at Eton College, where he was provost, and fished with him on the Thames. A letter of 1639 from Wotton to Walton suggests a visit and a casting of lines,

My Worthy Friend. . . .

I shall write you at large by the next messenger (being at present a little in business), and then I shall set down certain general heads, wherein I desire information by your loving diligence; hoping shortly to enjoy your own ever welcome company in this approaching time of the Fly and the Cork. And so I rest,

Your very hearty poor friend to serve you,

H. Wotton

About the time when Walton felt ready to hand over what he'd compiled on the life of their mutual friend, Henry Wotton died suddenly, and the task of writing Donne's biography fell serendipitously in entirety to Izaak Walton. Walton explains that he completed the project himself only because there was a need for a record of Donne's life to preface the publication of the sermons. Walton wrote: "The world should see the best plain picture of Donne's life that my artless pencil, guided by the hand of truth, could present to it." Walton's second book was a life of his good friend Henry Wotton, and his third *The Compleat Angler*.

The Izaak Walton Museum, housed in a cottage where some maintain Walton wrote *The Compleat Angler*, was outside of Stafford in Great Bridgeford, and I managed to find it by midday. It was well attended, and beyond the sign that said:

STAFFORD BOROUGH COUNCIL

IZAAK WALTON COTTAGE

AUTHOR OF THE "COMPLEAT ANGLER"

ANGLING MUSEUM – HERB GARDEN

PERIOD ROSE GARDEN – PICNIC ORCHARD

ENTRANCE CHARGE £1.00

there were people in period costume, black and white outfits with big black hats. It was an attractive timber-framed cottage; white with black beams. Although it was purported to have been the cottage Walton lived in when he wrote *The Compleat Angler,* it was more likely the servant quarters for Walton's Halfhead Estate. The roof of the cottage was newly thatched, trimmed and layered in a beautiful pattern, the lawn was green, and the garden of period flowers and plants in bloom. I paid my admission and was given a pamphlet on Walton in which was printed a small map of the nearby River Dove with relevant landmarks related to Izaak Walton and Charles Cotton. Inside the first room hung a portrait of Walton late in life, a facsimile of the one in the National Portrait Gallery, London, with his full head of white hair and gentle demeanor. Across the room from the portrait was a table covered with strange tools, and behind it stood a man in period costume who could have passed for a wax model. When I determined for certain that he was living, I looked at him and nodded my head to acknowledge he was there. I couldn't quite tell if he were the type of period costumer that even spoke to those of us in the current century or if he would pretend that he never had seen me. I got my answer when he spoke to me.

"So lad, you want your teeth fixed? Sit down in the chair and I'll check you out." I surmised then that he was a period dentist and having never had a cavity I wasn't about to let him show me what they used those horrible tools for. I wanted to tell him about fluoride toothpaste, but I assumed he would just say, "fluoride?" He saw that I was reluctant to become part of the act, and just went through each tool and told me what they were used for: to drill, to pull, to crack. I was trying to knock him out of character. I've always considered such people eerily out of their minds, and they scared me. "Wow," I said, "must have hurt back then."

"When lad, a fortnight ago when I pulled Mr. Oldy's molar?"

"No, back in the seventeenth century," and reluctantly, realizing I didn't want to play his game, he came out of it and put his period tool which he held in his period hand on the period table.

"You bet it hurt," he said, "and no anesthetics either."

I told him that I was in England to study Izaak Walton, and he told me that I should talk to a man named Bruce Brainthwaite, who was outside. "He's tall and thin," the dentist told me, "and he's got a big black hat on."

I said goodbye to the dentist and went into the next room, a gift shop of sorts where

I bought an annotated copy of *The Compleat Angler*, edited by Dr. Jonquil Bevan—a name unfamiliar to me at the time, but which I would soon come across many times.

I stowed my new copy in my backpack and happily walked up the narrow stairwell to the second floor. On the far wall was a display of stuffed fish and fishing tackle, rods and reels of all kinds, and above it a timeline of notable fishing books and their publication dates. I wrote down the names of the few fishing authors that preceded Walton on the inside cover of my new book, and moved into the next room. A video was running on a continuous loop. Assuming it was on Walton, I sat in the dark room to watch it. The video was narrated by two gentlemen who introduced themselves. One was Tony Bridgett, whom I would be fishing with the next day, and the other an old man named Bernard Venables. During the course of the show they talked about Walton while fishing the Dove with fly rods and later tried fishing nearby Shallowford Brook with seventeenth-century tackle similar to the equipment Walton describes in the *Angler*. I watched it twice.

On my way out of the museum I saw a black-and-white photo of a small, quaint, storybook-looking stone building.

I recognized it, I'd seen it before numerous times—what was it? And suddenly those images I'd dusted off in the Yale Library, century-old etchings and woodcuts, all came into my head. It was built by Izaak Walton's friend Charles Cotton and sat on a small piece of land, a peninsula by some accounts, on a turn in the River Dove. I'd read that Walton used to visit Cotton at his home in Beresford, and the fishing house had been built as a place to recline and talk after a day of fishing. Cotton held a deep reverence for the man he called "father Walton," and Walton considered him an adopted son. Cotton describes the house in a 1676 addendum on fly-fishing he wrote for the fifth edition of *The Compleat Angler*.

> I will tell you that my house stands upon the margin of one of the finest rivers for trouts and grayling in England; that I have lately built a little fishing house upon it, dedicated to anglers, over the door of which you will see the two first letters of my father Walton's name and mine twisted in cipher.

This little fishing house, almost chapellike in appearance and "dedicated to anglers," was the Holy Sepulchre for fishermen, the object and cornerstone of my pilgrimage. Etched and drawn representations of the fishing house varied considerably. This was the first time I'd seen photographic evidence of it. A caption under the photo read "the fishing temple."

Outside the cottage now, in the garden, I began to walk to my car and spotted the tall, skinny man whom the dentist told me to see. "Are you Bruce?" I asked him; I would have called him Mr. Brainthwaite, but I was more certain about the Bruce part.

"Bruce Brainthwaite," he said, and I told him the dentist recommended I see him, which sounded kind of quackish, and that I was doing my senior thesis on Izaak Walton.

"It might behoove you to visit or correspond with Dr. Jonquil Bevan at Edinburgh University," Brainthwaite advised, his big black hat casting a shadow as wide in diameter as many trees do.

"Yes," I said, "I just bought her extensively annotated edition of the *Angler*."

"Well," he said, "she's one of the foremost Walton scholars alive." He proceeded to tell me a brief life of Walton. "He may have written *The Compleat Angler* in this cottage, or on this site at least; the original cottage burned nearly to the ground. Walton moved away from London here to the countryside during the English Civil War because he was an Anglican and a Royalist, a supporter of King Charles, and Charles was soon to get his head cut off. Some maintain, including Jonquil, that *The Compleat Angler* is code for The Compleat *Anglican*. If it weren't for the war, *The Compleat Angler* might never have been written."

It would take some brushing-up on my English Civil War history after returning to the States before I would fully understand the ramifications of this association. Brainthwaite recommended I get a copy of Bevan's own book, *The Art of Recreation,* which was one of only two critical books ever written on *The Compleat Angler* in English. And the more I thought on it, the more relevant a visit to meet her myself in Edinburgh seemed; after all, how complete would a passage in the wake of Walton be without a meeting with the subject's preeminent scholar. I cheerfully stowed these thoughts away and spent the rest of the day following the cryptic map of relevant sites on the Walton Museum Pamphlet.

Among the sites on the "Staffordshire Trail" were St. Mary's Church, Stafford, where Walton was baptized, the cottage I had just left, Shallowford Brook which I'd just driven over, where Walton used to fish, St. Peter's Church in Alstonefield where Cotton and Walton went to worship, and the "fishing temple." The pamphlet said that "the story of Walton's life is obscure," and that during his lifetime his most popular works were the five biographies he'd written. It also alluded to the idea that Walton may have known John Milton, the writer of *Paradise Lost*, 1667, which I found satisfying because I quite like Milton, though I hadn't read of their association in any other source. I supposed it was possible that they may have met, though there was no evidence to support or refute the possibility.

In order to accomplish any respectful pilgrimaging this day, I at least had to find the River Dove and contemplate its reflections. I decided to try and search for "Viator's Bridge" in Milldale, which is mentioned by Charles Cotton in his addendum to *The Compleat Angler*. The addendum on fly-fishing, Cotton tells us, was hastily written in ten days and modeled after Walton's style of dialogue between Viator and Piscator. Cotton's Piscator said to Viator of Walton and his work:

> Pisc. My opinion of Mr. Walton's book is the same with every man's that understands anything of the art of angling, that it is an excellent one, and that the fore-mentioned gentleman understands as much of fish, and fishing, as any man living: but I must tell you further, that I have the happiness to know his person, and to be intimately acquainted with him, and in him to know the worthiest man, and to enjoy the best, and the truest friend any man ever had; nay, I shall yet acquaint you further, that he gives me leave to call him Father, and I hope is not yet ashamed to own me for his adopted son.

Cotton exhibits in his continuation of Walton's dialogue the same kind of genteel pastoral hospitality that his "father" did. Cotton details several landmarks in the conversation along the River Dove. These landmarks still survive, one of which was the bridge I was searching for in Milldale. I marked where I thought the bridge should be on a detailed topographic map I'd purchased of the Dovedale area. Cotton's character Viator says of the bridge, "why, a mouse can hardly go over that bridge: 'tis not two fingers broad."

My first glimpse of the Dove was near Milldale. Crossing the river on a one-lane stone bridge, I parked the car and walked to the stream. As with the Wye, the Dove was gentle and crystal clear with trout visibly feeding in the current. I had parked near a small lot for a public footpath that followed along the Dove. Many of England's rivers, I came to find, had public paths along them for walking, and walking only. In most cases trout streams are private and to fish them one needs to belong to a club or know an owner. The fishermen who belonged to private clubs were often bitter about the public footpaths because people walking by, as well as their leashless dogs who often jumped in, disturbed the fishing. But ironically, after fishing several of these streams, I found that the footpaths actually improved the catch rate in fishing because the trout, conditioned to having visitors along the banks, were less wary. I noticed that when the trout saw me they would stop feeding, and even hide, but when I turned around a minute later standing twenty or so yards upstream or down, I saw that my lumbering by them had caused only a momentary disturbance and that feeding had promptly resumed. Some trout, especially those who are fed bread by old ladies and kids, and, I confess, me, are even less easily spooked, and stand their ground and continue feeding even if you flail your arms over them.

There were only two cars in the public access lot, and the lot was beside another lovely garden, bees zooming about the many-colored flowers. An old gentleman sat in one of the cars with the window open. He seemed idle enough to possibly be an angler, so I watched him. Eventually, he got out of his car, put on his spectacles, and, opening the "boot," took out a fly rod and started to thread the line through the guides for a bit of fishing. I had my rod in my car and it was jumping out of its tube for an opportunity to fish the Dove. I found it strangely disturbing that this man was able to fish this stretch of river and I wasn't. I walked over to him to talk about the fishing and ask if he knew where Viator's bridge was.

"Fishing been good lately?" I asked.

"Fair," he said, "depends on how many bloody people are trafficking up and down the river. My wife is off on a walk now picking flowers. I fished this morning and didn't get any."

"I did pretty well on the Wye the other day," I said, "and fished the Wharf yesterday and we did well there too."

"What kind of flies did you use?" he asked in a gentle curmudgeonly fashion, and showed me a small caddisfly that was tied to his line.

"Something like that," I said looking at his fly, "but mostly on a small brown nymph." He opened his box of nymphs to give me a look and I didn't see any that resembled what I'd been getting them on—they were all too big.

"I spent all last night tying flies at the bed and breakfast where I'm staying in Alkmonton," I said, "I'll run to my car and get some for you." He nodded and said he would like that. When I returned with my box of flies he was putting on his hip waders. I opened the box and gave him four flies. He thanked me and put on his hat, but really, thanks wasn't what I was after; I was hoping he'd say, "Well young man, why don't you come along and fish some, haven't you a rod?" But he didn't ask me and didn't offer me any flies from his own box; he only sauntered off and over a fence with a sign on it that said **"PRIVATE: NO FISHING."** I didn't ask him where Viator's bridge was because he would only have been privy to that knowledge if he'd read and had an interest in *The Compleat Angler*. I assumed he hadn't because if he had, he would have been aware, in part at least, that angling was about exchanging ideas and sharing draughts of friendship, and would have asked me to come along through a small moss-covered gate to a private part of the stream where even the footpathers could not tread.

The bridge at Milldale was just around the bend, two stone arches spanning the Dove. It was narrow, and two people walking side by side across it would have been just shy of comfortable. It was made for me to cross, and Walton's ghost in front of me. I didn't have any illusions about how many of the stones on this bridge were original, though some must have been, but Walton at one time may have occupied this same space and looked into the Dove, most certainly in the company of Charles Cotton. The water was shallow off the bridge here and no fish were visible. The path that went up over the hill after you crossed the bridge was the one that Cotton purportedly traveled on with his family every Sunday to services at St. Peter's Church in Alstonefield. I didn't take the footpath; it could have been several miles to the church. Instead, I got back in my car and navigated the narrow roads to Alstonefield.

The fifteenth-century parish of St. Peter's stood tall, though not intruding on the rolling green hills, and when I say rolling I mean that if you dropped a marble off the tower it seemed that it would probably roll, if the inhibiting stone walls stood aside, all the way to the North Sea. The land was green and smooth. The church was surrounded by a fortress of gravestones of different sizes and shapes. The stones were dark because they were backlit by the late afternoon sun. I went in through the church doors quietly, and a group of people were seated near the altar, at a small service or meeting. Not being a conventionally religious person, and not having attended many services as a child, I felt little spiritual connection to this church or any other for that matter. This was not a haven for me, a place that settled my heart or where I felt close to God. To me it was just a dark and musty place with unkempt pews. I tried to imagine what attending services would have been like for Walton and Cotton as I walked to the oak pew still bearing the Cotton family arms. Walton and Cotton may have been seated here together at some point. Was I missing something? It was always pleasant for me to go out fishing on a Sunday morning on a stream near my home, knowing that while all the poor brainwashed sheep were in church I had it figured out; I was enjoying God's creation firsthand. I had always remembered a line I'd read printed on a birdbath in my neighbor's yard back in Connecticut: "A kiss of the sun for pardon/a song of the birds for mirth/one is nearer God's heart in a garden/Than anywhere else on earth." I didn't sit down in St. Peter's, I only stood in the muted light coming through the windows, thinking about my faith or lack of it. If *The Compleat Angler* were at least in part code for the Compleat *Anglican*, was Walton saying perhaps that good anglers were also good Christians? To me, Walton's book seemed to suggest that fishing itself was a religion because the greatest peace that he experienced, the place he felt closest to God, was on the trout stream. Though admittedly slanted, this was my interpretation. For Walton, angling was an art practiced by honest, pious, and gracious men which bordered on religious faith. And Cotton, by virtue of the name he gave his house on the Dove, "the fishing temple," had realized this too.

The day was waning and I still had not yet seen the fishing temple. Somewhere near the town of Hartington I stopped to look at my map. Just as I had pulled over, I saw an old farmer in suspenders walking with the aid of a cane near the road. He was on his side of a stone wall. I greeted him and asked if he'd ever heard of the fishing temple that Charles Cotton built on the Dove.

"Oh, well, yes, why, hm." I let him think it through, as the calmness of the day did not encourage haste. His arthritic hands kneaded the hard gnarled top of his wood cane polished by his palm, and his head remained tilted toward the green ground for some time. He looked up finally and through me, one lazy eye hid by its squinting lid, and one very blue. "I've heard of Cotton, lived near Beresford, poet fisherman. The little building, it's on the bank of the Dove from what I've been told." And with some effort he extended a finger over my shoulder indicating where he thought it was. I said goodbye and he turned and walked away. I didn't have enough information on the fishing temple to find it, so I retired to my dairy house accommodations for a nap. When I woke, I took out my watercolors and painted in the front garden, trying to find the red that glowed on the brick of the barn from the setting sun. And then all was dark.

"Look for my gold Audi," Tony Bridgett had told me, "I'll be parked across from the Esso gas station on the main road outside of Leek." Ten A.M. was our rendezvous time and I made sure I was early, anticipating that I would have trouble finding the Esso station, as these small towns were nearly impossible to navigate by car. I'd searched the town of Leek pretty thoroughly by 9:30 A.M. and found two Esso stations. Ping-ponging from one to the other until 10 A.M., I spotted Bridgett's Audi and parked. I walked up to his car, the engine running, and he motioned for me to get in.

"So you want to go fishing on the Dove?" he said to me sitting there. He told me to follow him to a car park on the river near the town of Ilam. I felt like I was being given instructions for some covert operation. Once at the car park, Bridgett again motioned for me to get in his car; this time I brought a copy of my trout book to give to him. "Oh," he said, "you've done a book on fish; how wonderful."

He asked if I would inscribe it, so I did, "to Tony Bridgett, who took me fishing on the Dove," though of course we had not fished yet. It was a self-fulfilling prophecy.

Bridgett talked for one solid hour about Walton's history and some of the people who studied him. Jonquil Bevan at Edinburgh was a name he mentioned. I asked Bridgett if it might be worth my trying to meet Bevan. "I met her for the first time last October," he said, "at a dedication of the renovation of Silkstead Chapel in Winchester Cathedral, the site of Walton's burial." He continued by telling me that she is certainly the individual who is most intimate with Walton's life and writings and that it was entirely worth my while to meet her, adding that he would call her himself and give her some background on me and my interests.

So Bridgett began: "Walton was born in 1593 in the town of Stafford and later moved to London to get apprenticed into the drapery trade. He later became a kind of research assistant for Sir Henry Wotton who at the time was writing a preface to the publication of John Donne's sermons, a short life of John Donne, the late poet and Dean of St. Paul's Church. And, Sir Henry Wotton died, you see, and Walton knew John Donne, so he finished the book that he'd pretty much written anyway under Wotton. So began Walton's career as a writer. He later expanded the preface to a full biography of Donne, and called it the *Life of Donne*. So it was by accident really that he ever began to write in the first place." Bridgett told me that he was a retired policeman and had devoted much of his life and retirement to studying the "good book," as he called it. Though he was a native of Staffordshire, he had a bit of what sounded like a Scottish accent with pauses and inflections in strange but appropriate parts of his narration. The word that seemed to carry the most emphasis and which he pronounced most interestingly was "book" in which the "oo" sounded like the "u" in "duke." I continued to listen to him, carefully too, because really at this point in my journey I hadn't known a whole lot about Walton's life. "So Walton's first book was the life of Donne published as part of the sermons in 1640, and in 1651, he went on to write a biography of his friend who had died, Sir Henry Wotton. Now, Walton says that the seed for his third book, *The Compleat Angler,* which was published in May of 1653, was planted by his late friend Wotton who was a fisherman himself and had always planned to write a book on fishing. About this time, 1641, to the Restoration in 1660, England was very turbulent as the country was in the midst of a civil war. Did you hear about the bomb that went off in Manchester the other day?" he asked me.

"Yes," I said, "I was in Manchester the day it happened."

"Well, that bomb was set off by the IRA and all these bloody problems are aftershocks from that civil war." I confessed my ignorance concerning the English Civil War. I later read a good deal about it.

"Now they think that at this time, Walton, who had been living in London, escaped the troubles brewing there and moved to Stafford. That is where he wrote the 'good book.'"

The biographical summary that Bridgett had given me that day fishing the Dove served as a backdrop to the numerous biographies that I would later read.

"Undoubtedly," Bridgett told me, "the most thorough biography of Walton was written by a man named Arthur Munson Coon as his graduate dissertation for his Ph.D. at Cornell University." I asked Bridgett where I might be able to find a copy of Coon's biography. He told me it had never been published and that it existed in manuscript form at the Cornell University library.

Needless to say, in the months after my trip I became increasingly interested in Walton and read several biographies of him, the best of which, or at least the one that seemed most "thorough," as Bridgett had said, was the one written by Coon that I obtained through interlibrary loan from Cornell.

I will pause now in the late morning of this day to continue the narrative of Walton's life and times which I began on the bridge in Stafford over the small tributary of the River Sow. And though mayflies are hatching on the gentle Dove and trout and grayling are eager to rise for them, the sun will wait for us until the life of Walton has been provided as a veil through which to read his books and to see his streams. I encourage you to shoulder your rod momentarily. We will resume our fishing when the story has been told, and will be better off for it.

Fishing Temple on the River Dove

4
The Life of Izaak Walton
and an Adventure

Coon's thesis of 1938, entitled "The Life of Izaak Walton," had been shipped to my local library from Cornell University, and when I checked it out I felt strange carrying it away with the knowledge that this could be the only copy. I held it, bound in its tattered black cover, the text typed by hand on very thin air-mail type paper. There were four hundred pages of it and only twelve names in sixty years of those who had borrowed it.

I was eager to pore over it, and as I began to read, I wondered why Coon had taken an interest in Walton for the subject of his graduate thesis. Fishing had provided my introduction to Walton; was Coon a fisherman too? But after turning the last of four hundred pages I saw very little indication of what compelled Coon to choose Walton, though the gentleness of his tone suggests that the author's affection for the old fisherman was great. But I found while reading Coon that more personal attention and reflection finds its way into those passages concerning Walton's family life, which Coon could no doubt identify with, having just recently become a father himself. Coon's autobiographical sketch that prefaces "The Life of Walton" mentions that he was married in 1934 and his wife bore him twins, Nancy and Tucker Townsend Coon, to whom he also dedicated his thesis. Also it is mentioned that in March of 1938 his left arm had been amputated. After reading the thesis, I called Bridgett in England and asked him why he thought it had never been published. He said that he thought Coon was having serious health problems at the time and never pursued publication. Other Englishmen I later talked to, who coincidentally knew Bridgett, advised that I not rely on an ex-cop as my academic reference. Well, well, resentment lives in every corner of our lives. Incidentally, Dr. Bevan also finds Coon's unpublished thesis the most thorough life of Walton to date.

I cannot say more strongly that Walton's pious demeanor and propensity for making friends were the qualities that shaped his life and writings. He was always described by people who knew him as gentle and humble, and the circle of friends that he developed were loyal to him. The members of this insular circle were, as Walton calls them, "brothers of the angle," held together by their common interest in angling and their faith of Anglicanism. Coon's representation of Walton, though zealously thorough, is for the most part lean and pleasant to read. He by no means was the first biographer of Walton, but his is the more current. Other biographers of note, in succession, were Anthony à Wood of 1691, who had actually corresponded with Walton while he was alive, William Oldys, Sir John Hawkins, Reverend Thomas Zouch, Philip Bliss, Sir

Harris Nicholas, Richard le Gallienne, R. B. Marston, E. Marston and Andrew Lang. Sir John Hawkins wrote the first extensive life of Walton. It has proved to be the one most frequently reprinted among those which preface the over four hundred separate editions of *The Compleat Angler*. By Coon's time many aspects of Walton's life had come to be accepted as "tradition." Coon says that "tradition" in biography is "a notoriously irresponsible oracle," and as a result of much hard work in dusty church archives in small English towns, he dispels some of the biographical errors that tradition helped develop. But because Coon's research was so thorough, he felt the need to give accounts of leads that he followed concerning Walton's life—leads which often came to dead ends. His recording these loose ends makes the text slightly muddy and tedious at times. In an effort to facilitate the reading of this life of Walton, I have distilled the work of several biographers. And there are certain assumptions I make in this work. For instance, there is a record of an Anne Burne, Walton's mother's remarried name, having been buried May 23, 1623, at St. Mary's Church, Stafford. Coon would leave it at that factual statement, since the possibility exists that it may have been a different Anne Burne and not Walton's mother at all. But I take the liberty to say simply that Walton's mother died May 1623 and was buried at St. Mary's, Stafford.

Because Walton is a legend and I wish to perpetuate his legacy, I present the biographical information this way, so it reads like a story and not like the records in the register of St. Mary's. History or biography cannot avoid aspects of fiction, because by the very nature of selecting elements from the past, through these subtractive and deductive processes, we are creating fictions.

Among the names you will become acquainted with in these pages are Anne and Gervase Walton, King Charles I, and John Donne; the events you will become familiar with are civil wars and deaths of friends, tragedies and joys that may parallel yours. Walton left us no journal of his every day as his contemporary Samuel Pepys did. What he has left from his own hand are a few letters and verses of poetry, five biographies that he wrote of his closest friends and people whom he admired, and *The Compleat Angler*. Much of his social life has been divined from what he tells us in these written works. The rest is inferred from what his friends wrote about him. But part of what makes Walton so appealing is that we know so little about him, and we can fill these gaps in his history with our imaginations.

The overwhelming picture that we have of Walton is of a humble, tolerant, and gentle man. That he left no written accounts of his own life behind only perpetuates this belief.

Coon says "no matter what we do, in biography we must always see one man through the medium of another man." It comes as no surprise that we see Walton reflected in his five biographies of others. I write on Walton's life for similar reasons that Walton wrote the lives of his five contemporaries: because I admire him and don't want his brilliance to fade. As I write about Walton's life, my own intimations shine through. The things I choose to select in telling Walton's life are those that interest me and are most relevant to my own condition and concerns. I don't think this is done selfishly, it is only that part of why we read and write is to learn about ourselves, and our favorite works and authors are the ones we most identify with. The souls of authors survive in their books long after their bodies have gone, and when we read these works we displace the dead with living bodies—our own.

It seems only natural that Walton, in writing Donne's biography, selects to report those parts that are of concern to him, that he identifies with or that bring him joy. Coon very well understood the process that Walton went through in writing the *Life of Donne* and, for that matter, his four other *Lives* as well as *The Compleat Angler*:

> No matter what we do, in biography we must always see one man through the medium, not of an impassive microscope, but of another man, with all his aberrations of mentality and disposition. Walton was a pious man. He chose to write about Donne partly because he saw in Donne a pious man. Shall we, then, be surprised if the *Life of Donne* emphasizes Donne's piety?

Shall we be surprised, then, that I have become fascinated with Walton because he has helped me understand myself and that digging into him and trying to understand what shaped him and made him is in the end an inquiry into my own spirit? Should you be surprised if I might be disappointed in Walton because of his temperance because I occasionally enjoy being intemperate? So too, it is understandable that Coon, in writing his graduate dissertation on Walton's life, gives special attention to the time in Walton's life that parallels his own.

The following account is of the moment in "Life of Walton" that most closely parallels Coon's. An admitted digression on my part, I show it because it is essential in making the point that biography cannot help but reflect autobiographically. Coon may not even have been aware of what he was doing when he strayed in his account of Walton's life to recount our London draper's participation in procession during a pageant in honor of the Lord Mayor. It is a small, imagined cross section of Walton's life, poignant and helpful in our developing picture of Walton because it shines through Coon's sympathies. "London's Tempe," as this particular Lord Mayor's day was called, was a party in honor of Sir Thomas Campbell's having been chosen the new mayor of the city.

> It is pleasant to think of Walton amidst the merriment and gaiety of this occasion. He had been married, happily no doubt, for three years. His marriage had been blessed by two children, little Izaak, now almost two and John, born the previous summer. His business was prospering; he was advancing in the estimation of the Ironmonger's Company, and in that of the parish. Only a few years and wife and children would be dead, his abode and business changed, his life completely upset by the Civil Wars. But all this was hidden from him on Lord Mayor's day, 1629, and he must have waved happily to his wife and children as the procession passed their station, while Rachel tried to induce little Izaak to wave a chubby hand in return at big Izaak, fearful and unrecognized in costume.

Coon creates drama here, a calm before the storm, and wonders unquestionably to himself what storm awaits his own wife and two newborn children, Nancy and Tucker. So in Walton's *Life of Donne* we see aspects of Walton, as in Coon's "Life of Walton" we see aspects of Coon, and in my life of all of them you see aspects of me. Biography is a continuum that helps ease the inevitability of our mortal world.

I pay homage with this brief continuation of the "Life of Walton" to Coon and the work he did that went unsung, as well as to those who preceded him and those in the future who will pick up Walton for the first time and bring a new life to him.

> *Immortal Walton! may thy flame still burn,*
> *And duteous pilgrims crown thy sacred urn,*
> *Lov'd as thou art, the future age shall show*
> *Thy cherish'd lineaments with brighter glow!*
> *May the fresh homage that shall yet be paid,*
> *Be grateful incense to thy gentle shade;*
> *Nor honours cease, e'en when thine altar rears*
> *The heaped applauses of a thousand years!*

What Tony Bridgett had said about Walton becoming a writer by accident seemed like an accurate account of things. We could at the very least say that an unforeseen group of circumstances led to his career as a biographer. Walton's first published literary effort, besides short commendatory verses in praise of the printed works of his friends, was a biography of the poet and preacher John Donne.

By the time the *Life of Donne* was published in 1640, Walton had left his occupation as draper and devoted himself full time to writing. Its success no doubt furthered and firmed the relationships with other eminent clergymen and prominent minds he had begun to develop himself. Coon rightly calls Walton the "first professional biographer," though he adds that writing really was an avocation for Walton and not a professional pursuit at all. Walton later joked in his introduction to *The Compleat Angler* that in writing about fishing he was making a "recreation of a recreation."

Biography before Walton was primarily hagiography, or the biography of saints. Izaak Walton was, if not the first, then one of the earliest biographers. In that medium, he was certainly an innovator. When he included some of Donne's letters in a later edition of the *Life of Donne,* he became the first to use primary sources in biography. He even attempted to reconstruct conversations in his biographies. "I have been so bold," Walton says, "as to paraphrase and say what I think he whom I had the happiness to know well, would have said upon the same occasion." Margaret Bottrall, a Walton scholar, explains that Walton's use of dialogue in his biographies was "an artistic principle enabling him to add life and variety to his narrative."

As we know that Walton was a pious man, it is not surprising that much of the *Life of Donne* is concerned with the doctor's religious activities. But we should keep in mind that, as a member of Donne's parish, having heard his sermons on many occasions, it was the pious side of the man with which Walton was most familiar. Later, Walton tells us indirectly that he did not quite fancy Donne's poetry. In Walton's own copy of Donne's poems, now at Houghton Library Harvard (Harvard also is in custody of Walton's will), he made corrections which Dr. Bevan tells us were "intended to regularize Donne's meter."

In *The Compleat Angler* Piscator remarks of the poems of Marlowe and Ralegh that "they were old fashioned poetry but choicely good, I think much better than the strong lines now in fashion in this critical age." The following lines by Walton appeared in the second edition of Donne's poems and were printed below an engraving of a portrait of an eighteen-year-old Donne.

> *This was for youth, Strength, Mirth and wit that Time*
> *Most count their golden age; but 'twas not thine.*
> *Thine was thy later years, so much refined*
> *From youths Dross, Mirth and wit; as thy pure mind*
> *Thought (like the Angels) nothing but the Praise*
> *Of thy Creator, in those last, best Days.*
> *Witness this Book, (thy Emblem) which begins*
> *With love; but ends, with sighs and tears for sinns.*

On reading these lines it becomes apparent that Walton did not approve of Donne's early poetry, which was mostly about love and often subtly lewd, or can we say, penetratingly graphic. Walton asks the readers almost to dismiss the works of Donne's early years and, selfishly, focus on the pious verses that so captured Walton himself. Though I would like to picture Walton as occasionally wild, not unwilling to wax excessive, engage in drunken revelry, or at least able to laugh out loud, as it turns out he was actually quite temperate. Coon notes "Walton probably distrusted and avoided hilarity with something of a Quaker spirit." Bevan has suggested that Walton's own works have suffered from a paucity of critical attention because of his criticism of poems "now in fashion," which included Donne's. She expands thusly:

> Walton's distaste for "strong lines" was not at all aberrant in his time, but it has done his reputation great disservice in the present century. Admirers of Donne find it hard to forgive Walton his deafness to Donne's poetry, and as a result insufficient credit has been given Walton for the intensity and exuberance of his love for verse and his delighted insistence in sharing his favorites with his readers.

We see in the *Life of Donne* Walton's interest in literary ability, a good deal of humor, and love—all infused with gentleness, which contributes to an overwhelmingly calm effect. We want to believe that Walton is like his writing; a man who, in the face of all his personal tragedies, could maintain a calmness and peace sublime for this earth. Coon says, "Walton introduces us to the world as he sees it." I tell you all this because Walton's was a good way to see this world, and I admire him as a model individual. It is his simplicity and compassion in the midst of his complexities that carried him, his ability to appear artless while being artful.

Perhaps my favorite lines in Walton's *Life of Donne* concern Donne's secret marriage to a young gentlewoman, the niece of Lady Ellesmere, while Donne was acting secretary to the Lord Ellesmere. The young woman's father, Sir George More, had tried to separate them by removing his daughter to Lothesley, "but too late, by reason of some faithful promises which were so interchangeably passed, as never to be violated by either party." Walton continues:

Many arguments were used to kill or cool their affections to each other: but in vain; for love is a flattering mischief, that hath denied aged and wise men a foresight of those evils that too often prove to be the children of that blind father; a passion, that carries us to commit errors with as much ease as whirlwinds move feathers, and begets in us an unwearied industry to the attainment of what we desire.

To me this passage proves to be one of the most beautiful attempts to articulate that inarticulable and unattainable love in a single sentence.

Two years after Walton's wife Rachel died in 1640, he would have seen civil wars erupting in his England. In 1643 Walton left London. He later wrote in his biography of Bishop Sanderson that he had found the city "dangerous for the honest man to be there." "Honest men," to Walton, are Anglicans, members of his faith. In order to understand *The Compleat Angler* we must understand the times during which it was written. Everything had fallen apart in Walton's world. His angling trip, physically walking from London and her troubles to the countryside, is a journey into normalcy and stability as well as fantasy.

A brief summary of the events of the civil war is necessary to understanding why London was a dangerous place for Anglicans in the 1640s.

The outbreak of war in the summer of 1642 plunged the kingdom into years of civil strife and bloodshed, culminating in the beheading of Charles I in 1649. The orderly round of civic life was shattered, and Walton's whole world was turned upside down. The major crisis which helped precipitate the Civil War was not really of English making but arose instead from the king's efforts to foist his own brand of high Anglicanism upon his puritanical Scottish subjects. In 1637, Charles and his government took the momentous, and as it proved disastrous, step of trying to introduce a new and Anglicized prayer book in Scotland, where most of the people were strongly attached to Presbyterianism. Charles was a firm believer in his father's maxim—"No bishops, no king"—and it was perhaps inevitable that he should try to bring the Scottish church more in line with that of England. But Charles proceeded too fast and with too little regard for the sensibilities of his Scottish subjects, and the result was rebellion.

Charles's first attempt to bring his Scottish subjects to heel, the First Bishops' War of 1639, ended in an inconclusive stalemate. His second attempt the following year, known as the Second Bishops' War, was mounted in the teeth of growing opposition in England and a severe financial crisis—the costs of war were exorbitant and his subjects resented it. In the spring of 1640, Charles called his first parliament for eleven years in the hope that it would grant him sufficient funds to defeat the Scots. But the two Houses of Parliament—the Commons and the Lords—would only agree to vote him money if he would consent to scrapping most of the religious and financial innovations he had made between 1629 and 1640, a period know as his Personal Rule. Enraged, Charles dissolved Parliament, which, having sat for just one month, was appropriately called the Short Parliament. With no money in his treasury and low morale among his troops, Charles could not prevent the Scots invading northern England in August 1640. He was now entirely at the mercy of his discontented English and Scottish subjects, who forced him to call another parliament. This second parliament convened in November 1640 and sat almost continuously for the next thirteen years, thus becoming known as the Long Parliament.

The meeting of the Long Parliament unleashed a torrent of reform which swept away many of the innovations and abuses of the Personal Rule. Charles was at first powerless to resist this outpouring of reformist zeal—a measure of just how unpopular his policies had been during the preceding eleven years. But, as the leaders of the Long Parliament began mounting an attack upon the Church of England itself, the king gradually gained support from those, such as Walton, who were deeply attached to episcopacy and the Anglican liturgy. Future Royalists like Walton were also deeply alarmed by the apparent willingness of the parliamentary leadership to use popular demonstrations to intimidate their political opponents. Nowhere was this tactic more in evidence than in London, where huge and often riotous crowds gathered outside Westminster Palace (where Parliament sat) to shout abuse at the bishops and courtiers as they attended House of Lords. And it was not just members of the aristocracy and the gentry, the elite of the propertied classes, who were disturbed at this spectacle of the mob interfering in national politics. Many London masters and small businessmen also believed that rousing the common people from their accustomed political torpor could have only one result, the destruction of all private property and the unleashing of chaos. For men of property in the seventeenth century, democracy was virtually synonymous with anarchy.

Walton would have been among the first Anglicans to have suffered as a result of the wave of Puritan militancy which swept London after the calling of the Long Parliament. In 1640, he had been elected to the vestry, or administrative council, of his parish church of St. Dunstan's-in-the-West. St. Dunstan's contained an unusually large number of Puritans, and with the Long Parliament in power and no episcopal authority to keep them in check, they quickly seized their chance and took control of the vestry and set about introducing a more Puritan form of worship. They may even have gone so far as to strip the parish church of all relics of popery, such as stained glass, ornate carvings, and images of the cross and crucifixion. This Puritan coup in St. Dunstan's was soon to be repeated in many other parishes across London. To Walton's eyes such developments must have seemed tantamount to sacrilege and a profaning of all that was holy and decent in church worship.

Over the spring and summer of 1642, both king and Parliament set about raising armies, and by the autumn fighting had broken out across the country. Although many people remained neutral in the war, most would probably have had a preference for one side over another. Their reasons for sympathizing with either king or Parliament were many and varied. In general, though, most Puritans and those who feared that Charles was the dupe of domestic and foreign Catholics sided with Parliament, whereas most of those whose attachment to the Church of England and sense of allegiance to their anointed sovereign outweighed all other considerations remained loyal to the king.

Although Walton may have owned some property and was known, at least to his fellow parishioners, as a gentleman, he belonged in fact to the upper middle classes and was therefore, in social terms perhaps, not quite a typical Royalist. Being a gentle and passive man, he did not actively take sides. Yet in his devotion to all things Anglican he was very much in the Royalist main-stream, and in one respect at least he had something in common with those contributing to the king's cause—his love of angling and other rural sporting pastimes, which many Puritans equated with lasciviousness and idleness.

The onset of war and its terrible cost in lives and money was felt particularly by Londoners. Parliament relied heavily on the city to supply much of the money and manpower it needed to fight the king. As a leading member of the Ironmongers' Company, Walton may well have been under considerable pressure to contribute to the parliamentarian war chest or else face fines as a neuter and malignant. In addition, Parliament and the Puritans continued to strengthen their grip on civic religious life, purging Anglican clergymen, practically outlawing Anglican worship in some parishes, and destroying superstitious images. Not surprisingly, a steady stream of Royalist refugees left London after 1641, and in 1643 Walton joined this exodus. Walton comments on the political climate of these years in his biography of Bishop Sanderson:

> The Presbyterian party of this nation did again, in the year 1643, invite the Scotch covenanters back into England: and hither they came marching with it gloriously upon their pikes and in their hats, with this motto; "For the Crown and Covenant of both Kingdoms." This I saw, and suffered by it. But when I look back upon the ruin of families, the bloodshed, the decay of common honesty, and how the former piety and plain dealing of this now sinful nation is turned into cruelty and cunning, I praise God that He prevented me from being of that party which helped to bring in this covenant, and those

sad confusions that have followed it. And I have been the bolder to say this to myself, because in a sad discourse with Dr. Sanderson, I heard him make the like grateful acknowledgement.

The last record of Walton being resident in the parish of St. Dunstan's was on May 3, 1643. It was no doubt emotionally a difficult relationship for Walton to sever. He apparently had little trouble physically making his exodus. As Coon points out "it was easier for Walton to disappear than for others, as he was now a widower with no living children." From London, Izaak most likely moved to Stafford, the place of his birth, or otherwise lived with eminent Anglican clergymen friends in the countryside, becoming one of many of that faith who were exiles in their own nation.

During the years until restoration of the monarchy in 1660, Walton made several visits back to London. One such instance was his appearance as an overseer of Thomas Grinsell's will in 1645. In 1647, aged fifty-four years, he returned again to marry his second wife, thirty-five-year-old Anne Ken, in Clerkenwell, north London. As with Walton's first wife Rachel, Anne was from a distinguished family, the eldest daughter of the London lawyer Thomas Ken. Anne Ken's stepbrother, Thomas Ken Jr., became a friend of Izaak's and later bishop of Bath and Wells. Thomas also became famous for writing hymns, and he and Walton—who shared proclivities for music—may have spent time singing together. Izaak and Anne's first child, also named Anne, was christened in Clerkenwell, March of 1647. In February Walton's wife bore another child, a son, Izaak, who died June of the same year, being the eighth child that Walton had lost. In September 1651, Anne Walton bore the third and last child, also a son, and also named Isaac. But this Isaac lived and even survived his father and namesake. Walton recorded the birth of his son, as he did many other things, in the pages of his prayerbook.

A footnote in Walton's career as Royalist, writer, seamster—and occasion of another trip back to London—was his delivery of a crown jewel called the "Lesser George" from Stafford to the Tower of London. The following incident is related in Ashmole's *History of the Order of the Garter*.

> Soon after the battle of Worcester, September 3, 1651, when Cromwell defeated the King with a loss of six thousand men, and all their baggage, and a garter which belonged to his Majesty, formed part of the spoil, and were brought to the Parliament a few days afterwards by Major Corbet, who was despatched by Cromwell with an account of his victory. The Sovereign's lesser George was, however, preserved by Colonel Blague, who, having taken shelter at Blore Pipe House, two miles from Eccleshall in Staffordshire, then the residence of Mr. George Barlow, delivered the jewel into that gentleman's custody. In the ensuing week, Mr. Barlow carried it to Robert Milward, Esquire, who was at that time a prisoner in the Garrison of Stafford, and Milward shortly afterwards gave it into the 'trusty hands' of Izaak Walton to convey to Colonel Blague, who was confined by the Parliament in the Tower of London. It is said that Blague, 'considering it had already passed so many dangers, was persuaded it could yet secure one hazardous attempt of his own'; and having made his escape from the Tower, he had the gratification of restoring the *George* to the King.

That Walton was able to deliver the jewel safely and avoid its interception by parliamentary forces is a testament to his genial nature and ease with friendship, or negotiation. He must not have been considered threatening to the parliamentary forces in London. Though Walton by nature was nonconfrontational and noncontroversial, this account leads us to inquire whether he may have been a more active participant in the events of his times than has been previously acknowledged.

As horrible as it may sound, the tragedies that Walton experienced up to the point when *The Compleat Angler* was published in 1653 in his sixtieth year were essential to his development as a writer. On this subject Coon remarks "surely the peace and quiet notable in Walton's writings was not attained without suffering on his part." I think that Coon, who had himself experienced tragedy and loss by this time in which he wrote of Walton, at least that of losing his arm to amputation, realized that in order to write as calmly and normatively as Walton had, you needed some measure of understanding concerning its extreme opposite. We can all identify with Walton, because by the time we are old enough to read him we have on some level experienced tragedy. Walton's account of the events leading up to the bloody civil wars in his biography of John Sanderson are revealing in this sense.

> Some years before the unhappy long parliament, this nation being then happy and in peace (though inwardly sick of being well) namely in the year 1639, a discontented party of Scots Church were zealously restless for another Reformation of their Kirk Government.

What Walton says here is that the people of England were tired of living in peace, they were "sick of being well." Walton realized that humans cannot be content during extended periods of peace, that they become bored with it. The only way you can truly appreciate peace is to have experienced war. Walton may have been disturbed by and hesitant to record his acknowledgment of this paradox, that peace alone does not contentment bring, because it is fundamentally anti-Christian. I think that at the time he wrote *The Compleat Angler* Walton was in the process of revising, if reluctantly and with some deal of pain, his own views on religion. His faith becomes problematic when he realizes that the heaven he aspired to is precisely such a peace, and there is nothing keeping him or any of his peers from growing bored with that place when they get there. These doubts were swimming in Walton's head, I am sure of it. But Walton had likely justified heaven to himself, as others have, with the thought that "up there" we encounter a whole new set of rules. The best that we can achieve on earth is a pleasant median between tragedy and happiness that is called contentedness. Charles Cotton dedicated a poem to Walton called "Contentation." The title simply means to be content, and the poem is about what being *content* means, through what method we achieve contentation, cast through Cotton's incensed exclamations about the turbulent events of the times. That he dedicated this poem to Walton suggests that it may have been a common theme of their conversation. These are only four of thirty-two stanzas.

> *'Tis contentation that alone*
> *Can make us happy here below,*

The Complete Angler

And when this little life is gone,
Will lift us up to heaven too.

Who from the busy world retires
To be more useful to it still,
And to no greater good aspires,
But only the eschewing ill.

Who with his angle and his books
Can think the longest day well spent,
And praises God when back he looks,
And finds that all was innocent.

Untrodden paths are then the best,
Where the frequented seem unsure,
And he comes soonest to his rest,
Whose journey has been most secure.

Cotton, in this poem, has a preoccupation with heaven. I would like to think that by his sixtieth birthday, when Walton had finished writing *The Compleat Angler*, he had come to realize that the heaven he sought could at times be achieved on this earth, and more specifically on the trout stream. And the more Walton revised *The Compleat Angler* and expanded it (it went through five editions in his lifetime), the closer he came to realizing that angling was his religion and that through angling he could achieve a form of immortality as great as the ideal he held of heaven. Bevan says quite rightly in her book *The Art of Recreation* that for Walton, "angling seemed more a kind of moral vocation than a sport."

In the flyleaves of a 1655 edition of *The Compleat Angler*, which appears to have been Walton's copy, are written the following lines in Walton's hand. By this point in his life he may have acquainted himself more securely with classical languages because the lines are in Latin. They are provided here in English.

> In infaelicitate felix Va soli
> *Happy in misfortune. Go alone.*
> Nunquam minus solus quam cum solus
> *Never less alone than when alone.*
> Qui bene latuit bene vixit
> *Who endures well, lives well.*
> Ictus piscator sapit
> *The Angler feels the blow (thrust or wound).*

If these are in fact his lines, we can see here that Walton had drawn inwardly to confront his tragedies. In the last of the four perhaps he meant Anglican to replace angling, because certainly during this time, when the Puritans were taking over his country, the Anglicans would have felt the wounds of their nation.

The link between angling and Anglicanism is perhaps nowhere more consummately made than in the association of his art with that of its patrons—the apostles. This association is well articulated by Bevan, who endeavors to explain that by emphasizing the apostles as the earliest anglers, and modern day Anglicans the followers or successors, Walton is returning to a primitive Christianity while revealing an argument against Puritanism.

> The era of the Apostles and their successors, the Church of Fathers for the first 500 years following the Institution of the Church by Christ, was known as the era of Primitive Christianity and the Primitive Church. 'Primitive' in this sense means 'earliest, original', and the Primitive Church, the Christian Church, in its earliest and purest times. The Primitive Church offered therefore, in one way, an alternative to the Puritan ideal. Two things made these ideals incompatable:
>
> 1: That the Primitive Church represented an ecclesiastical golden age in the past, while Puritans had a millenarian tendency to look forward to the near future; and
>
> 2: that the Primitive Church emphasized historicity, and the historically derived authority of the present-day bishops descended from it.
>
> Whatever the Primitive Church had enjoyed was in the past and, for most Puritans, largely irrelevant; what mattered to them was not revelation handed down from others but direct revelation to Christian professors in the here and now. . . .

The Anglican claim under James I, Charles I and again after the Restoration, to identification with the Primitive Church, was important to the Anglicans who were struggling for survival during the interregnum. Indeed, it was not difficult for them to think the parallel even closer than it had been, since Anglicans (like early Christians) were now threatened and oppressed.

What is fascinating to any angler about all this is that a return to primitive Christianity, and that visionary glimpse of the apostles casting their nets in Galilee, could also be interpreted as a return to nature. By 1655, "a year which had seen considerable tightening of measures against Anglicans and Royalists," the year in which Walton may also have scribbled the solemn lines in Latin above, "brothers of the angle" were being pushed out of their houses of worship. It was a time, as I see it, when primitive Christianity was most appropriate as a model for their condition, being that worship would have to have been performed in the countryside. This is well expressed by Hammond, staunch proponent of the episcopal cause, in his book *Of Schisme,* 1654, "the night-meetings of the Primitive Christians in dens and caves are as pertinent to the justifying of *our* condition, as they can be of *any*."

Perhaps the best and most evocative message concerning this inevitable turn toward nature and the simplicity of the early Christians was in a letter of 1655 from Bishop Duppa to his friend Sir Justinian Isham, "who had been imprisoned upon suspicion earlier in the year, but was now released." (as quoted in Bevan)

We are yet suffered to offer up the public prayers and Sacrifice of the Church, though it be under private roofs, nor do I hear of any for the present either disturbed or troubled for doing it. When the persecution goes higher, we must be content to go lower, and to serve our God as the ancient Christians did, in dens, and caves, and deserts. For all the world is His chapel, and from what corner of it soever, we lift up our devotions to Him, He is ready to listen to the lowest whispers of them.

These powerful words make Walton's journey out of London to the River Lea, which provides the text for *The Compleat Angler*, even more relevant and metaphoric. Walton is leaving the city's turmoil and returning to the simplicity of the primitive Christians—choosing an exercise such as fishing so as to meet on a level with the meek and quiet, thankful apostles. There can be no doubt that this is what Walton is doing.

Venator says in the first chapter that he has always looked on anglers as "simple men." Piscator responds:

for my simplicity, if by that you mean a harmlessness, or that simplicity which was usually found in the primitive Christians, who were (as most Anglers are) quiet men, and followers of peace; men that were so simply-wise, as not to sell their consciences to buy riches, and with them vexation and a fear to die; if you mean such simple men as lived in those times when there were fewer Lawyers; I say Sir, if you take us Anglers to be such simple men as I have spoken of, then my self and those of my profession will be glad to be so understood.

It is simple men that are simply contented and find happiness in a drop of dew because they are thankful for what they have and are not concerned in always getting, getting, catching, and corrupting.

It seems clear by now that Walton meant to make the association between Anglican and angling and so too between anglers and primitive Christians. Such views of his fishing book and its ties to his religion are not easily revealed for a reason: they were meant to be hidden because of persecution of Anglicans by Puritans during these hard times. But reading Walton this way on its dual levels, as fishing book and Anglican polemic, is like taking a trout out of water and holding it up to the light—there was color when it was under water, sure, but so much more detail is revealed when it is held aloft to the sun and truly examined.

It is going one step further to say, which I do, that Walton considered the act and pursuit of the art of fishing in itself to be a religion. That is melding the whole package. And although Walton was perhaps one of the first to strongly consider angling as faith, twentieth-century novelist Rose Macaulay expanded wonderfully on the relationship between Anglicanism and angling in her 1956 book, *The Towers of Trebizond*. The story is narrated by the character Laurie, who tells of her travels with her Aunt Dot and a chantry priest from their English home through the Turkish countryside in an attempt to establish a High Anglican mission there. Writes Macaulay:

> It is not strange that our family should have inherited a firm and tenacious adherence to the Church of our country. With it has come down to most of us a great enthusiasm for catching fish. Aunt Dot

maintains that this propensity is peculiarly Church of England; she has perhaps made a slight confusion between the words Anglican and angling.

However this may be, our family have been much given to this pursuit. Inheriting the fish-ponds of the Sussex abbey which they so warily angled for and hooked in 1539, they took for their crest three pikes couchant, with the motto "Semper pesco"(fish always), and proceeded to stock the abbey ponds with excellent carp, which they fished for by way of recreation and ate for dinner in the fasting seasons. Those of the family who took Holy Orders, brought up from infancy to this pastime, continued to practice it assiduously in the various pleasant livings which came their way. One of them, rector of East Harting in the late eighteenth century, wrote in his journal (published in 1810) that he prepared most of his sermons while thus engaged; he thought that his vocation as fisher of men was assisted by miming it out on the river banks, and each fish that he landed caused him to exult greatly, as if he had captured a soul. When they nibbled at the bait, he prayed; when they got away, he repented of his own unworthiness that caused his hand to fail, and took it as divine correction. Subsequently he became bishop, but did not cease to fish.

By and large, the more they fished, the Higher they grew. And the more tenaciously and unswervingly Anglican they were, the better they fished.

My aunt, therefore, had inherited a firm and missionary Anglicanism; she had also inherited a tendency to hunt fish.

An American named Norman Maclean raised in the trout country near Missoula, Montana, had similar intimations on angling as faith. His father, a proud Scot, was not Anglican, but a Presbyterian minister, and impressed upon his two boys a love of fly-fishing. The well-loved lines in the opening of Maclean's celebrated book, *A River Runs Through It,* read: "In my family there was no clear line between religion and fly fishing."

We have to give credit to Walton for recognizing the therapeutic and religious qualities in his contemplative recreation. I wonder if Walton ever considered skipping services and hours-long sermons to fish a trout stream on a Sunday morning, like myself and Mr. Bridgett were about to do. Forgive me if I have been a bit long winded, but let us resume our day of angling, as really it has just begun.

By the time I took my first cast it was about eleven in the morning, and my great big English breakfast of eggs and ham and grilled tomato was giving way to a churning and distracting hunger. But this urge for food was temporarily usurped by excitement when Tony pointed in the Dove to a beautiful grayling finning in an eddy behind a growth of the small, light, green-leafed starwort. The water, upwelling at intervals from cold springs, was very clear, and you could feel a cold dampness when you came near it. Tony told me the pool on whose banks we stood was called Lover's Leap pool. It flowed at the foot of a big cliff that cut the glare from a noonday sun.

We had walked along a well-worn footpath to get to this pool, as if through a tunnel of lush green foliage. The banks were lined with a big broad-leafed plant, its great green leaves shaped somewhat like rhubarb, with long stems, but bigger, rounder and greener, dripping greenness. Some of the leaves were probably two-and-a-half feet in diameter. "That's butterburr," Bridgett said when I asked him. "Why don't you have a shot at that grayling? And use the butterburr to conceal you as you make your cast."

Bridgett had not seen me fish yet, and I wanted to perform well under his supervision and tutelage. So I crawled down the bank and measured off some line, letting it pile by the butterburr at my feet. My little brownish gray nymph was secured on the line and I cast it to the grayling, up four feet or so ahead of him so it would drift by his head and be seen by those glassy black eyes. On the second cast he took my fly and used his great colorful arcing dorsal fin to make resistance with the current. Eventually he glided in, and I admired the reds and blues of his great dorsal fin, his silver scales and small black spots. I unhooked and released him, and watched as he disappeared in the weedbeds.

"Well done," exclaimed Bridgett, scratching his forehead with the butt of his rod. "Your first fish on the River Dove, and a noble fish indeed." And Bridgett went on to recite as best he could from memory what Walton had said of the grayling.

> The French value the grayling so highly, that they say he feeds on Gold, and say that many have been caught out of the River Loire, out of whose bellies grains of Gold have often been taken. And some think that he feeds on Water-Thyme, and smells of it at his first tak-

ing out of the water; and they may think so with as good reason as we do, that our smelts smell like Violets at their being first caught; which I think is a truth. Aldrovandus says, the salmon, grayling and trout, and all fish that live in clear and sharp streams, are made by their mother Nature of such exact shape and pleasant colors, purposely to invite us to a joy and contentedness in feasting with her.

Bridgett and I headed up the stream, stomping the overhung greenery in the path. We saw two small fish rising for flies at the next turn. "Have a go at them, why don't you," he said. So I took my little brown nymph off the line and tied on a small imitation caddis fly that floated well on the surface. I cast it to the closer of the two, and the fish rose and took the fly and leaped out of the water, all five inches of wild brown trout.

"Another fine fish," said Bridgett, who was now casting just upstream of me, his blond amber bamboo rod making lazy arcs against the greens. He was nearly concealed by the elephantine leaves of the butterburr. We returned to the footpath, and neither of us took another cast the rest of the day. I was content with the thought that I'd caught a native descendant of trout that Walton had.

"I'm sorry we didn't exactly hit the mayfly hatch right," said Tony. "You know it should actually be called the June fly, as it hatches more often during the beginning of that month. Do you know why that is?"

"No," I said.

"Because in Walton's time in England they used the Julian, or Old Style calendar, whereas today we use the Gregorian Calendar, which is ten days ahead of the Julian."

Bridgett wore wading boots that came up to his hips, and a long-sleeved plaid shirt with a red cap. His hair, which spilled out from under his cap, was mostly white, but looked like it once had been red, graying late as red hair does. As Walton had, Bridgett carried his flies and fishing gear in a shoulder bag. And when we reclined by a fence on the banks of the Dove in the sun to watch the pool for rising trout, I happily realized he used his fishing bag to carry something else that Walton often did too: food. He undid the two leather buckles on his bag and pulled out two cheese sandwiches for each of us, and a thermos of coffee with milk. I nestled back against a fence post. It was not the pack lunch that Walton had recommended, that of dried beef, radishes, and ale, but when Bridgett handed me a sandwich as a gesture of companionship, to slake the hunger and ease conversation, I felt that he could just as easily have been Walton. Sitting there in the grass, munching my sandwich and drinking coffee poured from his thermos, I told Bridgett what I'd been thinking—that he had been kind to take me fishing and how quickly anglers could become friends. He sipped his coffee and squinted in the sun.

"They knew how to live," he said, and I got to wondering how many people I knew back in the States who would have taken a stranger on their private trout stream after a single phone call.

Bridgett talked in the manner of Walton—used Waltonisms in his speech. The spirit of Piscator had occupied him and I was pleased to be his scholar. He seemed bitter that his England had neglected Walton in recent years. "I know more Walton enthusiasts in the States than I do in England," he said. "The greatest collections of Walton's works are not in England, they are in libraries and private

Small trout under the butterbur

collections in America. You have all the money, I suppose, over there, and are buying it all up, and no one in England apparently cares to see it go."

Bridgett asked if I knew what *angle* I thought I might take on *The Compleat Angler* for my senior essay. I told him that part of it would be an account of my fishing Walton's waters and the people I met along the way.

"The English are all too apathetic," he broke out all of a sudden, putting his sandwich down. "They don't care about anything. That's what I like about America; when an American orders something at a restaurant and it's undercooked or he doesn't like it, he sends it back. An Englishman would never do that." This reminded me of what David Scott had said somewhat cynically the other day about all Englishmen being "thin." Two other fishermen walking by stopped for a chat, interrupting Tony's monologue. Tony introduced me to them as his "friend from America," and remarked to them how he'd noticed young anglers from other countries, namely America and Germany, were excellent at casting a fly. When the two anglers walked on upstream, Tony said to me, "You can never tell an Englishman how to cast—even if he were holding the rod at the wrong end." Bridgett finished his sandwich and his coffee. He went on to tell me how he'd helped found an organization called "the friends of Walton," and asked if I would like to join. For ten pounds a year I would receive their newsletter, which contains articles on little-known facts about Walton as well as events coordinated by the museum and cottage trust where I had been yesterday. I gave him the ten pounds as we sat there in the sun.

"Walton was a simple man like me," said Bridgett, tilting his round face to the ground of the footpath. He almost seemed embarrassed to have made the comparison, as if Walton might be listening to us as we walked along his stream. I came to thinking about what being "simple" meant to Bridgett—what simple meant to me—simple in education perhaps, or simple in occupation. I had always considered myself a simple person, that I dressed simply and talked simply, that I didn't use ostentation to convey my feelings, that I probably would not need a good deal of money to live the way I wanted to live. To some degree I considered myself a minimalist and told myself I would try to subsist on the least that I could—to live as a Thoreauvian, my father's ideal, by the Yankee motto:

> *Eat it up*
> *Use it up*
> *Make do*
> *Or do without.*

I have come to enjoy fishing with the least amount of tackle possible, a handful of flies, two in particular: a small gray or brown nymph wrapped with gold or copper wire and a small dry fly, a caddis or emerging caddis which also passes for a mayfly. This is partly the result of my friendship with an old Yankee minimalist outdoorsman named Joe Haines, whom I later wrote a book about called *Joe and Me*. I tend to wear mostly the same clothes, fishing at least, as what I wear has become one of the few constants in my life. But then again, there is the side of me that likes fine things—the look and feel of a fine

English tweed or a beautifully made fly rod—that side that occasionally indulges in the reading of overly academic poetry. I'm not so much of an idealist that I shun making money, and I feel that those people who do shun it are those who don't make any. The most comfortable situation to be in is to *have*, and to know that you have, all that *you* need. Perhaps a minimalist with means is more of what I had in mind. I strive for the ability to be outwardly simple, while fostering interior complexities that shine through in simple ways. There is a simple pleasure in knowing that all you need to bring to the stream for a day of fishing is a rod and a shoulder bag with a bit of lunch, lines and flies. But achieving this "simplicity," through which contention is more easily achieved, takes years of patience and planning. Walton was able to achieve it because of where he'd come from and what he'd been through. As we read *The Compleat Angler* we see that Walton struggled with materialism, issues of making money, and what was required to achieve "contentation." Though he shuns the chasing of riches, he realized that money was essential in achieving his "simple" pleasures.

Contentation is achieved through a rare combination of elements that join to create a path to pleasure. These elements, which fall through the funnel and filter of contentation—simplicity, a certain wealth in spirit and pocket, a mixture of active and passive submission to God, and thankfulness for the gifts we've been given—all fermented and distilled may produce some drops of happiness. Bevan notes, "anglers are presented, not as mere possessors of certain skill, but as peaceable, quiet, meek-spirited men, who give their first fruits to the poor . . . and are the true possessors of the pastoral scenes they enjoy, even though they have no title to legal ownership of land." Walton enjoys fishing on the rich man's property, but does not want his troubles.

> As I thus sat joying my own happy condition, and pitying this poor rich man, that owned this and many other pleasant Groves and Meadows about me, I did thankfully remember what my Savior said, that the meek possess the Earth; or rather, they enjoy what the other possess and enjoy not, for Anglers and meek quiet-spirited-men, are free from those high, those restless thoughts which corrode the sweets of life; and they only can say as the Poet has happily expressed it:

> > *Hail blest estate of lowliness!*
> > *Happy enjoyments of such minds,*
> > *As rich in self-contentedness,*
> > *Can, like the reeds in roughest winds*
> > *By yielding make that blow but small*
> > *At which proud Oaks and Cedars fall.*

But, despite the difficulties the rich man may encounter as a consequence of his position, he concedes ultimately that riches can help "remove many fears and cares, and therefore my advice is, that you endeavor to be honestly rich or contentedly poor."

Walton's character Venator argues that since the poor have very little, what they do receive is more heartily enjoyed.

And I now remember and find that true which devout Lessius says, That poor men, and those that fast often, have much more pleasure in eating than rich men and gluttons, that always feed before their stomachs are empty of their last meat, and call for more: for by that means they rob themselves of that pleasure that hunger brings to poor men.

Venator goes on to say to Piscator along the same theme:

And I do seriously approve of that saying of yours, 'That you had rather be a civil, well governed, well grounded, temperate, poor Angler, than a drunken Lord.'

There would be no joy in angling if we caught all that we desired—if the challenge and chase were gone. Pleasure is all a matter of contrast, and in this sense Walton is like Machiavelli, who said "Contrast makes virtue apparent," or like Hesse, who through his character Goldmund wrote "Any life expands and flowers only through division and contradiction. What are reason and sobriety without the knowledge of intoxication? What is sensuality without death standing behind it? What is love without the eternal mortal emnity of the sexes?" For the most part, Walton continues to shun the life of the "poor rich man." Says Piscator to Venator:

No life, my honest Scholar, no life is so happy and so pleasant, as the life of a well governed Angler; for when the Lawyer is swallowed up with business, and the States-man is preventing or contriving plots, then we sit on Cowslip-banks, hear the birds sing, and possess our selves in as much quietness as these silent silver streams, which we now see glide so quietly by us. Indeed my good Scholar, we may say of Angling, as Dr. Butler said of Strawberries; Doubtless God could have made a better berry, but doubtless God never did: And (if I might be Judge) God never did make a more calm, quiet, innocent recreation than Angling.

We cannot ignore that Walton had been a businessman and endured years of prudence and frugality. By the time Walton had written *The Compleat Angler*, he had amassed a considerable fortune and was able to *afford* to live poor. At one time Walton very likely considered himself a "poor rich man," a man bound to his trade by monetary obligation. Walton could only understand and recognize the harmony of the scene among the cowslips because he knew what it was to be "swallowed up in business."

It should also be stated that Walton's achievement of riches by his own merit and not as a consequence of inheritance was a matter of considerable satisfaction for him. He says through the voice of Piscator "I would rather prove myself a Gentleman by being learned and humble, virtuous, and communicable, than by any fond ostentation of riches, or wanting those virtues myself, boast that these were in my Ancestors." The characters of *The Compleat Angler* are not judged by their social status—says Bevan, "rich or poor, they meet on terms of civil equality." Angling is for those who drink their wine from the bottle as well as from the box. In one of my favorite lines from the *Angler*, Walton humorously and deviously maligns the poor rich man, putting himself somehow above them, by trivializing their worth and the worth of the world, which is what fishing does, attributing the only envy he experiences to success in the pursuit of a cold-blooded animal—"I envy not him that eats better meat than I do, nor him that is richer, or that wears better clothes than I do; I envy nobody but him, and him only that catches more fish than I do."

Walton was not as idealistic as his lines on the pleasures of poor men may suggest. He had a very shrewd business sense and would probably have done well in today's markets because he knew, even then, that the surest way to make money is to use time to your advantage. That is, you are more certain to make money in the Stock Exchange if you can put the money in and keep it in, instead of speculating about ups and downs. Piscator instructs Venator in the art of fishing with a "dead rod," or fishing by leaving your bait in the water overnight.

> And let me tell you, this kind of fishing with a dead rod, and laying night-hooks, are like putting money to Use, for they both work for the Owners, when they do nothing but sleep, or eat, or rejoice; as you know we have done this last hour, and sat quietly and free from cares under this Sycamore.

Tony Bridgett, simple man, and I, continued along the stream until we got to a small bridge over the River Dove, at which point we turned around and headed back to where we had parked our cars. Bridgett explained to me that most of the fishable water on the Rivers Dove and Wye were the property of the Dukes of Rutland and Devonshire, on which there were two large estates: one called

Haddon Hall, a castle-like mound of rocks on the Wye, and the other called Chatsworth House. "Feudalism still very much has a presence in Derbyshire," Tony said.

Feudalism was basically an economical and political contractual relationship, between the lord who owned the land and the vassal who exchanged military service for use of the land. The Duke's legacy is several hundred years old and, according to the people of the peak and Derbyshire, many things still revolve around him. His own private water is fished by no one else, and several keepers work full time to manage the streams that he casts a fly into maybe only twice in one year—if that. The Duke leases some of the land to fishing clubs, allowing individuals who are less than deities to fish for trout. Angling was, in the seventeenth century, primarily a pleasure of princely types. As Cotton says, "anyone who can afford to angle for pleasure has somebody to land the fish for them." Walton elicits no such pretensions, most likely because of his humble background.

I followed Bridgett in his car through the narrow roads that scratch the endless Dovedale farms, to Beresford where Charles Cotton lived on the Dove. When we arrived in Beresford, Tony began to tell me about Cotton, the "adopted son" of Izaak Walton.

"Cotton was born into a low-income family and his father was a drunk, but he was part of a class of people who made it through life by charming others, by writing poetry and reading and such. Cotton married into the wealthy and old Beresford family of Beresford Hall, which is now in ruins by the River Dove, just up over the hill, in fact. But the family, by Cotton's generation, was land rich and money poor, and he was plagued by creditors most of his life. There is a cave not far from here where Cotton used to go to hide from his creditors." He pointed to our left to indicate where the ruins were, the Dove on our right. We carried no fishing rods because Bridgett had no rights to this water.

"Can we go see the ruins of Beresford Hall?" I asked.

"There's not a lot left to see," said Bridgett. "Usually when a house is abandoned and falls into ruin and disrepair, locals come and take stones and statues away to use for walls, or to make their own homes. Many of the homes in the Beresford area probably have stones from the ruins laid into their walls. I know the people who own the property, but it is a popular site and they don't appreciate a lot of visitors. I would have had to give them more advanced notice that we were coming."

"That's O.K." I said, and he resumed his discourse as if he were lecturing to a room full of people.

"Now the word *Beresford* is thought to have been derived from bear or berry, both of which were found with greater frequency in these parts during Cotton's time. Cotton became friends with Walton, both being Anglican, and in the fifth edition which came out in 1676, Cotton included his piece on fly-fishing." He took a red bandana out of his shirt pocket and wiped his forehead.

As we passed several dark shaded pools, occasionally seeing a trout or grayling splash or rise to take a fly, Bridgett preached a not-entirely-coherent narrative of man's relationship to nature. It was dark between the high walls of rock that engulfed the Dove, and Bridgett was getting somewhat poetic, telling me that when he sits in his office all he need do is close his eyes and he's on the banks of the Dove again. The smells of spring were diverting my attentions.

What was it like for Walton, fishing here in his eightieth year, casting and dappling a fly or bait in this dark hollow on a small stream by the base of a cliff? This was a treasured nook and somewhat fearful, and the closest I've come to wishing I could see a dead man walk. Did Walton actually believe he was going to heaven? I'm disappointed if he did, or maybe I'm disappointed because I don't. I thought about what it would be like to be in a war, and then picked up on Bridgett's discourse again. He was talking about "chain reactions" in the environment, that fertilizing fields had promoted weed growth, beyond healthy amounts in the stream and that the weeds use up oxygen in the water and there is less oxygen left for trout. He told me that when he was a kid things seemed more pristine, but I could not have imagined a better-managed trout stream anywhere than this gentle Dove.

We enjoy fishing in part perhaps because it gives us a perspective on the order of our existence. The angler pursues the trout and the trout pursues and kills other smaller organisms, as insects and other fish. Both Walton and Cotton understood this order. Cotton expounds in his poem "To my dear and most worthy Friend, Mr. Isaac Walton."

> *There whilst some bush we wait*
> *The Scaly people to betray,*
> *We'll prove it just with treach'rous Bait*
> *To make the preying Trout our prey.*

The next site Bridgett pointed out to me was a series of stepping stones across the river that he said "Walton and Cotton may have laid to cross the stream on." He also pointed to a path that he said Cotton and his family would travel on, on their way to Sunday services at St. Peter's Church in Alstonefield.

Just a couple hundred yards upstream the forest opened up, the dark cliffs ahead began to subside a bit, and there was revealed a pool.

"It's pike pool!" I said. It was absolutely amazing, it looked just like the etchings I'd seen in the old editions of *The Compleat Angler*, etchings from the eighteenth century of this very same pool. There is a large monolithic rock that juts out from the stream bottom in the middle of the pool. The pool was called pike pool because this long skinny rock was said to resemble a pike jumping out of the water. Seeing pike pool made the text of *The Compleat Angler* very real. Cotton mentions it in his piece on fly-fishing and describes it in detail. I felt somewhat like I do when I see a constellation in the sky and recognize what it is, using the same imaginative powers that those ancient people used when they named them.

We turned from the pool to a hill behind us, and Bridgett pointed to stones overgrown with vines that made a cryptic staircase. "Beresford Hall is just up there. Cotton probably used these steps to come down to pike pool to fish. There is a scene in the *Angler* where they are called to dinner and Cotton asks his friend if he would like to take the long way or the short way home, and his friend chooses the long way, so they go to it, and these steps are probably the ones they took." Bridgett went on to tell me that the Beresford family, into which Cotton had married, was an old one that fought in the Battle of

Agincourt in October of 1415 with arrows, and that the bows for the arrows were made from ancient yew trees like the ones on the hill. Not these exact yews, presumably.

"Cotton may have planted these yews because yews are ancient trees. You see, besides being a poet and writer on angling with a fly, Cotton wrote a book on the planting and cultivation of orchards: *The Planter's Manual* of 1675." I sensed this consistent element of continuity in his voice, that he treasured the old pieces of history that were still left and drew on them as aids in his narrative to connect the past world of Walton's and Cotton's to ours. "Knowing the English, they will demolish all these features soon," he said. "That's why I've taken it upon myself to photograph them for posterity." It is evident from Cotton's poetry that he too had a unique and profound love for this Dovedale country and the Peak, the now national park which surrounds it. In his poem "Wonders of the Peak," Cotton describes the River Dove and its valley and certain recognizable landmarks such as a giant cave where an outlaw named Poole was supposed to have lived in hiding. This is one of the many places that Bridgett showed me on this day. Cotton also describes the beauty of Chatsworth, seat of the Duke of Devonshire, which still stands. He expresses a general disgust for the political climate of the times in the first stanza and contrasts it to the peaceful "nook" in which his fabled river lies.

> *'Twixt these twin-Provinces of Britain's shame,*
> *The Silver Dove (how pleasant is that name)*
> *Runs through a Vale high crested Cliffs o'ershade;*

By her fair progress only pleasant made.
In this so craggy, ill-contrived a Nook
Of this our little world, this pretty Brook
Alas! is all the recompense I share
For all th'intemperances of the Air.

I followed Bridgett across a small bridge just upstream from pike pool. He stopped and stood at the crest of a little hill with his chest out as if he were about to stake claim on a great discovery. "And there my friend is Cotton's fishing temple," he pronounced. But all I could see of it was a small piece of roof through a mass of late spring foliage. "I wish I could take you over to see it, but I'm afraid it's on private property and the owners try to have as few visitors as possible, as they don't want many people to know where it is. In the winter it is a good deal more visible." Oh great, I thought, disappointed in Tony's lack of spirit, I'll come back in winter just so I can see it through a bunch of leafless trees. This is just the kind of display of indifference that he had criticized in the English people, but then again he was one, and I was an American. Bridgett of all people should have understood that I'd come across an ocean to see this thing and I was not going to leave until I touched it. He could feel my disappointment, but said only, "That is the best I can do for you because the house is on private land. You could walk to the stream and see it from the back there," he pointed, "but there are a good deal of bushes. I could mail you a photo of it." I looked down the hill from the footpath—not wearing waders, I had only my shorts on—and the ground was solid with a grove of stinging nettles, their little prickly stems just waiting for me to brush against them so they could watch my skin immediately pock up with little itchy bumps. This descent to the fishing temple was suddenly a hazardous and now much more exciting, appealing, and adventurous affair. Bridgett looked at the shorts I was wearing and, sensing I was determined to take the most direct route, suggested, "You might like to return to your car and put on long pants."

He told me that one of the greatest moments of his life was being invited to see the fishing house and to go inside and have a picnic lunch there. "It was the culmination of everything," he said. He also said he'd managed to get a friend and famous English fishing writer named Bernard Venables a day of fishing on this piece of the Dove. "Venables," recalled Bridgett, "fished here at this turn in the Dove and caught a trout in its shadow. Venables said to me, 'that is one fish I will never forget.'"

I felt that Bridgett and I had shared something unique this day—a mixture of a mutual love of Walton and Cotton and the green land we all have tread—and I felt that he did too.

"I encourage you to call me for Jonquil Bevan's number and that you contact her and visit her in Edinburgh before the end of your trip. You will be coming north from Hampshire if I heard you correctly, and I would be pleased if you will accept the hospitality of my wife and myself at our home for two or three nights on your way to see her. I also recommend you call Bernard

Venables, England's oldest and most venerable writer on angling. I will contact him and tell him he should expect to hear from you." I told Bridgett that was one of the kindest offers I'd ever heard and that if I encountered no hindrances I would be pleased to accept. We shook hands and parted ways.

I drove off back to Alstonefield and Ashbourne and there in town had a dinner of fish and chips served on a day-old newspaper. I could only hope the fish was that fresh. As popular as fish and chips might be, they did not really exhibit the essence of what I admired about England.

It had been a glorious day, much like the ideal fishing day in May that Cotton describes in a poem dedicated to "my dear and most worthy Friend, Izaak Walton."

> *A day without too bright a beam,*
> *A warm, but not a scorching sun,*
> *A Southern gale to curl the stream,*
> *And Master half our work is done.*

I sat on a table outside in the late evening sun thinking about the day, stacking vinegar and red sauce (ketchup), on to my chips (French fries) and fried haddock (a northern Atlantic fish related to cod, also called scrod), pondering this, England's equivalent to American fast food, while trying to decide whether I should return to Beresford to trespass in order to touch Walton and Cotton's fishing temple. Thinking I did not want to be earmarked an "apathetic American," I decided to do it. I think in Bridgett's subtle English way, he had suggested I trespass; at least, that's the way I justified it.

Really though, there was no doubt as to whether I would do it; it was more that I feared what I might get from it, or rather, what I might *not* get from it. Sometimes when the sun comes low in the sky and you are in a foreign country alone with no immediate connection to anyone who knows you or what your purpose for travel is, you just begin to doubt everything, or you think, "what the *hell* am I *doing*?" and the fish and chips are settling sufficiently heavy in your gut.

I stared out into the street from my small greasy table, pondering the desertedness of the narrow stone streets of Ashbourne in this seemingly depressed quarter of town. I began to think of the irony behind the fish I'd just eaten, advertised as *haddock*. The traditional fish of "fish and chip" fame is the cod. This fish, the cod, of England's most notably English dish, was distinctly American to my thinking. It was the abundant cod fisheries off Georges Bank that built the "codfish aristocracy" and the Boston we know today. But cod was traded with Europe and the Caribbean at a time when British trade acts had mandated that America should not be involved in overseas commerce with anyone but the mother country. England's attempted crackdown eventually led to America's independence, the beginning in a long series of losses incurred by the massive British empire that had been controlled remarkably from a tiny island in a cold ocean.

So, methinks, revved up with American nationalism, having just consumed white flakes from the large-mouthed, bottom-dwelling fish that caused England's debacle, I'll do it my way. I took my Volkswagen rental to full throttle through the meadows of the afternoon. I parked by the Dove where Tony and I had before, with that peculiar feeling I get when I return to a place that I thought I might never see again. But somehow, as I put on my waders, it was different this time. I forded the trail along the Dove through an opening in an old wooden fence.

As an angler, entering these sacred grounds where sport fishing as a recreation had its popular genesis and resurrection, I felt as those on pilgrimages must when they enter the old city of Jerusalem through the Jaffa Gate and walk the stone alleys through the Christian Quarter to the Holy Sepulchre— through the Arab Markets hung with rugs and sheep heads to the Dome of the Rock or through the Jewish Quarter to the Wailing Wall. This is the spiritual mecca for anglers, and to walk it alone in a communication with the self and imagination makes it that much more profound.

That sheltered nook, that hollow and cliff-sided glen through which I walked, was much darker than it had been several hours ago. Now that the sun was no longer overhead, the cliffs made long shadows that swallowed up the headwaters of the dim and almost imperceptibly gurgling Dove. The atmosphere on the path, as I walked in my waders, camera around my neck, without a rod, was consummately gothic, and the rays of light shone through parapets on the cliff walls like lights through cathedral windows. Here by pike pool I could hear the lines I'd read from Charles Cotton's piece as spoken by the haunting ghosts of foregone fishermen. Cotton's two characters are a traveler (Viator) and the fisherman (Piscator).

> Viat. "But what have we got here? a rock springing up in the middle
> of the river! this is one of the oddest sights that ever I saw."

Pisc. Why, sir, from that pike that you see standing up there distant from the rock, this is called Pike Pool.

So it was, the moss-covered monolith, soberly echoing my silent presence there. I moved on up the path and crossed the Dove on a small footbridge. I passed the yews that Cotton may have planted and the stairs up the hill he used to take back to Beresford Hall.

Coming to the rise and turn on my narrow way, where the top of the fishing temple's roof was barely visible through the trees, I stepped over the wire fence that marked the public path and stomped down a hill of high nettles. The nettles came nearly to my shoulders, with great leaves and stalks covered with stinging needles. My bare arms took pain and I shrugged it off as part of this rite. The bitter, itching bumps honored proof of my faith. Through bushes and brambles I made it to the bank of the Dove and lowered myself into its waters. It was a slow and deep pool, the water up to my chest, that led to the fishing temple which sat on a small peninsula. I pushed a small wake that blurred the temple's reflection. Its entrance, enchantingly small, appeared through a tight weave of branches. I crossed the Dove, and on hands and knees, well worn from my poaching days, I crawled into a clearing onto a soft and manicured green lawn. There it was, the shrine to all fishermen, and the object of my pilgrimage. To its stone facade I clambered, and touched it, and through its small glass panes I saw the round marble table where Piscator taught Viator to tie a fly, holding the hook in his hand for a vise. Over the door I saw the words carved in stone *Piscatoribus Sacrum*, and the initials of Charles Cotton and Izaak Walton "twisted in cipher." I sat at the edge of the clearing and watched the door to see if it might open.

Pisc. But look you, sir, now you are at the brink of the hill, how do you like my river, the vale it winds through like a snake, and the situation of my little fishing-house?

Viat. Trust me, 'tis very fine, and the house seems at this distance a neat building.

Pisc. And now, sir, you are come to the door, pray walk in, and there we will sit and talk as long as you please.

Viat. Stay, what's here over the door? Piscatoribus Sacrum. Why then, I perceive I have some title here; for I am one of them, though one of the worst; and here below it is the cipher too you speak of, and 'tis prettily contrived. Has my master Walton ever been here to see it, for it seems new built?

Pisc. Yes, he saw it cut in the stone before it was set up; but never in the posture it now stands; for the house was but building when he was last here, and not raised so high as the arch of the door. And I am afraid he will not see it yet; for he has lately writ me word, he doubts his coming down this summer; which, I do assure you, was the worst news he could possibly have sent me.

Viat. I am most pleased with this little house of any thing I ever saw: it stands in a kind of peninsula too, with a delicate clear river about it. I dare hardly go in, lest I should not like it so well within as without; but, by your leave I'll try.

Within the walls of the fishing house, sitting at the round marble table in the manner of the most pleasant days at Camelot, Cotton gives instruction on fly-fishing to the traveler.

Fly-fishing, that is, the art of fishing with an artificial fly, was nothing new in 1676—it had its origin several centuries before in Macedonia. Claudius Aelianus, a Roman who wrote the Natural History *De Natura Animalium* in the second century describes the Macedonian way of fishing on the Aliakmon River near modern day Thesoloniki, Greece. Their method was to tie red wool and two blue-gray feathers from a cock's wattles about a hook and use this fabrication to catch black-spotted fish: trout. Centuries later, Dame Juliana Berners described how to tie twelve different flies in her *Treatise of Fishing with an Angle* of 1496. The twelve flies of Dame Juliana are copied in Walton's *Compleat Angler*. But Cotton ultimately deserves credit for the first modern directions on how to tie artificial flies and fish with them. His instructions are as relevant and useful today as they were when he wrote them hastily in March of 1676. His ingredients to tie flies are charmingly obscure and often sound like the ingredients of a witches brew: "the down of a hog's bristles, the hair of an abortive calf, the whisks of the hairs of the beard of a black cat, the dubbing of a black spaniel's fur." Mixed in with these recipes are wonderful descriptions of the gentle appearances of the diaphanous winged mayflies that come off the water in May and June. "May is the month that affords more pleasure to the fly angler than all the rest," says Cotton. Walton agreed with this sentiment, for in *The Compleat Angler* he quotes Henry Wotton, saying that he would rather live one May than twenty Decembers. Cotton explains how the green-drake mayfly, perhaps the largest and most beautiful of the mayflies, got its name. "His tail turns up towards his back like a mallard; from whence, questionless he has his name of green-drake." Cotton adds, "The stone-fly and green drake are the matadors for trout and grayling, and in their season kill more fish in our Derbyshire rivers than the rest, past and to come, in the whole year besides." They did not only use imitations of the flies, on occasion they used the flies themselves. Cotton gives instruction on how to impale two live mayflies on a hook and dapple them on the stream's surface for trout. But Cotton prefers to catch trout on artificial flies, especially ones that he has made himself. He says to his new friend Viator, "a trout taken with a fly of your own making will please you better than twenty with one of mine." It is appropriate to mention here that in America, *mayfly* is the generic term for insects of the order Ephemeroptera, family Ephemeridae. In England "mayfly" is what they call the largest of the ephemerella species. It was called the mayfly because it hatched from its nymphal stage during that month; now the mayfly hatches most profusely in Derbyshire during the first week of June, due, as we now know, to the calendar change.

There are of course differences in the way we fish today. In Walton and Cotton's time they used rods of fir wood that were a minimum of fifteen feet long, and no reels. To the tip of the rod was tied a tapering length of braided horsehair for line. Flies were not cast in the sense they are today, but "dapped," or "dappled," just laid on top and sometimes skittered on the surface.

I stood from the spot of grass where I had been sitting, and carried pipe smells from Cotton's pipe and the sounds and sights of the Dove all the way to my bed and breakfast in Alkmonton. I tied flies through the last moments of twilight in the lady's garden, and contemplated clipping beard whiskers from the lady's black house cat to wind into my creation. When it was dark, I climbed up the stairs and lay my head on the pillow with the distant sounds of bleating lambs.

St. Peter's Church, Alstonefield

5

Holy to Fishermen

The Derbyshire countryside and her streams had personified the images conjured from my readings of *The Compleat Angler*, but the river of Walton's book is not the Wye or Dove, it is the Lea, which enters the Thames in East London. I considered a trip to London to see the Lea, now wrapped in the boom of post-WWII sprawl, an essential ripple in the wake of Walton, and I was headed there via Oxford to trace the steps of Piscator and Venator.

It was with satisfaction and contentedness that I left my dairy house in Alkmonton, the morning sun glowing red on the rich Derbyshire brick of the barn. I had planned a brief visit to Oxford to stay several days with Michael Suarez, a Jesuit priest and friend of Steve Parks who lived at Campion Hall, and navigated the motorway maze a good part of the day to the city center.

I parked my rental on High Street two hours before I was to meet Michael and searched around for Campion Hall. I went into a secondhand bookshop and picked up a free pamphlet of all the antiquarian booksellers in town. The locations of the booksellers were marked on a good general map of the city. Having found Campion Hall on a narrow side street off St. Aldates called Brewer Street, just down from Christ Church, I started to walk toward what I figured was the center of "campus," down the High Street.

The general layout of the university was similar to what I'd experienced at Yale, as if to say that Oxford was a copy of Yale. This is certainly not the case, Oxford came way before and Yale modeled its "college system" after Oxford. The school is divided into what they call colleges, residential areas for students, poised as fortresses about small manicured courtyard lawns. As I walked by the entrances to these colleges, University, Magdalene (pronounced Maudlin) and some of the more famous ones I'd heard of, I noticed they were charging admission to get inside. One pound to see a college courtyard? The students, of course, as I'd come to notice, did not pay, and unless you exuded tourist juices it was no problem to walk in gratis. I had no trouble infiltrating several, looking very much like the student I was; worn shoes and a backpack. The lawns inside of the colleges were exceptionally well kept; trimmed as tight as golf greens. The English students generally looked like American students and exhibited no pretensions in dress or manner that I could see. Toward six o'clock a few couples here and there were obviously heading off to dinner somewhere nice, wearing tweed blazers and patterned summer dresses, walking arm in arm. It was a pleasant day in May.

I walked in and out of several bookshops, looking mostly for fishing books. A few antiquarian booksellers had handsome editions of *The Compleat Angler*. At Blackwell's I purchased a small anthology of various English fishing writers—fifteenth century to the present—and stowed it in my backpack. I also found a copy of the Jonquil Bevan book entitled *Izaak Walton's* The Compleat Angler: *The Art of Recreation* that the man at the museum and cottage trust had suggested I read. It was not simply an annotated copy of *The Compleat Angler,* as was the one I had purchased at the museum, but a book of criticism and unlike any I had previously heard of or seen. At a glance it proved very enlightening and thorough. I was very excited to have it.

I stopped in an art store and bought some tubes of watercolor paints in pigments I was running low on. I passed by the Oxford Botanic Garden opposite Magdalene. They call it simply "the botanic," and it was overflowing with variously colored roses.

To quell the rumblings in my stomach, I bought a sandwich and lemonade at a little food store, walked into Christ Church College, and sat down near a fountain of Mercury, watching the afternoon light glow on the sandstone walls. When I'd finished eating I pulled out the copy of Bevan's book I'd just purchased and began to read it. The title page described her as "senior lecturer at the Department of English Literature at Edinburgh University, Scotland." Early on in the book I learned that *The Complete Angler*, more popularly *The Compleat Angler,* was spelled two different ways in the first edition of 1653, as it seems the two were interchangeable.

What came as a welcome surprise to me—that is, what the first chapter revealed—was that Izaak Walton had several ties to the very Oxford College in which I sat: Christ Church. Eminent clergyman George Morley, later Bishop of Worcester and then Winchester, whom Walton became friends with in the 1630s and with whom he shared his final years, was once Dean of Christ Church. Morley, M.A. Christ Church 1621, was four years Walton's junior. In 1668 Izaak Walton's son, who shared his father's name (though distinguished by a *c*, in place of *k* and an *s,* in place of a *z*: Isaac) became a student at Christ Church, likely as a consequence of his father's connections there. Bevan noted that Isaac's tutor at Christ Church "was Richard Allestree, who had acted throughout the interregnum as a Royalist agent until his imprisonment in Lambeth Palace in 1660; Izaak Walton presented to him several of the different editions of his *Lives*, and these are still at Christ Church."

As it turned out, just around the corner from where I was sitting, in the library of Christ Church were several volumes signed in Walton's own hand. "I must make plans to see them tomorrow," I thought. I closed my book, and as it was 7:30 on the clock tower of the college, and time for me to go meet Michael Suarez, I walked to the great doors of Campion Hall and rang the bell.

I could not decide if I enjoyed or was shocked by the American accent with which Michael greeted me at the big door on Brewer Street, cut in a drab marvel of masonry. He was entirely pleasant, from New England, athletic and of priestly posture, and led me silently, wrapped in his black collar, through dark halls and the center courtyard and garden.

Michael came with me to get my car, which had been parked on the High and we moved it to a small space beside Campion Hall behind a locked gate.

On our walk to the car, Michael told me a bit about Oxford. All students apparently have a "tutor" who works with them intimately in their studies. I told Michael that I had just been up in Derbyshire tracing the steps of Izaak Walton and Charles Cotton for my senior thesis in English Literature.

"Cotton was a great, though neglected poet," said Michael. He studied English Literature, mostly poetry, was a poet himself, and was currently prospecting for a job at an American Jesuit University.

Later in the evening I ate dinner in the refectory at Campion with Michael and a group of other intellectual powerhouse Jesuits who were from different parts of the world. They had set a buffet of cold salads, and it was extremely good. Over dinner I explained to Michael and the other Jesuits sitting with us that I was doing my senior essay on the Anglican/angler and literary great, Izaak Walton. They asked where I had been and where I was going. I prefaced all explanations of my trip by saying that this was a spiritual pilgrimage I was on. With an air of intellectual arrogance, one or two of the Jesuits seemed to have an "isn't that quaint," attitude toward my study of this happy little inconsequential "fishing book," partly because, I felt, they saw Walton as a man who never received a proper education. But as soon as I offered *The Compleat Angler* in its historical context as the Compleat Anglican, one said, "yes, yes, how fascinating. It does not make sense that the author of the *Lives* is the same as the author of the *Angler*, unless you take into account that *angler* may be, at least in part, code for Anglican."

I had a copy of the *Angler* with me and introduced them to some of the language in the book and passages that could be read as allegory, the one following in particular:

Pisc. I shall put on a boldness to ask you Sir, Whether business or pleasure caused you to be so early up, and walk so fast, for this other Gentleman hath declared he is going to see a Hawk, that a friend mews for him.

Ven. Sir mine is a mixture of both, a little business and more pleasure, for I intend this day to do all my business, and then bestow another day or two in hunting the otter, which a friend that I go to meet, tells me, is much pleasanter than any other chase whatsoever; howsoever I mean to try it; for tomorrow morning we shall meet a pack of Otter dogs of noble Mr. Sadler's upon Amwell hill, who will be there so early, that they intend to prevent the Sun-rising.

Pisc. Sir, my fortune has answered my desires, and my purpose is to bestow a day or two in helping to destroy some of those villainous vermin, for I hate them perfectly, because they love fish so well, or rather, because they destroy so much; indeed so much, that in my judgment all men that keep Otter-dogs ought to have pensions from the King to encourage them to destroy the very breed of those base Otters, they do so much mischief.

Ven. But what say you to the Foxes of the Nation, would not you as willingly have them destroyed? for doubtless they do as much mischief as Otters do.

Pisc. Oh Sir, if they do, it is not so much to me and my fraternity as those base Vermin the Otters do.

Auceps. Why Sir, I pray, of what Fraternity are you, that you are so angry with the poor Otters?

Pisc. I am Sir, a brother of the Angle, and therefore an enemy to the Otter: for you are to note, that we Anglers all love one another, and therefore do I hate the Otter both for my own and for their sakes who are of my brotherhood.

"Yes," said a round Jesuit from Pennsylvania, "I see, that is untypically strong language for Walton. And why should he hate otters so strongly? I see, yes, the otter could be viewed as code for an individual of the time with an amphibious nature, unsure of their allegiances to the King and changing from camp to camp." He was right; such people, particularly Puritans who had broken the sacred oath of duty to the sovereign, would have been scorned by Walton. Walton revises his phrasing in the line "I hate them perfectly, because they love fish so well, or rather, because they destroy so much." It is because they *destroy so much*," that he ultimately hates them—destroy perhaps the stability of the nation. "Very interesting," the Jesuit continued, "you know 'hunting the Romish Fox' or simply 'hunting foxes' was used from the Reformation onward as a term for hounding out the papists, suppressing or hunting out the Roman Catholic influence." The Puritans were big on Catholic and pope bashing, but the Anglicans, like Walton, did not so much mind the Catholics as long as they kept their noses clean. This is in keeping with what Walton said in response to Venator's comment that the Foxes do as much mischief as Otters; "if they do, it is not so much to me and my fraternity as those base Vermin the Otter do." Walton's "fraternity," what he called the "brotherhood of the angle," was a real-life circle of dispossessed Anglican clergymen, those who had lost their jobs and were disenchanted with the state of their England.

"It can be dangerous to read *The Compleat Angler* as allegory," another said, "but at the very least one should accept that Walton lived through some extreme times and that what he'd experienced couldn't help but seep into his writings, even a book about fishing."

After dinner, Michael showed me to my basement room, which he has the privilege of offering to guests, and gave me the mortice key, which turned a large slug of a bolt in the door. "Anytime between now and when my fellowship runs out," he said, "you are welcome to come to Oxford and use this room." In passing, I told Michael about the preface I'd been reading to the edition of *The Compleat Angler* I'd recently acquired, and about the books signed by Walton in the Christ Church College Library. Upon my mentioning the name of the woman who had written the preface, Michael said, "I know Jonquil Bevan; I had lunch with her just last week." It seemed all too appropriate that Michael introduce me to her. He did so through E-mail, expressing to Jonquil that he had a student friend from America who was very keen on Izaak Walton, expressing in addition that I had met Tony Bridgett and that he had suggested I meet her and perhaps had already contacted her for me about my interest in her work. Before we parted for the evening, Michael wrote a letter on Campion Hall letterhead communicating to the librarian of Christ Church that I was a "serious scholar," and that they should let me have a look at Walton's books. He told me he would call the library in the morning after our 8:15 A.M. breakfast.

I moved my bags from my rental car to the basement room. The dimming interior of wood-paneled Campion, with its great oil portraits of stern men, the statue of Mary with child quietly sitting in a dark niche, was eerie and solemn. I settled in my basement room and washed my hands and face. There were two small horizontal windows at the top of one side of the room, but it was now dark outside. It was nice to have a place to stay.

I awakened pleasantly, the sound of boys from the nearby cathedral school playing outside my window. Breakfast was refreshing and filling. The refectory was fairly quiet but for the sounds of spoons clinking on bowls and morning papers crumpling as they were creased and folded or pages were turned. But once the early-middle-aged Jesuits settled in and rubbed the sleep from their eyes, their mouths opened for things other than food; they stretched their jaws in yawn and even spoke. Michael told me a bit about his undergraduate years playing lacrosse at Bucknell and his year rowing for Oxford during the famed Oxford mutiny. When we'd finished breakfast, Michael bid me well; he was off to London for the day.

Being enveloped in observation of this postgraduate academic world had put me in a somber mood. I had always admired and looked up to academics and considered myself somewhat of an isolationist, holding at least this one property as essential to becoming one. But this world seemed so deeply solitary, and I could not help but be lonely. Perhaps they had some greater faith than I did, and that brought them joy. My only consolation for the loneliness I sometimes experience through the isolation necessary for study is that I feel as though I sometimes am in communication and even friendship with the author I am reading. I am never alone when I read Walton. And when I write, which is a solitary endeavor, I am comforted in knowing that I may make a friend with anyone who reads what I have put down.

As is normally the case, at my stepping out the doors of Campion Hall into the sun this solemnity fled my dark interior and my spirits were renewed. The new day has this power.

It was now near nine and I walked toward the Botanic Garden so I could enter when they opened. The fragrances of the flowers that preface the garden gates were abated by the morning chill, but I knew that they would be invited by warmer airs to permeate and travel, and probably even reach the Jesuits at Campion, hunched over little desks in study. I strolled among the roses until quarter after nine and then paid the admission and entered the garden. The garden is on the River Cherwell. The punt boats were lined up and tied to the bank and there was little activity on the river. As far as I could see, I was the only one in the garden. I saw great glass greenhouses and through their windows palms, and because I have always loved greenhouses I went in. When I entered greenhouses as a kid, walking among the greenery that overflowed those places, I occasionally took small clippings and stowed them in my pockets. At home I potted the clippings or put them in water until they grew roots. These clipping urges surfaced here in the botanic's greenhouses but I suppressed them. One greenhouse replicating a desert environment was filled with cacti, and I remembered someone telling me once while on a trip to Baja, Mexico that "only an Englishman could love the desert." The other greenhouse was lush and was filled with plants, each labeled with its native location, all from lost colonies of a collapsed British empire. Great dwarf palms grew there too, spreading their fronds frustratedly in far, unflinching corners of their confines. When I began to feel my space being compromised by walls and ceiling and had my fill of humid, soil-smelling, mossy air, I struck out onto the walkways that led one through the garden. I perused the grounds in admiration of the English and their ability to construct such well-tempered plant architecture. I've always struggled to determine which I prefer, these cultivated corners or the sportive wood run wild.

By about midmorning I'd had my fill of the garden, and headed back down the High to Campion Hall feeling particularly well primed for a nap. I let myself in through the doors of Campion and walked around the ground floor trying to remember which door led into the basement. Finally I discovered an old portly Jesuit with white hair and black priestly garb, his hands folded on his belly, snugly set in a big armchair facing a courtyard window. "Do you know which door leads to the basement rooms?" I asked. He looked up at me, taking one last breath of air coming in by breeze through a door to the courtyard and said pointing; "Go down the hall to the bottom of the great stairs.

Turn right at the statue of St. Ignatius and there you will find the door that leads to the bowels of the earth."

It was a lovely nap and at noon I walked to the refectory to eat with the Jesuits. I never saw more than twenty of them, though the dining hall could easily seat a hundred.

After lunch I walked back down the High to what they call Radcliffe Camera, a big round building, and sat on the steps there reading through *The Compleat Angler* and Jonquil's introduction.

At around two in the afternoon I walked over to Christ Church Library and presented my letter from Michael to the librarian. I was very pleasantly received there and was told to sit in a side room, that the books would be delivered to me. I had brought a pencil, as I know that librarians usually don't like you using indelible ink near high-value antiquarian books. After about ten minutes the same man came over and planted the books before me. They were each dedicated to Richard Allestree, who was Isaac Walton Jr.'s tutor at Christ Church. They each had Allestree's bookplate in them, "Regius Professor of Divinity," and the date January 18, 1680. They were small, leatherbound editions of Walton's collected biographies of John Donne, Sir Henry Wotton, Richard Hooker, and George Herbert.

From what I could read of Walton's aging hand, the brief dedication read "Hon Dr. Alestry, Iz: Wa." The four initials Iz: Wa was Walton's most frequent method of signing his name. The librarian told me that the several corrections made in the text were also in Walton's hand. I reread the introduction, Walton's apology for having written the *Lives*.

To the Reader

Though, the several Introductions to these several lives, have partly declared the reasons how, and why I undertook them: Yet, since they are come to be reviewed and, augmented, and reprinted: and, the four are become one book; I desire leave to inform you that shall become my reader, that when I look back upon my mean abilities, 'tis not without some little wonder at my self, that I am come to be publicly in print. And, though I have in those introductions declared some of the accidental reasons yet, let me add this to what is there said: that, by my undertaking to collect some notes for Sir Henry Wotton's writing the life of Doctor Donne, and Sir Henry's dying before he performed it, I became like those that enter easily into a law suit, or a quarrel, and having begun, cannot make a fair retreat and be quiet, when they desire it. And really, after such a manner, I became engaged, into a necessity of writing the life of Doctor Donne: contrary to my first intentions. And that begot a like necessity of writing the life of his and my honoured friend, Sir Henry Wotton.

These lines are important because they describe how Walton came to be published, but they also tell us something about the man himself. Such an apology seems as though it were crafted to draw praise or at least cushion failure, and I have a difficult time believing Walton was entirely genuine. If he weren't proud of what he'd done he would not have given out signed copies. Secretly, I think he was astounded by what he'd accomplished, and persistent apology makes the story of Walton's career that much more exemplary in the history of innovation in biography. I can identify with Walton's methods here. I have viewed much of my own life in the manner of this introduction, ever since my mom told me a story concerning my birth.

I am the second of two children in my family, my sister being six years older than I. But I'm really the third, or the third attempt, because my mother miscarried the first. If the first had been born healthy, then my parents would have stopped at two after my sister, and I wouldn't be around. So, really, I shouldn't be here in these hallowed halls of Christ Church College Library, but here I am looking out the somewhat lumpy and distortive glass of the windowpanes, into a honey-colored sandstone courtyard. I have always considered myself a "bonus child," and that consideration has made everything easier to handle somehow. It is that "I might never have even done this or been here in the first place" attitude that make disappointments more palatable. The same attitude excused Walton of failure, had what he'd written been only mildly accepted.

However he interpreted his own career, by the year 1680 in which he'd given these three volumes to Richard Allestree, Walton had enjoyed considerable success as a writer. By his eightieth year, all of his books had been printed several times—*The Compleat Angler* five, and his *Life of Herbert* more than ten. To the surprise of some anglers, he was celebrated during his lifetime more for his work as a biographer than as the author of his wonderful little book on life and fishing.

The two other books he presented to Allestree were separate volumes of his *Life of Sanderson* and his *Life of Richard Hooker*.

Filled with images of an aged Walton walking through the Christ Church courtyard, I put down the last of three slim and comfortable volumes and left the dim library.

I sat in Christ Church for a while, just sat and rubbed my hands together; then used them to support myself as I leaned back to look up toward the sky. A half hour later I walked out of Christ Church onto the main street through Oxford, St. Aldates. I found that everything closes at 5 P.M. so there was no chance of my getting a soda somewhere on my way back to Campion Hall.

I let myself in the front door and to my basement room. The boys whom I'd seen playing in the morning were now playing while they waited for their parents to pick them up. They had small cricket bats and tennis balls and wore blue blazers over white shirts; blue shorts and blue socks pulled up to the knee and white sneakers.

I napped until dinner at 7:30, when Michael and I had agreed to meet. Michael told me about his day and I shared mine. He had received word from Jonquil by E-mail and brought a print out for me to see.

Dear Michael

Your *Compleat Angler* student: do tell him to write to me directly if there is anything specific I can do. I'm going to Toronto 8 July – 19 August to work on Walton's *Lives*, but I'll be here until then. Winchester Cathedral is having a 'Walton Day' on 5 October, which he may like to know about. (Write to Canon Keith Walker.) He may also like to know that Walton left half of his books to his son, half to his daughter and her husband: the former moiety is in Salisbury Cathedral Library. The Salisbury Cathedral Librarian and Archivist, Miss Suzanne Eward, will probably be at the Winchester meeting. Tony Bridgett is excellently well-informed.

Jonquil.

This bit about the Salisbury Cathedral Library collection seemed like an excellent opportunity, and Michael drafted a letter of reference for me to possibly see if I might go there to see the books.

Dinner was mackerel, which I find to be a detestable eating fish.

The next morning at breakfast I read the Jesuits at my table the following passage from Cotton's addendum to *The Compleat Angler* in which he introduces us to the fishing house, and then asked them what their translation of *Piscatoribus Sacrum* would be.

> Viat. Stay, what's here over the door? Piscatoribus Sacrum. Why then, I perceive I have some title here; for I am one of them, though one of the worst.

I told them that I considered angling as my religion and this little fishing house on the River Dove as that place "sacred to fishermen."

"A man I met up north went so far as to call it the 'fishing temple,'" I explained.

Joe Munitis, Master of Campion Hall, and another American seated across from him came up with the following suggestions:

Holy to Fishermen

sacred for those who fish
for anglers only
dedicated to Anglers
holy to fishermen
sacred for fishermen

It seems as though, from the text, that Cotton had meant it to mean "dedicated to anglers." But *sacrum* for me held an intrinsically holy connotation, and we know where my bias lives.

Grayling taking a fly

6

Good Company Makes
the Way Seem Short

ith a warm cup of tea from the Campion refectory, riding
south out of Oxford along the English Motorway toward London, with
Winchester and the south of England on the journey's horizon, it seems an
appropriate time to give an account of Walton's life from the publication of
The Compleat Angler in 1653 when he was sixty to his death in 1683. Most of
those thirty years were divided between his friend Bishop Morley's residence
near Winchester and his daughter Anne's in Droxford fourteen miles south.
Both towns had very important features for an aging angler with a lion's share
of leisure: trout streams, in particular chalk streams, so named because they
emerge as springs from beds of chalk, or limestone. The River Itchen flows
through the town of Winchester and the River Meon through Droxford, both
of which are spring fed and crystal clear, with many trout. Says Walton:

And you know that Hampshire exceeds all England for swift,
shallow, clear, pleasant brooks, and store of Trouts.

As I would come to find out, Walton's descriptions still hold true, though
today these chalk streams are less full of wild trout and more often stocked.
Places like the lower stretches of the Test and Itchen, in the words of English
novelist David Profumo, are the kind of "chalkstream fly-factories where duns
drift down on a conveyer belt, and the water is as clear and cold as a
Stolichnaya Martini, and just as expensive."

In May of 1653, a small *octavo* (a book composed of printer's sheets folded
into eight leaves) volume was published by Richard Marriott of Fleet Street
London, the same publisher and friend of Walton's who had printed his *Life of
John Donne*, 1640, and *Life of Henry Wotton*, 1651. This first edition of *The
Compleat Angler* was not much larger than three inches wide and four long,
bound in full brown calf with six copperplate engravings of fish, a total of 246
pages. It sold for eighteen pence.

From what Walton told us, though he was notoriously unreliable with dates,
he began fishing at the late age of thirty-nine. We know this from a letter he
wrote in 1663 to fellow angler and author Robert Venables: "I have been for
thirty years past," Walton says, "not only a lover but a practicer of that innocent recreation of angling."

Perhaps the most significant political event during these thirty years of
Walton's life was the restoration of the English monarchy and, with it,
Walton's Church of England. The coronation of Charles II, symbolically
marking the Restoration, meant that Walton no longer had to practice his reli-

gion in secret. It is curious and revealing to parallel Walton's career as a writer to the political events of the period. By publishing the second of his biographies, the *Life of Henry Wotton,* in 1651 in the midst of turmoil, Walton put himself somewhat at risk of persecution because, says Bevan, he "insists on the friendship between Wotton and Donne and presents Wotton, Provost of Eton at the end of his life, as a promoter of implicitly Anglican teaching." Not until the Restoration, with the publication of the *Life of Hooker* in 1665, did Walton dare another biography. Later in the 1650s, when Anglican clergy were being fined, ejected from their livings, and even imprisoned, he turned to angling for his subject, but with a political bent; *The Compleat Angler,* as we have discussed, even if mildly, is code for the Compleat *Anglican.* Walton refers to fishermen in his book as "brothers of the angle," peace-loving men who "study to be quiet" (I Thessalonians, 4:11). The principles held by the "brothers of the angle" concern noncontroversial and nonconfrontational attitudes, and Walton infers that the same qualities that make a good Anglican also make a good angler, and vice versa I suppose. Walton wrote his last three biographies after the Restoration in 1660. We could perhaps conclude, though it would be trite and unnecessary to do so, that if there had never been a civil war in England we would have no *Compleat Angler*—trite, because we could say the same thing about any book with respect to its times, as no books come out of vacuums. I say it only to emphasize that very few readers of Walton have considered him in the context of his times, and though it is not essential to understand these times in order to enjoy the book, such an understanding brings greater depth to it.

In Walton's "to the reader," he is predictably self-effacing, and adds as he does in his preface to the *Life of Donne* that that it was no real choice of his, but necessity which led him to write *The Compleat Angler.*

> Sir, This pleasant curiosity of Fish and Fishing, had been thought worthy the pens and practices of diverse in other Nations, that have been reputed men of great learning and wisdom, and amongst those of this Nation, I remember Sir Henry Wotton has told me that his intentions were to write a Discourse of the Art, and in praise of Angling, and doubtless he had done so, if death had not prevented him; the remembrance of which hath often made me sorry, for if he had lived to do it, then the unlearned Angler had seen some better Treatise of this art, a treatise that might have proved worthy of his perusal, which I could never yet see in English.

Walton tells that the idea for the book on angling was planted by Henry Wotton. He also says that he felt there had been no good book on angling, in the language, later displaying unusual confidence to the effect that he filled this void with *The Compleat Angler.* Walton says "though this discourse may be liable to some exceptions, I cannot doubt but that most readers may receive so much pleasure or profit by it, as may make it worthy the time of their perusal, if they be not too grave or too busy." There is no mistake that Walton himself is *Piscator* because he tells us: "the whole discourse is, or rather was, a picture of my own disposition." By addressing himself as one of the characters or even both Piscator and Venator, Walton is indirectly talking about himself and his own ideas. He could have conveyed much of the same information without the dialogue, but the indirect method is in keeping with his humble nature. But I would be hesitant as a reader to attribute Walton's claims of reluctant authorship in his preface entirely to his modesty. Portraits of ladies are often rendered with the lady looking away as a device to allow the viewer of the portrait to admire them. Sometimes modesty and expressed humbleness is used deliberately to invite praise. You may have seen portraits of noble men inviting admiration this same way, by gazing away to some diviner thought, with a phalanx of dogs at their feet looking up dotingly at their master on whose conscience the universe is seated.

In editions subsequent to the first, *The Compleat Angler* is prefaced with commendatory verses from friends and literati. Some of these verses are from individuals whom Walton praised in his past writings. Charles Cotton, for instance, praises Walton publicly and Walton praises Cotton. Although today such practices could be seen as strangely underhanded, in Walton's time such displays of mutual admiration and love seemed in every way to be genuine. The following commendatory verses were contributed by Robert Floud to the second edition of *The Compleat Angler*. Robert Floud was one of Walton's brothers-in-law.

> *This book is so like you, and you like it,*
> *For harmless mirth, expression, art and wit,*
> *That I protest ingenuously 'tis true,*
> *I love this mirth, art, wit, the book, and you.*

Walton may have used as models for his *Compleat Angler* such books as the *Treatise on the Nature of God*, 1599; and *Herasbachius's Husbandry*, 1597. Bevan tells us the *Arcadia* of Sir Philip Sydney and Erasmus's *Colloquies* may have served as models for Walton's book. Bevan also notes that the sermons of Walton's friend Henry Valentine, two in particular from his "Four Sea-Sermons," of 1635 "show some striking parallels with *The Compleat Angler*." Lucian's first century A.D. dialogue *The Fisherman*, in which the poet sits on a parapet of the Acropolis equipped with the rod of a Piraean fisherman with bait of gold and figs to catch philosophers, may have influenced Walton. Plato's dialogue *The Symposium* also bears resemblance to the structure of *The Compleat Angler*, only the discourses in the *Symposium* are on love, not angling, and they drink more in the *Symposium*. Walton makes mention of Lucian as well as Socrates (the primary interlocutor in the *Symposium*) in *The Compleat Angler*. From Virgil's *Eclogues,* 37 B.C., and the tradition since Theocritus, Walton adopts the pastoral, perhaps the idea for dialogue, and the "broad beech tree," under which Piscator replaces Tityrus. Bevan tells us that Walter Scott had praised "the beautiful simplicity of Walton's Arcadian language," and Hazlitt considered the *Angler* "the best pastoral in the language." Walton most likely used as a model for his *Angler* a book of 1577 entitled the *Arte of Angling*, which is written as a dialogue between the piscator and viator, the same characters that open the first edition of Walton's book. We might as well mention the King James Bible as an influence on Walton's style, as the *Angler* in places is replete with the same soothing continuum of *and*s, not to mention the fact that the piscatory form is appropriate for his sometimes pious agenda because of its adaptability to religious allegory—"fishers of men." Though some have criticized Walton for cribbing, and he did, it is important to realize that Walton, or any author for that matter, had many influences, a fact which should not distract from his own originality. Lucian says on this subject, "as for these very works of mine, where else did I get them but from you, culling your flowers like a bee and putting them on display for man."

In Walton's "to the reader" he makes it clear that there are two distinct parts to the book. The "pleasant part," which displays his humor, mirth, and philosophies, and the "more useful part," that which is concentrated with practical angling instruction. The "pleasanter part" gives us insight into Walton's demeanor.

> I wish the reader that in writing of it I have made myself a recreation of a recreation; and that it might prove so to him, and not read dull and tediously. I have in several places mixed some innocent, harmless mirth; of which, if thou be a severe, sour complexioned man, then I here disallow thee to be a competent judge. I am the willinger to justify the pleasant part of the discourse.

> Next let me tell the reader, that in that which is the more useful part of this discourse, that is to say, the observations of the nature and breeding, and seasons, and catching of fish, I am not so simple as not to know, that a captious reader may find exceptions against something said of some of these.

The fishing instruction, on how to properly raise maggots or tie flies, or recipes on how to cook pike or chub, while completely relevant for today's angler, are only a small part of what makes the book great. Below are two of my favorite passages from the *Angler*. I provide them as means of introduction to Walton's prose, that is, if you have not already read Walton.

Piscator and Venator are fishing for chub and their angling is interrupted by a rain shower. Piscator is speaking.

> But turn out of the way a little, good Scholar, towards yonder high honeysuckle hedge: there we'll sit and sing whilst this shower falls so gently upon the teeming earth, and gives yet a sweeter smell to the lovely flowers that adorn these verdant meadows.

> Look; under that broad beech-tree, I sat down, when I was last this way a-fishing, and the birds in the adjoining Grove seemed to have a friendly contention with an Echo, with an Echo whose dead voice seemed to live in a hollow cave, near to the brow of that primrose-hill; there I sat viewing the silver streams glide silently towards their center, the tempestuous Sea; yet, sometimes opposed by rugged roots, and pebble stones, which broke their waves, and turned them into foam: and sometimes I beguiled time by viewing the harmless Lambs, some leaping securely in the cool shade, whilst others sported themselves in the cheerful sun: and saw others craving comfort from the swollen udders of their bleating dams. As I thus sat, these and other sights had so fully possessed my soul with content that I thought as the poet has happily expressed it:

I was for that time lifted above earth;
And possessed joys not promised in my birth.

This passage describes a spiritual, almost metaphysical encounter for Walton, an almost omniscient life-awareness—a reflection of his own inevitable condition cast in his surroundings. His sentences are at times unending and watery, which are charmingly appropriate given that Walton is very often expounding on the immortality of the stream and her mortal inhabitants. The next passage is quite different, describing not the relationship between Walton and his world and the out-of-body experience of streamside subconscious, but a large-scaled minnowlike fish called a chub, and how to catch it.

Go to the same hole in which I caught my chub, where in most hot days you will find a dozen or twenty chevens [another name for chub] floating near the top of the water, get two or three Grasshoppers as you go over the meadow, and get secretly behind the tree, and stand as free from motion as is possible, then put a Grasshopper on your hook, and let your hook hang a quarter of a yard short of the water, to which end you must rest your rod on some bough of the tree, but it is likely that the chubs will sink down towards the bottom of the water at the first shadow of your rod, for a chub is the fearfullest of fishes, and will do so if but a bird flies over him, and makes the least shadow on the water: but they will presently rise up to the top again, and there lie soaring till some shadow affrights them again: I say when they lie upon the top of the water, look out the best chub, and move your rod as softly as a snail moves, to that chub you intend to catch.

This passage to a great extent is written in iambic meter, and with very little editorial license could be broken into blank verse, or an iambic pentameter poem. A certain calm and peaceable music played in his head that was reflected in his writing; who but Walton could make fishing for a chub so romantic and magical? The next passage is perhaps my favorite in the whole book.

Pisc. I have another bite: come Scholar, come lay down your rod, and help me to land this as you did the other. So, now we shall be sure to have a good dish of fish for supper.

Ven. I am glad of that; but I have not fortune: sure, Master, yours is a better rod and better tackling.

Pisc. Nay, then take mine, and I will fish with yours. Look you, Scholar, I have another; come, do as you did before. And now I have a bite at another: Oh me! he has broke all; there's half a line and a good hook lost.

Ven. Aye and a good Trout too.

Pisc. Nay, the Trout is not lost, for pray take notice no man can lose what he never had.

The line of real concern here is "no man can lose what he never had," which taken metaphorically could apply to *losing* a wife or a child or England *losing* the American colonies. As we have seen, by the year 1653 when the *Angler* was written, Walton had experienced great loss. Perhaps he had been wondering too what his life had amounted to and his lack of control in situations of death and civil war. In the end, Walton discovers, through increasing disillusionment with his country and times, that there are very few things that we ever, indeed, have. Most things in the world, especially those things which we rely on for emotional stability—a friend, lover, a relative—are perishable, combustible, and fickle. But through the medium of fishing, Walton can express this sentiment without too much pain, because fishing is a safe, albeit frustrating, way in which we experience failure and learn from it; safe in the sense that we are not damaged irreparably by the "loss" of a fish.

In 1658 when Walton was sixty-five, the second edition of his *Life of Donne* was released; not as a preface to Donne's sermons but as a separate work, somewhat expanded. The book had been very favorably received, and the second edition included, as subsequent editions of the *Angler* had, verses commending the work. The following lines were written by a Royalist poet friend of Walton's named Alexander Brome.

> *By thee fish die; by thee dead friends live,*
> *As from oblivion and the grave set free,*
> *Names, whom thou robest with immortality*
> *For he that reads thy Wotton and thy Donne*
> *Can't but believe a resurrection.*

The subject of immortality frequently surfaces in the wake of Izaak Walton, and these commendatory verses are replete with such mentions. It is the idea that Walton has preserved for future generations, the lives of these much loved people, that seems to fascinate the readers. As I have remarked, though some may disagree, immortality and how it is achieved is a central theme in his little book on "fishing." And though he was indeed a humble man and may have wanted no monument built over his grave, Walton likely knew and was satisfied with the thought that through the success of his books he had immortalized his friends, yes, but also himself. But still, Walton doubts his achievements; "I had thought time had made this relation of Donne so like myself, as to become useless to the world and content to be forgotten." This line is even more self-deprecating than usual and contrasts highly to the modest optimism he expressed about his work in *The Compleat Angler*.

As mentioned, the landmark political event of the second half of Walton's life was the Restoration of the monarchy, the return of Charles II. On May 29 of that year, Walton penned verses commending a collection of his friend Alexander Brome's poems (note commendatory verses by Brome on Walton's *Angler*). Perhaps better than any other, these lines show Walton's sentiments at the time of Restoration. The poem is presented as a conversation between a man and woman, Damon and Dorus.

> *Damon: Hail happy days! Dorus sit down:*
> *Now let no sign, nor let a frown*
> *Lodge near thy heart, or on thy brow.*
> *The King! the King's returned! and now*

Let's banish all sad thoughts and sing
We have our laws, and have our King.
Dorus: 'Tis true, and I would sing, but oh!
These wars have sunk my heart so low
'Twill not be raised.

Sort of a gloomy answer to "hail happy days!" These lines well express the two sides of Walton; the one that shows joy at the king's return and the one that knows that some miseries can make irreparable marks on the spirit. It seems those war times were very difficult for Walton, and knowing this, the outwardly cheerful *Compleat Angler* begins to show muddy and miserable undertones. One of the few places that Walton can go for solace is to the shade of that "broad beech-tree" that he mentions in his fishing book, where he shelters from the grimness of showers.

Walton's second wife died in 1662, about which time we find that Walton had moved from his residence, whether it had been London or Stafford or both, to the area near Winchester in the south of England. In 1661 and 1662 he was acting as personal steward to his friend Bishop George Morley in Worcester. It was rumored that during the times of the civil wars, the staunch Royalist Morley was in hiding at Walton's residence in Stafford. Shortly after Morley preached at the coronation of Charles II, he may have asked his aging friend if he would like to come live with him in the south. The term *Restoration* not only described the return of the monarchy and bishoprics but in many cases the cathedrals ravished by parliamentarians needed physical restoration and renovation. Such restoration is something that Walton may have supervised as steward.

1662 not only marked the death of Walton's wife but also that of John Donne's son. It is interesting to note that Donne's son left in his will "all writings under my father's hand to Mr. Izaak Walton."

On the grave of Walton's second wife, in the Virgin Mary Chapel in Worcester Cathedral, was written:

> *Here lieth buried so much as could die of Anne Walton*
> *A woman of remarkable prudence*
> *and of the primitive piety; her great*
> *and general knowledge being adorned*
> *with such true humility, and blest*
> *with so much Christian meekness; as*
> *made her worthy of a more memorable monument*
> *She died. Alas that she is dead!*

In April of 1662, George Morley was translated from the bishopric at Worcester to that of Winchester. Walton went with him and lived with him there. Winchester is a lovely town through which the River Itchen winds. For the next twenty-one years until Walton's death, he likely fished the Itchen. To this day there are trout in the very center of town.

Walton's fourth book, his *Life of Richard Hooker*, which appeared in 1665, he dedicated to Bishop Morley. In the dedication Walton mentions that he had written the book under Morley's roof, which confirms he had been living with Morley. Hooker's *Life* was unique among Walton's biographies because unlike the lives of Donne and Wotton, Walton had not known Hooker as intimately as he had his other friends whose lives he had immortalized. The general consensus is that the *Life of Hooker* is more seriously written than the previous two. Walton says in his research that he conversed with many people who had known Hooker intimately and made inquiries "of his person, his nature, the management of his time, his wife, his family, and the fortune of him and his."

On June 12, 1668, Walton's son matriculated at Christ Church, Oxford. At this point Walton was seventy-five.

In 1670, Walton released his fourth biography, that of George Herbert. As with Richard Hooker, Walton did not know Herbert, he only saw him once at the funeral services for Herbert's mother in 1627. One of the most admired passages in all of Walton's *Lives* is that in which he describes Herbert's courtship and marriage. As with the moment in Donne's life quoted above, Walton strays to give his own intimations on love. Herbert's future wife had fallen in love with him unseen, solely by the recommendation of her own father, who admired Herbert as a young man. Says Walton:

> This was a fair preparation for a marriage; but, alas! her father died before Mr. Herbert's retirement to Dauntsey; yet some friends to both parties procured their meeting; at which time a mutual affection entered into both their hearts, as a conqueror enters into a surprised city; and love having got such possession, governed, and made there such laws and resolutions as neither party was able to resist; insomuch, that she changed her name to Herbert the third day after this first interview.

The year 1670 also marks the publication of Walton's four collected biographies under the title *Lives*: Donne, Wotton, Hooker, and Herbert. This collection was dedicated to Morley as well, as Walton felt indebted to him for his friendship and hospitality. Walton says in a preface to *Lives* that his biographies are: "an honor due to the dead, and a generous debt due to those that shall live and succeed us." Walton must have been proud of his collected *Lives* because by Coon's accounts he gave away at least twenty-two copies, signed to friends and family.

It is known that Walton had a lease on some property in London near the Cross Keyes in Paternoster Row. We know this because some time after the historical fire that ravaged London in 1666, he had petitioned the Court of Judicature Touching Houses Burnt in London and was granted permission to rebuild on the property. Coon says that Walton may have lived here occasionally after 1670. In 1672 Isaac junior received his bachelor of arts degree from Oxford; he would later return to Christ Church to take his MA. Also in 1672 the best-known portrait of Izaak Walton was painted. It is by Jacob Huysmans (1633–96) and it hangs in the National Gallery in London. Walton's daughter Anne, who was born March 11, 1648, would have been twenty-four by this time. During his final years, Walton divided his time between the canonry at Winchester, Bishop Morley's townhouse in Chelsea and palace at Farnham Castle, and the hamlet of Droxford where Anne lived with her husband William Hawkins, who was the vicar of Droxford. When he visited and stayed with his daughter, he fished the nearby River Meon. Walton also probably visited his son, who in 1678 became chaplain to the Bishop of Salisbury. Also in 1678 Walton's fifth and final biography, the *Life of Sanderson*, was published.

The preface again is very apologetic. "I wish both for the readers and Dr. Sanderson's sake, that posterity had known his great learning and virtue by a better pen, by such a pen, as could have made his life as immortal as his learning and merits ought to be." We learn the most about Walton from this *Life*. Coon says, "he is old now, and allows himself the luxury of including more of himself in his work."

Very little survives of Walton's written works in manuscript form. Among the surviving manuscripts, mostly letters and inscriptions in books, is Walton's will, written in his own hand. It was drafted on August 9, 1683, during Walton's ninetieth year.

> In the name of God Amen I Izaak Walton the elder of Winchester being this present day in the 90 ninetieth year of my age and in perfect memory for which praised be God: but considering how suddenly I may be deprived of both do therefore make this my last will and testament as followeth.

In his will he gives his title to the London property on Paternoster Row to his daughter and her husband. He gave his son Isaac his right and title to a lease he held from the Lord Bishop of Winton on Norington Farm, as well as right and title to land near Stafford, but if his son failed to marry before the age of forty-one, then the land would go to the town of Stafford where Walton was born: "for the good and benefit of some of the said town." Walton specifies that the books in his personal collection at Winchester and Droxford should go to his daughter, and that his books at Farnham Castle should go to his son. The books that

Walton gave to his son are now in Salisbury Cathedral Library. Walton gave various directions for his monies to be distributed among the less fortunate, the poor, mostly of Stafford. Through reading the will, we are supplied with our final image of the genuine and humble Walton. He ends his will with the lines "I desire my burial may be near the place of my death: and free from any ostentation or charge, but privately: this I make to be my last will."

Izaak Walton died at the house of his son-in-law in Droxford on December 15, 1683. Walton's bloodline died shortly after. As he had predicted, his son Isaac died unmarried at sixty-nine, and his daughter Anne had two children, neither of whom bore their own.

But Walton's England and his writings were very alive in my head as I left my rental behind at Heathrow and took the tube into London and its flowering gardens at intervals along the Thames.

This is as appropriate a time as any to quote Charles Cotton and perhaps the best commendatory verses to Walton's works; these were published in the second edition of the collected *Lives* of 1673. They speak to the strength of Walton's power of friendship.

> *But, yours is Friendship of so pure a kind,*
> *From all mean ends, and interest so refined,*
> *It ought to be, a pattern to mankind.*
> *For, whereas, most men's friendships here beneath,*
> *Do perish with their friends expiring breath,*
> *Yours, proves a Friendship living after death.*

Good Company Makes the Way Seem Short

But, my dear friend, 'tis so, that you and I,
By a condition of mortality,
With all this great, and more proud world, must die;
In which estate, I ask no more of Fame,
Nor other Monument of Honor claim,
Then that, of your true Friend, to advance my name.
And, if your many merits, shall have bred
An abler pen, to write your Life when dead;
I think, an honester cannot be read.

London

The storefronts on Fleet Street in London were dim, their doors closed. As any civilized society should, the English celebrate the arrival of the loveliest month of the year in holiday. And living up to the occasion, the sun came out in splendid form after a long, wet April. Izaak Walton chose May as the month in which to set *The Compleat Angler*. It is on the May Day holiday that his book begins—a Londoner walking from his home with his fishing rod meets a stranger on his way to the River Lea—and the rest of the book engages us in the dialogue between them, an instruction and conversion of the stranger to the gentle art of angling.

I stood on the corner of Fleet Street and Chancery Lane near the Temple Bar where Walton had at one time enjoyed a glass of ale, on the same corner where he lived and his business as a linen draper prospered, on the same block that his church, St. Dunstan's-in-the-West, once stood, where he met his first wife Rachel Floud and the poet John Donne, who was responsible in many ways for Walton's career as a writer. Fleet Street, once the hub of London publishing, not far from where *The Compleat Angler* was printed by his friend and publisher Richard Marriott, is very different from what it was in the mid-1600s.

I was staying with a classmate of mine named Margaret who had graduated Yale and was studying at the London School of Economics. Her apartment was near the southwest corner of Hyde Park and had become, whether to her joy or her chagrin, the London stopping point for classmates on European excursions. I had recruited Eli, another friend from school and boarder at Margaret's flat, to join me for a day in the footsteps of Walton to bring credence to the line in his *Angler,* "good company makes the way seem short."

I had managed, craftily and contentedly, to swallow anyone and everyone who came within conversing distance of me in a discussion about Izaak Walton. But Eli had already been in London several days and since he had seen all the obligatory London sites, he was game for this less conventional tour of the city I had proposed. The plan was to set off from the site of Walton's first London home on the corner of Fleet Street and Chancery Lane.

Eli and I walked from Knaresborough Place to the Earl's Court station and took the tube to the Embankment stop on the Thames. The crude map I had of greater London showed vaguely where the Lea meets the Thames and the roads that lead north to Tottenham where we planned to walk. According to the scale of the map, Tottenham was about six or seven miles north of Fleet Street, where our spiritual trip began. Hoddesdon, a town about seven miles further north of

Tottenham, is where Walton says they had their breakfast ale. "Well," I said to Eli, "they knew how to do it—they had beer for breakfast." And we mused on how Walton, living on Fleet Street or even a bit north in Clerkenwell where he later leased property, could have possibly walked the fourteen miles to Hoddesdon before breakfast. The text in the *Angler* from which our mental map was made is printed below. There are three characters in the opening dialogue of *The Compleat Angler*, Piscator (in Latin, the fisherman), Venator (hunter), and Auceps (falconer).

> Pisc. You are well overtaken, Gentlemen, a good morning to you both; I have stretched my legs up Tottenham-hill to overtake you, hoping your business may occasion you towards Ware, whither I am going this fine fresh May morning.

> Ven. Sir, I for my part shall almost answer your hopes, for my purpose is to drink my mornings draught at the Thatched House in Hoddesdon, and I think not to rest till I come thither, where I have appointed a friend or two to meet me: but for this Gentleman that you see with me, I know not how far he intends his journey; he came so lately into my company, that I have scarce had time to ask him the question.

> Auceps. Sir, I shall by your favor bear you company as far as Theobalds, and there leave you for then I turn up to a friend's house who mews a Hawk for me, which I now long to see.

> Pisc. Sir, we are all so happy as to have a fine, fresh, cool morning, and I hope we shall each be the happier in the others'

company. And Gentlemen, that I may not lose yours, I shall either abate or amend my pace to enjoy it; knowing that (as the Italians say) Good company in a journey makes the way to seem the shorter.

Summer was impending and London had seen this day its first full day of sun since the beginning of April. The day before you could hear the Londoners moaning about the weather, for though England is notoriously misty and damp it had been the coldest and wettest April on record since 1750. Every living thing had a want to explode in joy and anticipation of warm weather. Buds swelled and girls emerged in patterned summer dresses from brick and plaster row houses warmed by the sun. Eli and I decided that before we did anything we had to drink our morning's draught. We walked from the Embankment to Fleet Street and each had a pint of warm ale.

Eli asked me what I intended to do exactly in writing this book on Izaak Walton. I told him that this was my pilgrimage in the wake of Izaak Walton, patron saint of the philosophy and religion of angling. "Walton has been a much-neglected author lately," I told him, "and I hope to uncover some of his brilliance by resurrecting Walton through the medium of someone who is still alive—myself." In describing what kind of person Walton was and what he'd emerged from, his history and times, I explained to Eli how important the Anglican faith and his Christian life had been to him. "Walton thought that the same characteristics that make a good angler also make a good Christian. As he explains, the apostles were fishermen; meek, quiet and virtuous men." I told Eli that not many people knew that above being a pragmatic book on fishing, *The Compleat Angler* was a philosophical book by a literary artist and partly code for the Compleat *Anglican*. "Walton was a gentle man with a great gift for friendship." I intended to illuminate Walton's book and bring together critical interpretations of the text and biographical and historical information as well as, admittedly, to inject Walton's text with my own philosophies on angling and life, producing a kind of hybrid with modern relevance. I wished to breathe new life into his words and give a picture of our twin dispositions that would reflect the nature of all those inclined toward the gentle art of angling. Eli decided we should have another pint on this day in honor of Walton.

The sun and ale aided in our interpretation of the above opening lines. Eli perused my crumpled map and wondered how Walton, whom we will take as the character Piscator, the fisherman, and his new companion, Venator, could have possibly walked even from Tottenham to Hoddesdon, a whole seven miles, before breakfast. I suggested they rode on horses, "But," Eli argued, "Walton said, 'I stretched *my legs* up Tottenham-hill,' not his horse's legs."

"You're right," I said, "they probably just left really early."

None of the buildings in the vicinity of Fleet Street and Chancery Lane are as Walton would have seen them, save perhaps Lincoln's Inn, one of the four Inns of Court. The great fire in London, which ravaged much of the city in 1666, is partly responsible for the cosmetic transformation. Before the great fire, London houses were mostly of the timbered Elizabethan style. The upper stories of these buildings jutted out over the street, which facilitated the dumping of dishwater and anything else on passersby. Walton's church, St. Dunstan's-in-the-West, just east of

Chancery Lane on Fleet Street, is not as it would have been in the 1650s. St. Dunstan's was rebuilt in the 1830s, thirty feet from its original site. The medieval St. Dunstan's was likely erected before the Norman conquest, shortly after the death of St. Dunstan in 988. The church was backed by a large churchyard, now covered by modern buildings. It was in this churchyard that Walton's book was first published, by Richard Marriott in 1653. Walton met his first wife, Rachel Floud, in the parish of St. Dunstan's, and it was through his participation in the church that his literary career saw its genesis. Walton met the poet and priest John Donne through St. Dunstan's and witnessed Donne delivering his sermons. I closed my eyes and tried to hear if Donnes words still echoed through the London streets. "No man is an island, entire of itself; every man is a piece of the continent, a part of the main; If a clod be washed away by the sea, Europe is the less, as well as if a promontory were, as well as if a manor of thy friends or of thine own were; Any man's death diminishes me, because I am involved in Mankind; And therefore never send to know for whom the bell tolls; It tolls for thee."

I had wanted to see the memorial window to Walton that I knew was in St. Dunstan's, to the left of the high altar, erected in 1895 by the Angling Society, but the church doors were closed. There was a plaque on the wall of the facade that read:

> To the memory of Izaak Walton, born at Stafford, buried Winchester Cathedral, author of *The Compleat Angler* and the *Lives*. Walton resided for many years at Fleet Street at the corner of Chancery Lane west side, and between 1632 and 1644 was overseer of the poor, a sidesman and vestryman of this parish. He was also a member of the Ironmonger's Company.

The tablet and window at the Northwest side of this church were erected by some anglers and other admirers of Walton in the month of April 1895.

A note outside the door said that Holy Communion would be held at 12:30 on Tuesday. I would try to get there; that was tomorrow. Eli and I crossed the street to get a better view of the church at a distance. The great black taxis and double-decker buses roared on down Fleet Street past the statue of a great black griffin that adorns the Temple Bar Memorial, erected in 1880. I tried to picture Fleet Street through the ages and the churchyard, which had been the hub of the book trade where authors came to find publishers. The following is a description of what activity in the churchyard would have been like during Walton's time.

> At the far end of the long facade of St. Dunstan's, the street became a square where every kind of commodity was sold, but especially books. There were noisy street hawkers, side-shows with human and animal monstrosities, fire eaters and occasionally a bewildered exotic animal from Africa or India. Everywhere was confusion, gaiety, crime, excitement and misery.

The churchyard of St. Dunstan's is where Milton, the blind poet, came to find a publisher for his epic *Paradise Lost*. Milton was paid five pounds down for his book and five pounds on the sale of thirteen hundred copies of the first, second, and third impressions. The title page of his first edition of 1667 reads "printed and are to be sold by Peter Parker under creed Church near Aldgate; and by Robert Boulter at the Turks Head in Bishopsgate-street; and Matthias Walker, under St. Dunstan's Church in Fleet-Street."

Another illustrious character of Fleet Street who should not escape mention is Dr. Samuel Johnson (1709–1784), the most prominent literary man of his time. He was purportedly a great eccentric and resided at one time on Gough Square just behind Fleet Street. One has said "his laughter on occasions could be heard from Temple Bar to the Fleet Ditch." Dr. Johnson deserves mention in this account of Izaak Walton because without him it is possible we would not even know of the book *The Compleat Angler*. Johnson was a great admirer of Walton's and gave a copy of *The Compleat Angler* to an officer friend of his named Astle in which he wrote "A mighty pretty book, a mighty pretty book." *The Compleat Angler* had seen its fifth edition by 1676, but from 1676 to 1750, some seventy years, it had been out of print. It was in the year 1750 that Dr. Johnson recommended to his clergyman friend Moses Browne that he republish *The Compleat Angler*. Brown tells us in the introduction of this edition that he undertook the project of printing *The Compleat Angler* "at the invitation of a very ingenious and learned friend, Dr. Samuel Johnson, who mentioned to me, I remember, in that conversation, his design to write a life of Walton. I wish he had performed it." James Boswell, Dr. Johnson's good friend, wrote and published Johnson's biography in 1791, which still stands as the authoritative work for the life of this great critic. In the biography Boswell tells us that Dr. Johnson "talked of Izaak Walton's *Lives*, which was one of his most favorite books." Boswell continues by quoting Samuel Johnson as having said that among the five lives Walton wrote, "Dr. Donne's life was the most perfect of them."

So it was within this small area where Eli and I stood that Walton's career as a writer began, evolved, and was immortalized posthumously. Soaking it all in and watching the two great "giants of St. Dunstan's"—carved figures in an alcove that beat on a pair of bells, which Walton likely had seen (they are one of the few features that remain from the old St. Dunstan's)—we decided to start our walk to the River Lea.

Looking at the map, Eli and I chose a possible route to Tottenham up Lothbury to Old Broad Street to Liverpool Street to Bishopsgate and up Bishopsgate until it became the Kingsland Road and Stoke Newington Road. There were fewer sheltered courtyard gardens and Jaguars in these neighborhoods, and more industry and pavement the closer we got to the Lea. Much of what we saw was post-WWII sprawl and not the most scenic or clean. The pigeons were thinner and looked less healthy than those in Chelsea. On the map, the Lea looked as though it had been dammed and diverted in several places. The farther we walked from central London the more I revised our plans, mostly because I didn't think Eli would have enjoyed this journey, but he continued to impress me with his enthusiasm. We were encouraged by two women who whistled at us, playing loud music on a balcony over the street.

"They're whistling at you," I said to Eli.

We figured that Walton probably stopped at a few pubs on the way and we planned to also, but soon found that there were no pubs on the high road out of London. This area was peculiarly un-English by my understanding, as England is statistically composed of 94 percent white Anglo-Saxons. The Stoke Newington

Road may be the only place in the world where you'll see the Aziziye Mosque adjacent to the Stoke Newington Baptist Church. It was an intensely integrated community, and henceforth I referred to it in conversation with Eli as little Jerusalem. The truth was that these continuous rows of run-down flats did not have the charm or mystique of Jerusalem. Eli had to be back in central London for an early dinner with his expatriate uncle, and I promised him that all I wanted was to see the Lea at Tottenham and that we didn't have to walk back, but we could take the underground from Tottenham Hale Station on the Victoria Line. After a while I began to enjoy the richness and peculiarities of the communities we passed—the open fruit markets with oranges and star fruits and the many kabob take-out restaurants. We got a bit to eat in the Turkish Muslim quarter at the "kara deniz" kabob place, *kara deniz* meaning "black sea" in Turkish. Soon after, we came into a large neighborhood of Hasidic Jews, all dressed in black and riding bicycles, their long peiot sailing in the wind behind them. Each family seemed to own a used Volvo, as there was one parked in front of every flat, and I began to wonder if it was a ritualistic requirement for London Orthodox Jews until I spotted a used Volvo dealership just north of the town of Islington. And this brought to mind, oddly enough, a poem by William Cowper called "The Diverting History of John Gilpin," which is subtitled "showing how he went farther than he intended and came safe home again." But it wasn't for want that our situation turn out like Gilpin's that it came to mind, but because this poem, first published in 1782, makes mention of the area through which Eli and I walked, specifically the town of Islington and the bell at Edmonton, just north of Tottenham.

John Gilpin was a citizen
Of Credit and renown,
A train-band Captain eke was he
Of famous London town.

Tomorrow is our wedding-day,
And we will then repair
Unto the Bell at Edmonton
All in a chaise and pair.

I am a linen-draper bold,
As all the world doth know,
And my good friend the Callender
Will lend his horse to go.

What happens is that John Gilpin goes with his wife to Edmonton following the same course that Walton had taken a hundred years before and his horse becomes comically unruly and all their provisions for the day spill over into the road as the horse gallops on.

Thus all through merry Islington
These gambols he did play,
And till he came unto the wash
Of Edmonton so gay.

It is also curious and fun to note that Walton and Gilpin shared the profession of linen draper.

One could go on quoting like this, that is, alluding to poems about the specific countryside, because when writing on England, one thing is certain, someone has trodden the land before you and likewise has already written a poem about it. But bringing our past to present is what it's all about, since nothing is produced in a vacuum and we are a product of what has come before.

Walton's walk through the fields at Islington to the River Lea could only be expected to have changed in over 350 years having succumbed to the asphalt revolution. But the countryside Walton knew outside the M25 circular highway is remarkably intact. This is primarily the case because the land is private and in many instances still owned by the same families that owned the land when Walton was alive. Of Walton's worlds, London among them has likely seen the most change. From the fire of London in 1666 to the Industrial Revolution, the city is not much of what it was in the early seventeenth century. One need only look in a trash can to see that they were in a different century.

"All on the road to Theobald's," I said to Eli. The farther we stretched our legs up Tottenham hill to overtake Walton's ghost the more I wondered how he would have reacted to these changes. After realizing we were in Tottenham, and also atop a hill, we walked east to where we thought the River Lea should be. We had trouble finding the Lea among loud traffic and endless shops. The sky grew darker as clouds rolled over our sun and threatened rain. We were fairly spent from the walk and the dizzying multitudes of people. Walton must have been in pretty good shape considering he had another seven miles to go to Hoddesdon before breakfast.

The Tottenham Hale tube station was right near the River Lea on the map and it was adjacent to the station where I first glimpsed the river. The Lea flowed pleasantly on, immortal witness of her surroundings, echoing the refrain of Tennyson's poem "The Brook" narrated by the brook itself—"For men may come and men may go,/But I go on forever."

I thanked Eli for coming along, "good company makes the way seem shorter," I repeated, and paid his tube fare as a gesture of my gratitude.

We entered the station and waited for our train on the Victoria line. When it arrived we got in and plunked ourselves down in the seats. About a minute later a man came into our otherwise empty car. He was wearing a Barbour jacket, had two fishing poles with him and a shoulder bag that overflowed with tackle. He sat right across from us.

"Where have you been fishing?" I asked him.

"In a reservoir behind Tottenham."

"Is it the dammed Lea?"

"Yes."

"Were you fishing for coarse fish?"

"No, trout."

"Wow, there are still trout in the Lea?" I mused under my breath. "You came out of London on the tube to fish for the day?" I asked him this not for the benefit of his answer—the answer of course was obvious, but because my asking him such questions out loud helped me form the revelation that was coming to me very slowly; the revelation of this man and his parallel to Walton. The idea that the people of London could *still* walk from the city center for a day's trout fishing, or take the tube, enchanted me.

The following day, I convinced Margaret to join me for Tuesday services at St. Dunstan's-in-the-West at 12:30 P.M. The vicar greeted us near the door and I told him I had come for the services, that I liked to fish and wished to see the Izaak Walton memorial window. He told me that the Anglicans share the church with a Romanian Orthodox parish. I wondered what Walton would have thought of that. The vicar pointed to a great elaborate Romanian Orthodox iconographic screen to the left of the altar and told me that one could not see the window because it was hidden behind it. He led me to the screen and pulled a chair up next to it for me to stand on. Opening a small door on hinges in the screen, only about five inches square, he showed me that you could see the window through it. I hadn't imagined the Walton window as the most prominent feature of the church, but I didn't expect to find it concealed. But through the little hinged door I could see it. On separate panes of the great stained-glass window were images of the individuals whose biographies Walton had written: Henry Wotton, John Donne, Richard Hooker, George Herbert and John Sanderson. Thomas Ken, Bishop of Bath and Wells, famous hymn writer, and Walton's brother-in-law from his second marriage to Anne Ken, also figured prominently in the window. And in the middle stood Walton over the words "To the glory of God, and in the memory of Izaak Walton, author of *The Compleat Angler* and other works, born 1593 died 1683." It was slightly revisionist of the window maker to slight Walton's extrapiscatory achievements as "other works," but that was O.K. Also in writing below these figures in separate windows were the words Walton lived by, "love, joy, peace, modesty, patience, and diligence."

The services began promptly at 12:30 P.M. There were only two people present other than ourselves, a man and a woman in front of the church in business clothes who sat in different pews. The brief readings from the King James Bible of Matthew and St. John appropriately were about fishing. The passage from St. John chapter 21 is one that Walton cites in *The Compleat Angler*. I wondered if the passages had been chosen by the Reverend A. T. J. Salter for the benefit of the angler and Walton fan he knew sat in his audience. Imagine the dark interior of St. Dunstan's and the words from John echoing in the rafters, and that Walton had seen the same words and heard them read aloud.

> Simon Peter saith unto them, I go a fishing. They say unto him, We also go with thee. They went forth, and entered into a ship immediately; and that night they caught nothing. But when the morning was come, Jesus stood on the shore; but the disciples knew not that it was Jesus. Then Jesus saith unto them, children have ye any meat? They answered him, No. And he said unto them, Cast the net on the right side of the ship, and ye shall find. They cast therefore, and now they were not able to draw it for the multitude of fishes.

Next he read from Matthew 4: 17–19.

> From that time Jesus began to preach, and to say, Repent: for the kingdom of heaven is at hand. And Jesus, walking by the sea of Galilee, saw two brethren, Simon called Peter, and Andrew his brother, casting a net into the sea: for they were fishers. And he saith unto them, Follow me, and I will make you fishers of men.

> And they straightaway left *their* nets, and followed him. And
> going on from thence, he saw other two brethren, James the son
> of Zebedee, and John his brother, in a ship with Zebedee their
> father, mending their nets; and he called them. And they immedi-
> ately left the ship and their father, and followed him.

Margaret and I left before Holy Communion, admiring the tall and narrow
church exterior and enjoying the brilliance of the day. She was off to classes
and I was headed to a small establishment on Brook Street for lunch called The
London Flyfishers. I hailed a cab and enjoyed the ride in the big, old-fashioned
black car. Leaning back in the seat and watching the buildings and buses go by
I pulled out the tie I had in my pocket and put it on to make myself presentable
for lunch. In traffic on St. James Street I took my paperback of *The Compleat
Angler* from my shoulder bag and read the passage which begins the hunter's
education under the master Piscator, who provides as one of his opening arguments the fact that Jesus chose no less men than fishermen to be his disciples.

> Jesus found that the hearts of such men by nature were fitted
> for contemplation and quietness; men of mild, and sweet, and
> peaceable spirits, as indeed most Anglers are: these men our
> blessed Savior, (who is observed to love to plant grace in good
> natures) though indeed nothing be too hard for him, yet these
> men he chose to call from their irreprovable employment of
> Fishing, and gave them grace to be his Disciples, and to follow
> him and do wonders, I say four of twelve.

And it is observable, that it was our Saviour's will, that these our four Fishermen should have a priority of nomination in the Catalogue of his twelve Apostles, as namely first St. Peter, St. Andrew, St. James and St. John, and then the rest in their order.

The reading of this well-fashioned argument carried me to the door of the Savile Club on 69 Brook Street near Grosvenor Square and the American Embassy. I have always coveted and been enchanted by the fishing enclave or place where anglers gather within the city. It is through reciprocal arrangements with a club I belong to in New York City, aptly named the Anglers' Club of New York, that I have privileges at the Flyfishers.

I had made a date to have lunch with the new secretary of the club, Tim Boycott, who retired last year as commander in the Royal Navy. The Flyfishers club is now on the third floor of the Savile Club, appropriately, as I have mentioned, on *Brook* Street. The club was founded in 1884 "for the social intercourse of gentlemen interested in the art of Flyfishing." Their motto, which adorns several club mementos, is "piscator-non-solumpiscatur," or *It is not all of fishing to fish*. The club has been housed in varied locations around London since its founding, from the Arundel Hotel to Haymarket to Swallow Street, Piccadilly. The members are gentlemen interested in all forms of the art of angling with the artificial fly and pride themselves on maintaining an atmosphere of friendship that they consider unique among London clubs. One of the most outstanding features of the club is its library of angling books, which along with that of the Anglers' Club of New York, is one of the best in the world.

I took the small elevator to the second floor, which houses the club today, and a man dressed in black and white greeted me there and asked who I had come to see.

"Tim Boycott," I said, and he shuffled around the corner to get him. I heard a deep English voice produce the words, "Is it the American?"

Boycott was a very friendly-looking man with a ruddy face and a pleasant smile. He told me that my things would be safe in the coatroom and asked me what I wanted to drink.

"I'll have what you are having," I said.

"A spritzer then," he said, "right." I soon learned that Tim shared in common with the secretary who preceded him, Norman Fuller, the fortune or misfortune of not being an angler among anglers. He showed me to a small round table in the great yellow rococo room and we sat there with another older gentleman and drank and talked about salmon fishing in Scotland. The white wine spritzer was cool and refreshing. We were handed menus and I ordered the roast chicken. I had already briefed Tim on the purpose of my trip to England, and he relayed that information to our portly companion.

"James is doing a book on Izaak Walton," he said.

And on the way to the long table where meals are served, Boycott stopped to show me what was believed to have been Walton's creel, a black leather fish holder of Walton's period in a glass case. It is not likely that it belonged to Walton himself, but it is fun to imagine that this was so.

I was seated beside Tim at the long table and looked about the beautiful room whose walls danced with fishing books, Bracket paintings of salmon, and dead fish. It is a peculiarly English phenomenon to put their stuffed fish, their taxidermy, in glass cases. I suppose it matches the English temperament, as aestheti-cally, a fish hanging on a wall outside its case, as we have in America, would be free to roam around the room. Here, in this room, as well as this country, everything had its own space that it filled and filled no other. And I was content with this refinement and the great ten-pound trout in their little dioramas in glass cases. On the long table before my real *silver*ware was a beautiful silver-plated sculpture of Izaak Walton reclining by his creel with his fishing rod. It was all very dear.

"I hope the meal is up to the standards of the Anglers' Club of New York," Tim said.

"I'm sure it will be," I said happily, and he poured me a glass of red wine. I was becoming fond of drinking with lunch.

There were five other gentlemen at the table, most of them very old, and I was promptly introduced to them. The man at the head of the table said, "Oh, are you James Prosek?"

"Yes."

"I'm Roger Harrison, I believe I'm taking you fishing next week at Ovington Mill."

"Yes, through Victoria," I said. It was all so wonderful how it came together. Harrison, the current president of the London Flyfishers club was the chief exec-utive of the *Observer* from 1967 to 1987. Victoria Wakefield, whom I had met through Reece Howard at home, had arranged my fishing at Roger's water on the River Itchen. Our meeting at the Flyfishers club was by arrangement of serendipity.

"So glad you could come to lunch," he said as if he had expected me.

The clam chowder, as well as the roast chicken, was very good.

"Is it up to your standards?" asked Boycott, not realizing I had left my standards at home.

"Beyond," I said.

"Would you like some more red wine?"

"Yes," I said.

Tim told me that his days at Cambridge were the best years of his life. This statement concurred with most others who said similar things of their college years. We mused that his college at Cambridge had been constructed in the thirteenth century and mine at Yale in the twentieth. I realized how much of what we had in America had its foundation in English standards.

Englishmen in the company of an American like myself use the occasion as an excuse to vent grievances about their own country. Boycott began to talk reproachfully about the problems of English children from wealthy families. "They have no drive," he said—of course, there were exceptions.

Boycott told me that one of their members had started a small fictitious club called the Tyburn Society. The Tyburn, he explained, was a London river that used to flow full with trout until it met the Thames, but has been covered by the expanding city and now flows underground. Such stories breed enchantment in me, and other thoughts—that maybe there would be access to a place in the underground today, a hidden stream that still bred large trout. This society was probably just another excuse to get together and share each other's company as well as a drink. Walton would have approved; perhaps his ghost still fished it.

When we had finished lunch we returned to the round tables for an espresso. I showed Boycott and Roger Harrison some paintings I'd been doing for the book and they seemed to like them. I had a brief tour of the club. It would have been a treat to dwell in the library for several days. Boycott encouraged me to tell more American members to visit the club. I thanked him for treating me to lunch. He gave me a copy of the latest issue of a literary magazine the club publishes biannually called the *Flyfishers Journal*.

The old man whom we'd sat down with when I'd first come in joined us standing by the Walton creel in the center of the library. "I can't think there is a better club in London," he said.

"A typical day at the Flyfishers," said Boycott.

That night, after a good dinner at an Indian restaurant with Margaret and a few pints of beer, I went to bed. A great moon was generous with its light through my window. It loomed white, "It must be missing from a Constable painting somewhere," I thought, nodding off to sleep. "I hope they'll let me borrow it for the evening."

The next day I stood before Walton's portrait in the National Portrait Gallery, the only known oil that he sat for. It was on the top floor in room three, in a dark corner in a dim room. This was becoming a pattern, how Walton was shoved behind the iconographic screen or in a broom closet, but I supposed it fit his unassuming nature. Arthur Munson Coon, who wrote the most complete life of Walton, most likely stood here before this painting at one time. The same is true for Jonquil Bevan, the foremost living Walton scholar. What can the portrait of this "fisher of men" tell us about the man? It says the following below his portrait.

The Complete Angler

IZAAK WALTON 1593–1683

A London Ironmonger, Walton made enough money to retire at 50, and devoted the rest of his life to country pursuits, above all angling. *The Compleat Angler* (1653), full of pious contentment, expresses his gentle character. He also wrote biographies of Donne, George Herbert, Richard Hooker, and Sir Henry Wotton.

By Jacob Huysmans (1633–96)

Oil on canvas, signed with initials and inscribed. c.1672.

Walton would have been nearly seventy-nine years old at the time that Huysmans painted his portrait. I had just been next door at the National Gallery where I thought the portrait was, and found myself in the late nineteenth-century French wing, where squadrons of smiling schoolchildren sat in front of Seurat paintings with their paper and drawing pencils. This was a slightly more solemn scene, but there was something noble in Walton's gaze that lifted my spirits. For a man of seventy-nine, his hands were extremely young looking and slender, with an almost feminine delicacy, or at least had been painted to appear so. Perhaps gentlemen were supposed to have young hands, hands protected by leather gloves. In life, Walton's hands may have reflected the rigors of a tradesman, a linen draper. On his left hand were two rings, which I thought perhaps were bands representing his two marriages. His right hand was gloved and held a staff. That was about all I could ascertain from looking at this white-haired man, not stern and not frivolous.

It was a beautiful day outside the gallery, with some of London's normal gloom. Loitering on the steps of the museum, I looked out toward the enormous and ominous lions in Trafalgar Square, which looked as though they desperately wanted to rise from their haunches and snap at the multitude of pigeons that assaulted their noble backs. I pulled out from my shoulder bag the copy of the *Flyfishers Journal* that Tim Boycott had given to me. It was a literary journal, a collection of stories written by club members. I found one of the pieces to be of particular interest because it was about a ninety-one-year-old man I had plans to visit, near Pewsey in Upavon, whose name was Bernard Venables. It was suggested to me by Tony Bridgett, the man who had taken me fishing on the Dove, that I meet Venables at his home.

Bernard Venables is perhaps the best-known fishing author in England. His book *Mr. Crabtree Goes Fishing*, a series of cartoons of Mr. Crabtree, a pipe-smoking gentleman, fishing with his son Peter sold two million copies, topped only by *The Compleat Angler* in total sales for a "fishing book." But sadly, because Venables had done the drawings as a staff member for the *Daily Mirror* newspaper, he had no rights to them. When the *Mirror* collected and published Venables's work in book form in 1949, he never saw a penny from the sales. From the piece about him in the *Flyfishers Journal* and his prompt response to my letter, which I'd received at Margaret's address—"If I am able to be of any help regarding your book on Izaak Walton and *The Compleat Angler*, I shall be very happy"—I was developing a very pleasant picture of the man. Venables was now nearly ninety-two years old, an author and an artist, and I looked forward to meeting him. I stowed that thought away with the *Flyfishers Journal* and walked back to Margaret's to collect my things for my journey south out of London the next day.

Brown trout in the River Stour

7

The Trout in Our River
Are Larger

he tube took me to Heathrow, where I hired another rental car, into which I put my things and myself full of savory images that London and her refinements had left with me. The countryside south of London with the afterglow of density and movement danced in a unique sharpness that kept me from dismissing it as simply a mass of green luxury. Walton I am sure enjoyed this same immediacy of contrast, that which I now recognized in my own life as a necessity for richness and stimulation.

Though many of these stories do not involve Walton directly, I endeavor to paint a portrait of England as I have loved and seen it, hoping that because Walton and I share twin dispositions, if you will allow me to indulge in that comparison, the centuries of May breezes that have blown between us can at last be married. There is no better portrait of England and of Walton and all his ideals, there is no better study of Walton's philosophies in vivid motion, than a man I spent some days with on the stream in southeast England, a Sir John Swire of Selling, in Kent just south of London.

I had corresponded with Sir John by mail, before even coming to England. Victoria Wakefield had informed him of my interests and encouraged me to introduce myself to him early on, as she knew of his keen interest in Walton, the proof for which was the replica of Cotton's fishing house he'd built on his own River Stour. When I first contacted him he was in South Africa but mailed me a note promptly after his return, expecting me to come sometime in early to mid-May:

> I am not, I am afraid, a Walton expert, but I can tell you some-thing about the Dove and the best place from which to get a view of Charles Cotton's fishing temple, which is somewhat diffi-cult to approach.
>
> As far as coming here is concerned, I could show you what we have here on the Stour and, although it is a little early, it would be worth your trying for a trout. Depending on the weather, there is sometimes a good hatch of hawthorn flies at that time.

When I originally stopped just past the White Lion Pub in town as Sir John had directed, I walked up the path to a modest home called Luton *Cottage*. A man in sweat pants and a T-shirt came to the door. "Sir John Swire?" I asked.

"No," he laughed, "Sir John is in the house next door; Luton *House*." And he pointed to a gate and a small curvy drive below it. It was about 10:30 A.M. that I knocked on the door of Sir John's beautiful country home. It was large and redbrick with a jungle of flowers growing up the front wall by the gravel drive. Sir John greeted me at the door in three-piece tweed and a red wool tie. I'm certain he wore a tie every day. This was more the picture of Sir John I had in mind, and I don't think it would be inappropriate to say that a man in sweats and a T-shirt would have been a disappointment, for you can't have a name like Sir John Swire and greet the world as a couch potato.

He looked a bit startled, as it seems he had not expected me until afternoon but was quick to include and accommodate me. His granddaughter was coming over for lunch and I would join them, and after lunch we would perhaps try a bit of fishing. This was a lovely tall man, silver haired, in his early seventies, and noble looking with a somewhat pointed aristocratic nose and indented cheeks, an inviting though not always convincing smile, and great blue eyes. He was eager to help me with my bags and show me to my room, up a large staircase past many grave and dim oil portraits. My room overlooked the front drive; I had not seen the garden yet.

That settled, Sir John told me he had several things to do before the guests came, but he wasted no time in introducing his knowledge, or in his modest terms, his lack of knowledge, on Izaak Walton and the fishing temple built by Charles Cotton.

"Now," he said, walking me into his great library and to his desk, "I had done some research when I was building our little fishing cottage on the

Stour about the actual building on the Dove." He took out a topographic map of the Dove and showed me the site of the fishing temple. "It was owned by a Michael Collins, a doctor or some working-class sort, and his bailiff's name was . . ." and he proceeded to write down this information for me, though he added that the man who owned it had not been very accommodating. Sir John had almost suggested I go there myself without asking, which I approved of because I had already done so. I followed him into a great yellow room that overlooked the back lawn and he reached over a table to take a small oil painting from the wall. "I thought you might enjoy seeing this," he said, and turned it in the light. It was a 1799 painting by George Samuel of Charles Cotton's fishing temple, and on the back was inscribed its whole life history and a description of its interior. Sir John set me up at a desk in his library and told me that I could copy down the information from the painting at my leisure. "I should take you to the Flyfishers club in London to see their book collection."

"I was there for lunch just a few days ago," I said. "I have reciprocal privileges with my club in New York."

"Oh it's splendid isn't it? Did you by any chance meet our president Roger Harrison?"

"Yes, I'm fishing with him Saturday on his Itchen."

"Oh it is a lovely piece of river he has, but I think you'll find the trout in our river are larger. Roger has all wild fish, but he loves to fish our river; I believe he's coming to stay in two weeks. He is a very fine fisherman. I hope you'll have good things to tell him about the Stour."

Now Sir John was going to do a few things, and in the meantime I was welcome to walk around the garden; in fact, he'd suggested it.

I exited the house through two large glass doors that were open to the still, morning chill and started down a winding green path into which pink azaleas extended their blooming arms. I paused by a small fountain with lilies and a cherub statue and was startled by a woman with a hoe. Her name was Mim, Sir John's Kenyan gardener, and she looked at me as if she were the eyes of the garden. She said that she was preparing the garden for an open day on the weekend when the public could come and see the product of her labors. I inquired a bit about my host, finding gardeners and bailiffs the source of many answers, and she volunteered that she'd thought Sir John had earned his sirness through military service in World War II but wasn't certain. Sir John's brother had also been knighted.

I said goodbye to Mim and sauntered off down the path. I came to a small cage of cooing white doves, which seemed Edenic enough for this scene, and shortly after I saw Sir John heading to a small white house concealed in the garden by copper beech. I imagined this building was his office. In passing he said to me "I'm afraid the cherry orchard is past bloom, but you can walk through it to an eleventh-century church which is quite lovely." I walked off realizing I did not know what time it was. I haven't worn a watch for five years, but kept a clock in my shoulder bag, which is usually with me when I need to know the time. I hoped that I would not be late for lunch, not knowing what time lunch was.

I walked into this ancient cherry orchard and leaned on a cherry tree, fiercely recording in my journal all that I saw; gnarled cherry trunks with horizontal lines etched in them. It was a breezy day, and the sun came chaotically in and out of the gray clouds, towering over neon yellow fields of rape flower. Some clouds were purple and complemented the yellow. This was the most beautiful place on earth. Coming into the orchard, I just touched and was shocked by an electric fence. I should have known it was electric because it was ticking, but I was wildly excited and less than cautious.

I continued on and could see the church Sir John told me about. I passed it and walked clockwise in an arc that would eventually bring me back to the house. I came up along a wood, a thick dark wood, the kind that druids used to play their ritual games in; thick oak and beech woods prime for sorcery. Some kind of druids probably planted these trees to match a celestial engagement, and at midnight on full moons danced about them in black robes holding torches. And just as those thoughts were whirling about, my presence in the wood or near its edge flushed some giant wood pigeons whose wings in flight clapped, seemingly against each other and the branches, echoing loudly through the forest. In the end it seemed they startled me more than I them.

Above the wood was a field where a man was loading sheep onto a truck. I thought he might demand I explain my presence but he just kept on with what he was doing. I figured they were being taken away for shearing. Someone had told me most of the shearing done these days was by New Zealanders who came up from the southern hemisphere to find work during their winter, and they worked for cheap. I returned to the house by a pond of ducks and geese and a patch of bluebells beneath a great beech tree. I entered the house through the same doors into the big yellow room, and on my way to the library a woman appeared in the hall. She greeted me very warmly, a lovely tall, thin woman with a gentle French accent, "you are the angler," she said, "and you have come to stay with us." Her name was Moira Swire and she had great blue eyes.

I returned to the library to copy the text from the back of the painting.

Painted, George Samuel 1799 Engraved 1808

Illustrated: Izaak Walton's Angler 1808

Recorded: "Angling in British Art" by Walter Show Sparrow, page 133 as follows: "For Walton's Angler, in 1808, he (Samuel) made two small oil paintings, one of Cotton's fishing hut on the Dove, another of a roadside Cottage: these I have seen in Mr. Arthur Gilbey's Collection."

Collection: Mr. Arthur N. Gilbey, Esq. Folly Farm

To add to the tale of this pictorial pedigree I remembered seeing the etching of this very painting in the 1808 edition of *The Compleat Angler*, and it was the source of considerable joy for me to see the original. Having now seen the actual fishing temple on the Dove, several things struck me as unusual about this painting. For one, it looked nothing like the building now standing. The general configuration of the facade, a window on each side of the door, was true enough, but it was of a white, almost plaster color, while the current one is the color of the natural exterior stone. Now there are two possible answers to this problem, either the one standing is not authentic, or the painter, George Samuel, had never actually seen the cottage but had painted it from a description. I was more inclined toward the latter as I would like to think that what I saw was the real thing, and frankly the one there now on the Dove is more attractive. It is no doubt a beautiful little oil painting, painted on a dark reddish ground, which depicts two people standing before it and a small dog and a cow. And it is clearly on a river that looks much like the Dove, only, peculiarly, the house looks like it's on the wrong side of the river, or at least the door is on the wrong side. When facing the door of the building on the Dove now, the river is on your right—while in the painting, facing the door, the river is on your left. This is partly why I'm inclined to think the painter never saw the fishing temple. This is a more complicated theory, but if the painter intended his painting to be engraved, he may have painted the mirror image on purpose so that the reverse image when engraved would be correct. But it did not turn out this way because on the engraving, of which there was a copy glued to the back of the painting, the door is still on the wrong side of the building, or the river is on the wrong side, whichever way you want to look at it. To say the least there was a discrepancy between actual and depicted; we can leave it at that.

Also printed on the back of the painting was a short description of Charles Cotton as well as a description of the interior of the fishing house, which I had not before seen.

Charles Cotton 1630–1687

Charles Cotton, poet, friend of Izaak Walton and Sir Peter Lely, was an accomplished angler, and contributed a treatise on fly-fishing as a second part to the fifth edition, 1676 of Walton's *Compleat Angler*.

The Trout in Our River Are Larger

> In 1674, Cotton built his little fishing house on the banks of the Dove, and set over the door a stone on which were inscribed his own initials and Walton's "twisted in cipher."

> The room was wainscoted, and on the larger panels were paintings of angling subjects; in the right hand corner was a buffet with folding doors in which were portraits of Walton, Cotton, and a boy servant.

Shortly after I had finished copying all this down, Sir John came into the library. I showed him some paintings I had been doing of England for a book on Walton I eventually wanted to do. "Well I should think for your book you will need to find a different angle, as there have been several books on Walton and Cotton. Your paintings I assume will carry you, they are really quite extraordinary. And you are at Harvard I hear?"

"Yale," I said forcefully. And just then the company arrived.

Lunch was very good and I had my first glimpse of their great, green-walled dining room, which overlooked the garden. There were vivid and colorful paintings on the walls; it was all quite springy and pleasing. I was seated across from Moira, and to my left was the granddaughter seated across from her male guest, and at the head of the table was Sir John. Lunch was sole fillet wrapped up with something in it—wow, was it good. Dessert was shortbread with strawberries and rhubarb—very good, and a beautiful rosé Bordeaux. I asked if the rhubarb was from the garden; it was. There were two curious silver centerpieces on the dining-room table, one of Walton sitting on a stump with his fishing rod and creel and the other a milkmaid with two pails of milk hanging from a yoke over her shoulder. Since the conversation had not yet turned to angling, it didn't seem like the appropriate setting in which to ask where they had come from.

We had an espresso in the yellow room, and Sir John told the company that he and I were going fishing. I think he was glad to use me as an excuse to get out of the house. He suggested I use his rod because it was already rigged up with a hawthorn fly, which he said the trout should be hitting. He told me I needed no flies either, that he would bring them, and that all I needed were my waders. As we drove in his Subaru he explained that the hawthorn fly larvae eat the leaves of the hawthorn tree. "They are a black fly with transparent wings and two big legs that dangle down as they fly."

I had remembered reading about the hawthorn fly in *The Compleat Angler* and enjoyed being instructed on the fly by Sir John, as Walton's scholar had by Piscator.

> The small black fly, or Hawthorne fly, is to be had on any Hawthorne bush after the leaves be come forth: with these and a short line you may dap or dop, and also with a grasshopper behind a tree, or in any deep hole, still making it to move on the top of the water, as if it were alive, and still keeping your self out of sight; you shall certainly have sport if there be trouts; yea, in a hot day, but especially in the evening of a hot day you will have sport.

> Mr. Barker commends several sorts of Palmer flies, not only those ribbed with silver and gold, but others that have their bodies all made of black, or some with red, and a red hackle;

you may also make the Hawthorne-fly, which is all black, and
not big, but very small, the smaller the better.

Sir John told me that he would not fish, but simply walk with me along the
stream as I fished. Sir John still wore his tie, but now with a sweater, as it was
fairly chilly, and he had brought a tweed jacket which held all he needed in the
pockets. He wore an English cap; I quite liked the man. A picture of him
emerged then. My early impressions of the English upper class had been
pounded in me by the opinionated David Scott who insisted that the upper
class were ignorant and hid behind their money and their "splendids" and
"dottys." I also carried with me what I'd read in Hemingway, a line I found
quite funny that never seemed to expire; I think it was from *Green Hills of
Africa:* "the English upper class have fewer words than the Eskimo." But this
was not so with Sir John. It was clear just from talking to him that he had read
The Compleat Angler, which surprisingly few people had. I was repeatedly
impressed with his knowledge of books, plants, and fish, much of which
seemed to have developed from investigations into his own personal curiosities. Sir John knows a great deal about trees, a passion for them even, an
observation I'd made that was later validated by his river keeper Giles. I was
astonished that he knew the range of the indigenous fish of England, the
brown trout, and that its southernmost native stream was said to be the
Orentes River in Lebanon, a fact I am sure very few people are privy to. He
continuously pointed out things to me as we drove, a magpie or a ginger-
colored vixen that crossed the road in front of us, explaining their habits and
idiosyncrasies to me. He had a very extensive library of books, and I just got

this feeling that he'd read a good deal of them. He obviously had what Walton described as the qualities that make a good angler, "an inquiring, searching and observing wit." And even if he didn't know something and was making it up, at least he was convincing.

One of the most beautiful sites was coming down into the green valley of the fifteen hundred acres Sir John told me he owned, driving down a dirt road to the Stour, and seeing a cock and hen pheasant disappear into a small lake of bluebells, their heads then just above the surface of the blooming waters. The red on the cock's cheek was especially brilliant against the spring greens. And when we stopped the car near the stream, sounds of spring cuckoos, as Walton had heard, lingered among beds of purple-pink king's pence, yellow cowslips, and bluebells.

The trail of lawn along the river was enchanting and very well kept, leading its visitors through trees trimmed into tunnels. I followed Sir John, holding the fishing rod, downstream to a pool where he said a week ago that he had seen several good fish rising. I stood patiently behind him and after several minutes we'd marked two fish coming up under the branches of the overhanging tree. He said they looked as though they were taking hawthorn flies and suggested that I ease myself in the water and walk below the fish to get a cast upstream at them. He did not state any rules about the fishing, but I assumed it was understood that only dry fly-fishing was allowed. I was dismayed when I did not catch the fish after two good drifts over him, as I wanted to impress Sir John as he had impressed me. On the third cast the fish came up and I struck and brought him in. Sir John smiled and said it looked to be a wild fish and that I should let it go.

We walked upstream carefully, watching for any and all rises. Sir John spotted a trout coming up and I tried for him and spooked him with a less than great cast, but we returned at the end of the day to catch him. From that spot Sir John pointed out to me that the roof of his fishing house was visible through the trees and next thing we were upon it, a quaint building with two lines of hedgerows framing the entrance. "It is ten by ten by ten, as opposed to the one on the Dove that is fifteen by fifteen by fifteen." Sir John opened the door with a key and we went in. It was wood walled, and there were several pictures hanging, and, as there should be, a copy of *The Compleat Angler* on the shelf. Sir John said we would come back tomorrow and have lunch in the fishing house, and then he would leave me to fish, for he had a meeting at Kent University. "I'd like to acquaint you with the better pools so that you can come back tomorrow and fish them with more care," he said.

When we left the fishing house to walk upstream he left the door open. He pointed out to me that over the door engraved in stone instead of Walton's and Cotton's initials twisted in cipher were his and his wife's, with an *M, J,* and two *S*'s.

I told Sir John that I found the place to be wonderful and enchanting. Whenever I threw a compliment like that his way he seemed to divert praise by talking of something else along the same subject, but slightly different. He did not dislike praise, it did not make him uncomfortable; it was only he did not invite it, and when it came his way he did not beg for more. I wanted to tell him that he was one of the most un-full-of-shit persons I ever met, that he really knew his stuff, and that I was very impressed with his genuineness—how presumptuous of me to say such things about a seventy-year-old on first acquaintance—but somehow none of that seemed appropriate. I only said as we walked on upstream, "You are one of the more knowledgeable and passionate people on Walton I have met. It is clear that you've read him, and the whole thing with building your fishing house . . . it has been a pleasure to meet you." And I meant it. He sometimes, as now, walking along the path with his cane, cracked a small, boyish smile. "Yes, the fishing house has been quite a success, we are indeed pleased with it."

And as we continued fishing upstream, he never told me what to do or how to do it; he only made suggestions and was never brash. He was so polished at making suggestions, though, that they took on the force of undeniable orders, but pleasantly so, because I agreed with almost everything he'd said.

"There is a fish rising," he would say. "We might want to see if he is worth fishing for." Then the trout rose again. "Yes, it seems as though he might be worth a try. That," he tapped with his cane, "is the best way to step into the river, down the bank. The bank is steep so you may want to slide down it on your rump." The banks very often were lined with stinging nettles, and he saw my forearms were being stung and developing bumps; "I should think your sleeves would help," he said. And so, we fished on, and saw some fish rise, and I fished for them. I broke one off at the strike with a hasty pull and caught one other at the end of our fishing, the one I had missed before. The fish are brown trout and are mostly stocked, but they color up well after some time in the river eating natural foods. Sir John said they were raised from original River Stour stock. The fish are golden bellied and healthy and relatively sparsely spotted, which seems to be a characteristic of the southern England fish.

We stopped fishing at about six, and Sir John recorded our catch, the water level, and temperature in a small log he keeps in the fishing house. He's been keeping a log of his fishing catches, he tells me, as well as air and water temperatures since he was a boy. "I've been fishing since I was a boy," he said, "and not just for trout. I'm quite fond of pike actually. I was fishing for pike one day, just upstream here in one of the deeper pools with a spinner and I caught a salmon."

We locked up the house and walked on. "I should think things were not very different during Walton's time," he said.

"No," I said, "it is beautiful."

On our way in to the house, Sir John brought me around the corner to show me a painting he had commissioned of himself fishing the Stour with his fishing house in the background, and sitting on a bench by the house were two antiquated figures ethereally painted. As if it needed explanation, he told me that the two figures seated at the bench were the ghosts of Walton and Cotton. It was eerily pleasing, this painting, and added to Sir John's aura as an angler and Walton enthusiast.

I went up the stairs past all the grand oil portraits and down the hall on great colorful rugs to my room, and not knowing what time dinner would be, I lay down on my bed to read and fell asleep. It was more that I was not exactly accustomed to the procedure, but apparently I missed cocktails, as a voice coming up the stairs woke me—Moira Swire saying "We're going to eat dinner now if you'd like to join us." They were both showered and looking nice for dinner, and I was still in the clothes I had been fishing in; I wished I had show-ered as I would have felt a lot better. I stood by my seat at the dining room table until I was motioned by Moira to sit, as I said I did not know the proce-dure. I was attuned to Moira now, as she was eager to teach me procedure. Penny, the cook, brought the food in on a cart and put it on a table against the wall behind Sir John. We each got up then to help ourselves from the table of lovely roasted guinea fowl. Sir John filled my glass with red wine.

"Whell Jemes," said Moira lowering herself into her chair, "I hope you won't be leaving us tomorrow, but that you will stay another night."

"I told Victoria I would meet her tomorrow night, but maybe I can leave Thursday." Victoria Wakefield was expecting me at her home in Hampshire on Wednesday, but the invitation to stay another evening at the Swires' seemed so genuine, I was inclined to stay forever.

"Whell then you will stay."

She picked up her fork and knife, cut a small piece off a guinea fowl leg, chewed and swallowed, lay her knife across the rim of her plate and lay her fork, tines down, on the plate.

"Jemes," she said, "I am very intrigued by you, and I hope you don't mind but I'm going to ask you questions, as I always like to know who is staying in my house." She took a sip of red wine, and her blue eyes sparkled. "I am inter-ested to know how you have come to travel by yourself at your young age, yes it interests me greatly. You do not seem to be afraid of anything. To walk into the grand Flyfishers club with all that yellow rococo and come in for lunch. I greatly admire that in you."

I told her, as she already knew somewhat, that I had come to do research on Izaak Walton and wanted to meet Sir John because I was told by Victoria he had a profound love of Walton.

"And how did you get to know Victoria?"

"I met Victoria through a Yale Alumnus friend at home, Reece Howard who used to come over to England fox hunting. She seems like such a wonderful woman."

"She's delightful; and how attractive and beautiful she was as a young woman. And oh, she is so beautiful still. Tell me," asked Moira, "where do your parents come from?"

"My mother was born in Prague and my father Sao Paulo."

"How very interesting—how ever did they meet?"

"In New York," I said, which seemed explanation enough.

"But you do not live in New York."

"No, I grew up in Connecticut. But Connecticut is a suburb of New York."

"What is it like where you are from?"

"I'm from Fairfield County in Connecticut, a small town called Easton. There are many trees and good trout streams. I'm about an hour train ride to Forty-second street." Sir John added that he had been to Greenwich, Connecticut, and that he thought it was quite beautiful. Several questions later Moira asked, "and what is the name of your gardener?"

"Well," I said, "my father is retired and he enjoys doing most of the gardening."

"What sort of profession was he in?" asked Sir John, taking a forkful of guinea.

"He was a teacher; he taught astronomy."

"Had he gone to Yale?" asked Sir John.

"No," I said, "he went to a maritime college in New York."

"And your mother?"

"She teaches foreign languages."

"In the university?"

"No, to schoolchildren in New Haven."

Such inquiries pried into the essence of my status and breeding, and truthfully, it was one of the first times I'd experienced such discreet, though frighteningly direct analysis. My family history and my own pedigree had never been of much concern to me; in fact, I had always considered it a blessing that I knew little of the lives or achievements of my ancestors, for I had no one to answer to, no one to live up to, and no burden of history to carry. I did, however, take pleasure in the occasional vignettes my parents shared with me about my particularly intelligent engineer of a maternal grandfather from Trieste or adventurous, motorcycle-riding grandmother who owned a house in Lugano. They somehow gave me a right to visit these places and feel as though I was visiting a piece of me. Some of these scattered sketches were told to the Swires on my third glass of wine and fourth guinea fowl leg—the converting of property in Prague to diamonds before the communists came and took it—my Bible-minded paternal grandfather who left Europe for Brazil and worked in the leather trade—my paternal grandmother whose ancestors came from a mountainous region of Portugal, where trout no doubt lived. Though the knowledge of my family history is limited, I endeavored to paint a favorable and coherent picture, fearing that if I didn't, somehow I would be given reason to feel like a racehorse who had won the derby but was disqualified because of some flaw in his lineage.

"So," concluded Sir John, "you are not, as the Australians say, 'short of a crust.'"

"I suppose not," I said.

At no point did I feel the Swires' inquiries into my family history were rude or inappropriate. Both Moira and Sir John were very warm and generous people. Having your guests talk about themselves is a polite thing to do, as it makes them feel as though their lives are important and allows everyone to become better acquainted. It was simply that their questions had forced me to go somewhere inside myself where I had hardly ever gone, and never wanted to, to meet the ancestors I had always denied being a part of me. I recalled then some verses my father used to recite when feeling particularly appreciative of the country he lived in, from a poem called "America for Me," by Henry Van Dyke.

> *'Tis fine to see the Old World, and travel up and down*
> *Among the famous palaces and cities of renown,*
> *To admire the crumbly castles and the statues of the kings,—*
> *But now I think I've had enough of antiquated things.*
> *I know that Europe's wonderful, yet something seems to lack:*
> *The past is too much with her, and the people looking back.*
> *But the glory of the Present is to make the Future free,—*
> *We love our land for what she is and what she is to be.*

I did not know very much about Sir John or Moira and wasn't about to ask. I figured I would just find out. I just leaned back in my chair all full of guinea in the great green dining room as if I were reclining in some magnificent forest of renown.

"I am fascinated with you Jemes, that you have already been on so many adventures and that you tolerate the company of two old people like us at your age of twenty."

After dinner, Sir John and I had coffee in the yellow room. Sir John talked about some of his travels for business, and I couldn't understand much of what he said, partly because of the physical distance between us, partly because the English upper class are consummate mumblers. We discussed our fishing the next day and what time we would rise. I asked Sir John if he had read any of Walton's *Lives*, mentioning the names of some of the people Walton had written biographies of. "Oh yes, I know Henry Wotton, he was late provost of Eton where I went to school." And Sir John also knew of George Morley, whom Walton was good friends with, as Morley had once been associated with Christ Church, and Sir John was an Oxford man.

I alluded to the fact that Walton had come from humble beginnings, was a tradesman, and had somehow become part of a very tight and insular literary and intellectual circle and married into a good family. "But," Sir John said, "things were not quite so strict then."

At one point Sir John was mumbling something about a Kentucky Fried Chicken franchise in Hong Kong he'd been involved with and that they had "got out at the right time."

I then naively asked if he had owned the Kentucky Fried Chicken franchise he spoke of.

"Yes, we owned a hundred of them," he said.

Showers being more the exception than the rule in England, I was happy to have one in the morning. A luxuriant feature of English bathrooms is heated towel racks, which provide you with a warm and fuzzy welcome when you are cold, naked, and dripping. A good night's sleep had erased all concerns and cares. I dressed and felt the good feeling that clean clothes bring. I felt as a bottle of wine must feel as it is brought up from its cellar and decanted, lovingly poured from its dusty housing into cut crystal walls—leaving all sediments behind and given room to breathe. I skipped down the staircase, bright morning sunlight through the windows making the dim expressions on the portrait subjects smile, humming the tune to Walton's "Angler's Song."

> *Man's life is but vain; for 'tis subject to*
> *pain, and sorrow, and short as a bubble; 'tis a*
> *hodge podge of business and money, and care, and*
> *care, and money and trouble. But we'll take no*
> *care when the weather proves fair, nor will we*
> *vex now, though it rain; we'll banish all sorrow*
> *and sing till tomorrow, and Angle and angle again.*

I chose a seat in the big yellow morning room in which to feel gentle fragrant zephyrs coming through the door from the garden. I could hear Sir John's white doves cooing, and could feel the early wetness of the dewy lawn as if I were walking barefoot on it; it was an especially comforting spring green. I picked up from the table and read the big glossy pages of *Country Life*. Indeed, it was a bit too comfortable. I had contemplated wearing a tie to fish today, as Sir John had worn a tie yesterday, and the idea of fishing with a tie had always, in a naughty and indulgent way, appealed to me. But I wasn't wearing a tie, as I felt that it might keep that gentle hand of spring from tickling my Adams apple and perhaps finding its way to a place a bit closer to my heart. And there I sat, trying to articulate to myself the ineffable beauties of this season when the maid fluttered into the yellow room in her white apron to empty the waste paper basket.

"Lovely morning isn't it," she said pulling out the plastic bag from the pail and replacing it with a new one.

"Yes," I said, finding that a satisfactory first word for the morning.

"Especially for you," she added, and, smiling, walked out of the room.

Shortly after—enter, Sir John. Sir John greeted me and led me into the dining room for breakfast. We did not sit at the grand table, but a small round table by the window. Penny came in to ask if I wanted a cooked breakfast.

"No, that's all right," I said, "I'll pass on eggs."

Sir John told Penny that he would like our picnic lunch ready by 10:30 A.M.

"And what to drink, Sir John?"

"Cider."

We had homemade cereal with fresh whole milk, toasted homemade bread, and fresh-squeezed orange juice.

"The gooseberry jam is a favorite of mine," said Sir John, reading his paper.

"Mmm," I uttered in affirmation, "it is very good. What a beautiful day."

On the little round table where we sat, there was a curious silver statuette of Walton sitting on a stump holding a fishing rod.

"The Flyfishers club made an edition of these available for members and I bought one. It is quite nice isn't it." And Sir John got up and brought over the other statuette from the dining room table to show me. "This is the young milkmaid, Maudlin, in Walton's book," said Sir John. "My wife had it made for our anniversary." It is the only one of its kind, and depicts a young milk maiden with a yoke over her shoulder, from which hung two pails of milk. Her smiling silver face shone brilliant in the morning sun and made a nice complement to reclining Walton. I faced them towards each other so as to precipitate a conversation, as the interaction between Piscator and the milkmaids is one of the more delightful parts of *The Compleat Angler*.

Piscator and Venator's encounter with the milkmaid comes during one of the more rhapsodic and otherworldly moments in the book, and the basic idea is that the milkmaids' life is as carefree as any and fit for May's spring season. Walton gives the milk woman and her daughter, Maudlin, a fish in return for a song, the song he heard her sing when last he was this way a-fishing. The milk woman tries to remember what song it was,

> Pisc. No, it is none of those: it is a song that your daughter sung the first part, and you the answer to it.

Milk. Oh, I know it now, I learned the first part in my golden age, when I was about the age of my poor daughter; and the latter part, which indeed fits me best now, but two or three years ago, when the cares of the world began to take hold of me: but you shall, God willing, hear them both, and sung as well as we can, for we both love Anglers. Come Maudlin, sing the first part to the Gentlemen with a merry heart, and I'll sing the second, when you have done.

Walton concludes, after hearing the lines sung by young Maudlin, "I now see it was not without cause, that our good Queen Elizabeth did so often wish her self a Milk-maid all the month of May, because they are not troubled with fears and cares, but sing sweetly all the day, and sleep securely all the night." So were the discourses recounted before me on the breakfast table by these two figures cast in silver.

But wasn't that a romantic burial of the milkmaid's daily duties? Of course, for to romance the working man's life is the essence of pastoral.

Though I have already addressed to a certain extent Walton's "simple" ethic, which is the base philosophy of angling, it seems here a good time, in the presence of a household blessed with riches, to add to the pot of inner conflicts. Forgive me reader, for interrupting such a pleasant morning in one of our world's most pleasant places, but we have a good day of fishing ahead of us and won't want to be bothered by all this then. As I have mentioned, Walton struggles with materialism and the dual nature of money as both a harbinger of troubles and a provider of security. Near the end of the book the master concludes that the most important thing is to live with a meek and thankful heart; that an angler should endeavor to be

> humble and cheerful, and content with what his good God has allotted him: he has no turbulent, repining, vexatious thoughts that he deserves better: nor is vexed when he sees others possessed of more honour or more riches than his wise God has allotted for his share; but he possesses what he has with a meek and contented quietness.

Walton's Piscator lends many thoughts about why money does not necessarily bring happiness, calling those who are always chasing riches and have huge estates but no time to enjoy them, "poor rich men."

> Let me tell you scholar: I have a rich Neighbor, that is always so busy, that he has no leisure to laugh; the whole business of his life, is to get money, and more money, that he may still get more money and more money; but he considers not, that 'tis not in the power of riches to make a man happy: for, it was wisely said by a man of great observation, that there be as many miseries beyond riches, as on this side them: and yet, God deliver us from pinching poverty; and grant, that having a competency, we may be content and thankful. Let us not repine, or so much as think the gifts of God unequally dealt, if we see another abound with riches, when as God knows, the cares that are the keys that keep those riches, hang

often so heavily at the rich man's girdle, that they clog him with
weary days and restless nights, even when others sleep quietly.

As often occurs in *The Compleat Angler,* Walton takes the middle road,
steering from extremes. But he realizes, and has trouble justifying, as anyone
would, those that are in the grasp of "pinching poverty," those who are "short
of a crust." Walton shows glimpses of the fact, but does not say it outright,
that very often there is pleasure found in making money. There is a parallel I
often draw, between angling and business, which I think tells why a great deal
of successful businesspeople enjoy fishing. To catch and deceive a fish with an
artificial fly is not unlike making a presentation of an idea or creation to a
client. The good businessman persists, and, if he wins that client's account,
wins the satisfaction of capture, the money that follows being akin to eating
one's own catch. Investing your own money is much like cooking the fish
yourself, for you are nourished by the satisfaction that you can cook well.
Though Sir John clearly is a man who has riches and great estates and many
responsibilities, he is susceptible to Walton's label of the "poor rich man." But
Sir John is also a man who is content with what he has been given and is
thankful and loves the gentle art of angling; he seems to have followed the
advice that Piscator ultimately bestows upon his scholar.

> Well Scholar, I have almost tired my self, and I fear more than almost
> tired you: but I now see Tottenham High-Cross, and our short walk
> thither shall put a period to my too long discourse, in which, my
> meaning was, and is, to plant that in your mind, with which I labour

to possess my own Soul: that is; a meek and thankful heart. And, to that end, I have showed you, that riches without them, do not make any man happy. But let me tell you, that riches with them remove many fears, and cares, and therefore my advice is, that you endeavor to be honestly rich; or, contentedly poor.

Walton concedes that riches, while adding many concerns to one's life, also work to relieve them as they "remove many fears." Perhaps the most difficult position to achieve is that of being "contentedly poor." To my eye, one can only truly be contentedly poor if it was a choice to be so, or if one has no knowledge of riches, for otherwise one is too often plagued by thoughts of gaining riches and resents those who have them. Let's go fishing.

"I know a little brook in Kent that breeds trout to a number incredible, and you may take them twenty or forty in an hour."
—*Izaak Walton*

Sir John explained that he was very formally dressed this morning because he had a meeting at Kent University that needed attending. But he would take me to the river, and we would start, "a bit downstream from where we fished yesterday." There was some business he needed to attend to before we left, and he told me he would meet me at the bottom of the stairs at a quarter past ten.

Minutes later he passed me in the yellow room on his way to the garden with a small, maybe sixteen-gauge, double-barrel shotgun broken over his right arm. And so, Sir John walked his garden after breakfast as proud Ahab walked his deck, a man not mad or possessed, but a man who possessed a mad contentedness.

When Sir John was ready to go I carried the picnic basket, heavy with goodies, and the fly rod to the Subaru and put it all in the boot, along with my hip waders. We drove, as Sir John had said, to a lower beat on the Stour where it flowed beside a pasture alive with small lambs playing. We carefully stepped over the barbed wire and walked between the stream and a small lake where coarse fishermen patiently sat staring at the lines they had cast and left.

"What are they fishing for?" I asked.

"Carp, roach, or bream, but I think they do it to get away from their wives," he said and smiled.

Even though it was not very early, it was still morning, and every bit of that energy that comes with getting up and smelling that rested, careless, untainted air still swirled about our senses. In the company of Sir John, walking along quiet and contented with his cane, making sure to be observant so as not to miss even the slightest indication of a rise, which could have meant missing a big fish, I felt somehow as though I would really learn from and enjoy this day of fly-fishing. We walked upstream until we saw fish rising. And when we saw one we saw several. I was excited because it was so beautiful to watch a trout take a fly on the surface, and I knew that we would catch them, but I was more excited because I could see that Sir John was excited, and that even though he had been fishing for the better part of seventy years, there were elements of angling that never got old. I slid down the bank and used the hawthorn fly that was on the line from the evening before to try to coax the rising trout from the left bank of the stream to hit.

"I don't think they want it," said Sir John, "but we can try two or three more casts before we change the fly." I realized then that dry fly-fishing, for trout especially, is a great spectator's sport. It is very dramatic and you can see almost everything the angler does, sometimes more—the cast, the presentation, the drift, the take. I climbed up the bank to Sir John so he could select another fly for me to try.

Reaching in the pocket of his coat, which he put over his three-piece suit, he pulled out his small, nondescript box of dry flies. He handled his flies with great care, inspecting each of them before deciding which to use. I could tell by looking at him that he enjoyed the simplicity behind this exercise immensely. He pulled one small, upright, dry fly from the pile and handed it to me to tie on. I cut the hawthorn fly off the line with my teeth and handed it to him. "This is the French fly, I call it. It was tied with the stiff hackles from my father-in-law's prize gamecock." Sir John was very current in his selection of dry fly floatant, and other than two small containers with flies and a spool of 5X tippet, that is all he carried. But the item he owned that I was most impressed with for drying flies was a small, flattened, brown piece of magic that looked like a piece of suede. He would take my sodden dry fly and dap it on this thing and it absorbed the water from the fly. I tied on the fly and he pressed it in this soft cushion. "What is that?" I asked.

"Amadou," he said, "it's a very rare South American mushroom, and dried it works very well to absorb moisture from the fly." It did work well. He stowed it with his other goodies in his pocket. I later found out that amadou was once used by surgeons to sop up blood during operations, and it found its way into fly-fishing as a device to dry flies because many doctors engage themselves in the gentle art of angling.

On my first cast with the French fly, I hooked a very good-sized brown trout of about two pounds. Sir John handed me the net he had been carrying, and as I hardly ever use a net, I laid it gently on the bank. But after three misses with my hand, I was feeling particularly obtuse in denying Sir John's suggestion and picked up the net. "I think you'll find it's better with the net," said Sir John. If nothing else the net was a beautiful piece of engineering. The handle slid out from where it blocked the opening of the net and allowed you to land the fish at a fairly good distance. After I handed the net and fish to Sir John and he subdued the large brown with his cane, he handed the net back empty and advised me to clip it to my side. Several fish were still rising with some degree of regularity. Sir John asked me to cast the fly up on the grass near where he stood so that he could dry it for me with his magic amadou. One fish, whose head was protruding above the surface when he took flies, looked particularly large, and when I cast the French fly to him he nearly came up out of the water completely to take it. Sir John was amazed too. He was a hard-fighting fish, and I had trouble getting him close enough to put the net to him. "It looks to be about the same size as the last one," said Sir John when I handed him the net, heavy with the weight of the fish. There was a trout that looked even larger rising near the head of the same pool, but Sir John said we'd better move upstream and let it alone so that someone else could have a try at it. Sir John promptly gave the cane to the second fish, and the life fled from its gentle body, a clouded glaze coming to the eye. All in all they were lovely fish, well proportioned and a wonderful cream yellow belly much the color of the cowslips. The sun was gaining height in the sky as we walked on upstream, and we stopped to stow our brace of trout in the shade of some nettles. Sir John stomped the ground in one spot and advised I not let the trout actually touch the nettles. The fish were beneath a barbed-wire fence marked by a bit of wool, from a lamb who'd rubbed the wire just so. After fishing a bit more, or mostly watching the river, we retrieved the fish and walked to the car.

It was about 1 P.M. when we headed for the stretch of the Stour by Sir John's fishing house. We came through the fields of barley and past a large brick house that Sir John said Jane Austen's sister, to whom the author had written many letters, used to live in. We parked where we had last evening, not far from the fishing house, and I noticed a cage, which I had seen the day before, that I had not asked about. The cage had a crow in it, and I asked Sir John what its function was. It was a trap to catch crows, and Sir John pointed with his cane to show me that there were two separate chambers to it, and one held a male crow which apparently worked to attract another male crow who, out of aggression during this mating season, wished to spar with the other.

"Does it really work?" I asked.

"Oh yes," said Sir John, "Giles has killed twenty-three this month."

The air was sixty-eight degrees Fahrenheit, ten degrees warmer than it had been yesterday, and Sir John said it was "the first proper spring day." I carried the picnic basket with our lunch, and when Sir John had opened the door to the fishing house, laid it on the table inside. After a long morning of fishing I was very hungry, but subdued my barbaric desire to plunder the basket and followed Sir John's more refined lead. He opened one side of the basket and unpacked a ham and cheese sandwich on a homemade roll and set it on the table. Then he handed me a red-and-white checkered napkin, and I put it on my lap. Sir John pulled two mugs off the shelf of the fishing house and, opening a thermos, poured them full with hot watercress soup. We stood outside of the fishing house with our mugs in hand waiting for the soup to cool. Sir John spotted a kingfisher; it was very blue.

"You like birds?" I asked him.

"I'm very keen on birds," he said.

"I'd always wanted to see the 'bird of paradise' of New Guinea."

Sir John squinted at the river and then the sky with his mug in his hand. "I lived in New Guinea," he said, "It's a bit of a bore because they are up in the canopy and you can't very well see them."

We both drank our soup, and whether it was the recipe or the day, for which God had written a splendid order, it was the best soup I had ever eaten.

"We must tell Penny she did a wonderful job with the soup," he said, as it seems he'd been thinking the same thing.

I opened two of the bottles of cider for us, "Scrumpy Jack's—made with English cider apples," it said on the label. Sir John had only half a cider, as he said he had to drive. There were two still unopened, and he encouraged me to drink them later. They were pretty strong in alcohol, and with the sun I was already starting to feel it on the first one. Sir John next took a hard-boiled egg, and so did I, and we peeled them and threw the shells in the bushes and ate them. That hit the spot. Then we sat down in the house for our sandwiches and cakes, and I delighted in watching the crumbs and bits of flour and cake fall on the red-and-white checkered cloth and the table.

"I should think not much has changed here since Walton's time," Sir John said, taking the view of the world cropped by the door frame of the fishing house as his evidence in defense of this statement. "But our lunch is better." This is true, as Walton's streamside fare consisted of powdered beef, radishes, and warm ale. "We must remember to complement Penny on the watercress soup."

Taking a pencil, Sir John noted our morning catch in his record book in the fishing house. "I think we've kept enough for today," he said. "If you catch some more let them go, unless you get a really big one." I packed the stuff back into the picnic basket, one more cider and an extra sandwich. Sir John said that he would do some work in the fishing house in preparation for his meeting and suggested I walk downstream and start fishing. He said to be near the fishing house at 5:30 P.M., as that was when he would be by to pick me up. In the event that I ran into Sir John's keeper, Giles—his vehicle was parked up on the hill and he was assumed to be about—I was to relay the following messages:

- *Ask him about the permit.*

- *Tell him we saw a ginger-colored vixen.*

- *Compliment him on his wonderful work on the weir upstream.*

With that, Sir John handed me one of his little containers of flies and I was off to fish. But I did not make it very far down the path before I was intoxicated by the sun to the point where I could no longer stand. I laid the rod against some bushes then, and myself along the carpet of grass, and taking off my sweater and using it as a pillow, I fell to sleep. I'm not sure how long I slept, but when I woke the effects of the cider had subsided, and I was left only with that glow of heat on my cheeks, that blush of sun fatigue. By the time I returned to the fishing house Sir John had gone and I was alone on the Stour.

I fished upstream some, above and almost to the second bridge. I got one good fish from under an overhanging willow branch on the way upstream and let him go. Looking up I saw then, sitting on the second bridge, a lovely young woman with blond hair. I approached her, though I did not want to startle her, as she sat so peacefully there and had not yet seen me, and the river, spring fed, made no sound as it passed under her. I thought her shepherd dog would alert her to my presence, but it only combed the opposite bank, nosing the nettles. She finally saw me coming peripherally toward her and said hello. I told her I was visiting with Sir John Swire. She apologized for her appearance; her shirt was covered in white horsehair. She loved her horse. She lived in the house Jane Austen sent letters to. Her skin was white, though she must have been out in the sun. We parted and I walked upstream. I almost asked her if she might sing me a song.

I later told Sir John I'd met a lovely blond-haired girl sitting on the second bridge, and he told his wife Moira, "James met a milkmaid today."

On my way downstream I caught one other trout, and, coming to the fishing house a bit after 4:30 P.M., I leaned my rod against it and called it a day. I walked up into the wood behind the fishing house, finding it hard to resist the curiosities a well-mown path into a wood presents, and came to a pen of pheasants which I walked around, eyeing the colorful birds. And coming around to the fishing house again I saw Giles, or a man that fit Sir John's description of him: "not too tall and somewhat pudgy." "Hello," he said, "you must be James, Sir John's American friend." Giles had two young male assistants with him, Nigel and Tim, and they had spent the day snaring pike. He showed me the instrument of his art, which he held in his hand, as well as his day's catch which lay in the bed of his pickup truck.

"They are very good pike," I said. There were about half a dozen of them and they ranged in size between ten and twenty-five inches, long and skinny with white lines and spots on a green sea. Their big teeth shone when he opened their mouths for me to see. "They eat their share of trout," he said. I knew the general idea behind snaring pike and understood how the snaring device worked, but I asked him if he might demonstrate for me. "There are very few people who are skilled enough to do this," he said, as preface to his demonstration, "in fact I know of two; and I am one. The man who taught me is the other." He had a long, limber pole, of willow perhaps, and at the end was a loop of piano wire, a kind of running noose that tightened when you pulled on it around an object, much on the principle of a lariat. Giles demonstrated on an invisible pike in the Stour. First of all you must have very good eyes as you have to spot the fish in the water; you must also carry a great deal of stealth because you have to get close to the fish, and finally you have to possess a very steady hand to loop the noose around the fish without spooking it. "And you pull up on him when the noose is just behind the pectoral fins, because they act as a kind of barb to keep him from slipping off. I am most proud of that small one we caught," said Giles smiling, "because it takes a lot of skill to get the small ones."

Giles marched up to the fishing house and leaned his snaring rod on it. "You caught fish this morning?" he asked.

"Yes," I said and walked around the fishing house in the shade to show him the two trout we'd kept.

"They are good fish," he said, and suggested we clean them. I told him I would do it, and he gave me a knife. Crouching at the stream's edge I slit the fish open from their anal fins to the head, letting all the colorful entrails wind down the stream like waterweed.

"You are awfully quiet and unassuming for an American," Giles said to me. His two boys stood behind him quietly. "I quite like you already and I've only just met you."

"Thank you," I said, and laid the two cleaned trout on the grass by his feet.

"Have you enjoyed your stay with Sir John?"

"I find Sir John very amicable and understated. He seems to know what he's talking about in terms of plants and animals and stuff. I thought maybe he played understated as a courtesy, but it seems to be genuine." I suppose I was freely provoking Giles here, as I had heard so much about the vitriol the "working class" foster for the "upper class."

"That's the way he is," said Giles. "He is a wonderful man." He picked up the fish and put them in the shade again and I washed off his knife and gave it back to him.

"Do you know anything about Sir John?" asked Giles.

"No," I said, "I really don't know anything about him."

"Well he's practically more money than God. He's bloody loaded. By some accounts he is the fifth richest man in England. He's worth something like 1.6 billion [that's pounds]. But don't tell him I told you that."

"No."

I prodded Giles a bit about whether he held any resentment for Sir John, as I'd met a lot of people in England who resented the upper class.

"Well, I've never felt resentment," he said, "I love my job." That was clear, and what was also clear was that he loved Sir John. I shared the three messages Sir John wanted me to pass along. Giles beamed when I told him Sir John was pleased with the job he did on the weir upstream.

"I only wish you were staying longer," said Giles. "I could have given you a proper tour of Sir John's super estate."

When Giles left with Nigel and Tim, I retired to the fishing house to read while I waited for Sir John. On the far wall I noticed a small picture, a painting in which various buildings and fishing scenes framed a bit of text. The painting was made in memory of a friend of Sir John's with whom he attended Eton, and the text was what Walton had said of his friend Sir Henry Wotton, the late provost of Eton College.

> He was a most dear lover and a great practicer of the art of angling; of which he would say, "It was an employment for his idle time which was then not idly spent . . . a rest to his mind, a cheerer of his spirits, a diverter of sadness, a calmer of unquiet thoughts, a

moderator of passions, a procurer of contentedness; and that it begat habits of peace and patience in those that professed and practiced it."

This is what Walton had received from his friend Sir Henry Wotton; one of the best and concise descriptions and defenses of the art of angling. Sir John understood these words and lived by them; that is why he built this fishing house and that is why I liked him.

That night I showered and changed before cocktails. Dinner was lamb medallions and potatoes, a glorious fresh mint sauce, and, as far as my mouth was concerned, a very savory red wine. Sir John and I talked about the fishing we had together and the two great fish we kept, which Giles would smoke. "We caught the fish on your father's flies," said Sir John to his wife. Moira told me that her father is a great fisherman, though I thought he must be very old and not able to get out fishing any more.

After dinner in the yellow room, Sir John asked me how the fishing was in Montana. I told him there were many big trout in Montana. Moira and I had a discussion about the past tense of the word *dive.* I had used the word *dove,* and she said she had never heard that before; that the English used the word *dived.*

"Well, I'm fairly certain that *dove* is acceptable," I said. According to Sir John's dictionary, *dove* is past tense for *dive* in America only.

Sir John stood up and poured me a cup of coffee as I reclined on the couch, an action to which Moira responded in her subtle French accent, enveloping the room in her huge inquisitive blue eyes.

"Whell Jemes, aren't you spoiled."

"Yes," I said, "but I am grateful."

"Whell I suppose that is the right ansa."

I inscribed copies of my books for them and told them I was leaving at six in the morning for Bramdean. Before I went to bed Moira gave me a snack to be eaten in the morning and a kiss on both cheeks. She made me promise that I would at least ring them up when I was next in England—what an elegant woman she is—and in parting,

"My father would haf loved you Jemes."

Victoria's house

8

Fresh Sheets
That Smell of Lavender

It was in the southern part of England, in the county of Hampshire, that Walton spent the last thirty years of his long life. It is open, fertile farmland country, rich in limestone, with great spring-fed streams and lovely stone cities built around their cathedrals. It is the land laced with distant cuckoo calls and bluebell woods and riding and great estates and all the country sports we think of when we think of England. It's a land where men wear wool ties and tweeds to fish for trout because they respect the trout as a gentleman and where great gardens with their herbaceous borders have been kept for hundreds of years, giving credence to the word perennial. It is also where German pilots in World War II unloaded a lot of their bombs on the way back to Germany. But dim days which occasionally come to cloud such jewels as Hampshire make them shine that much brighter when May arrives and allow the land to show its spectrum of color. It is in Hampshire that I fell in love with England.

Gilbert White's book *The Natural History of Selborne,* published in 1788, has become synonymous with this countryside, as the town of Selborne where he was vicar and which he wrote about, is in the very heart of Hampshire.

> The parish of Selborne lies in the extreme eastern corner of the county of Hampshire, bordering on the county of Sussex, and not far from the county of Surrey. The soils of this district are almost as various and diversified as the views and aspects. The high part of the south-west consists of a vast hill of chalk, rising three hundred feet above the village, and is divided into a sheep down, the high wood, and a long hanging wood, called The Hanger. The covert of this eminence is altogether *beech*, the most lovely of all forest trees, whether we consider its smooth rind or bark, its glossy foliage, or graceful pendulous boughs.

And the town of Selborne was no more than twelve miles from my destination; Bramdean House, in the town of Bramdean, fifteen miles east of Winchester, the city in which Walton is buried.

My host for the next several days was Victoria Wakefield, an Englishwoman of local renown who was introduced to me by Reece Howard, a friend of mine and Yale alumnus from home.

It was on a cool Thursday evening that I arrived at Bramdean House. I drove past it the first time through because the entrance was so abrupt and narrow, and cars whizzed by as if the country roads were practice courses for the grand prix. There was a wall of magnificent hedges in front of the stately brick house that Arthur, one of the gardeners, later told me used to be trimmed to look like a procession of elephants. I had not known at the time that this topiary was supposed to conjure exotic rituals in exotic worlds, but it did to me then what no other enchantment has worked on me since, and I knew somehow that, behind the dark yews and light green box elders married by planning and trimming through centuries of growth, something magnificent lay. I drove into the small gravel drive on my second try and walked to a small back door, as the front door was much too grand to allow the entrance of a first visitor with no knowledge of what he was walking into.

The cook, Marguerite, answered the door and informed me, as I had already known, that Victoria would not arrive from London until morning. Marguerite helped me with my things.

"You've come to help, have you?" she said to the dog that wagged his tail looking up at her adoringly. The Wakefields' dog was named Mr. Growler— what Victoria called a Labradoodle—"he is rather an odd shape," she later told me, "as his mother was a French poodle and his father a Labrador." Mr. Growler, as well as Marguerite, showed me to my room on the second floor and the great bed with four posts and canopy that would be my place of rest and residence for the week. These were possibly the most proper accommodations I'd ever had. Marguerite said that she would have dinner ready for me at 7:30 P.M. The back door on the first floor was open to allow the fresh cool air to circulate the three-story home, and Marguerite encouraged me to walk through it and enter the walled garden that was the pride and joy of Mrs. Victoria Wakefield.

Though Victoria had never met me, nor I Victoria, her letter to me in expectation of my arrival was quite warm. It was also appropriately to the point. Reece Howard had described her as one of the kindest and most wonderful women he knew. She had made suggestions in her letter to me of several people I should write to in the area as a preface to my stay. I was formulating my impressions of her before we'd even met through the visage of what she had made here, or worked to keep, in this magnificent garden. I imagined her as the most beautiful flower in all England, brilliant and poised, striking and attractive, indeed, a flower with such merits but also with a stern pragmatism concealed in its structure.

Victoria employed a cook, a housekeeper, and two full-time gardeners, one of whom I was about to meet. The cook and two gardeners lived on the property in small outbuildings partially connected to the house. Arthur appeared, or materialized rather as an Oz character might, from behind a wall where he was helping train one of the small rosemary plants and its purple flowers to grow horizontally. Walton's friend and provost of Eton College, Henry Wotton, said of gardens that they should not be too formal but arranged in a "delightful confusion." This followed what I had known of English gardens or the English landscape ethic, that philosophically they strived to maintain a cultivated wildness.

Bramdean House is a Georgian home and garden built by Mrs. Catherine Venables in 1741. I read this later, in an article from a 1950 issue of *Country Life* in which the garden was featured. Mrs. Wakefield's mother, a member of the Lord Ashburton branch of the Baring family, founders of the second old-est bank in England, was the first in Victoria's line to own the house. Lord Ashburton, Victoria's uncle, was personal financial advisor to the Queen.

I introduced myself to Arthur and found him an entirely amicable fellow, as well as being pleasant looking. Expressing myself ignorant to the workings of such a beautiful and extensive garden as this, he proceeded to give me some background on its design and function.

There were three basic parts to the garden: the herbaceous border, or perennial flower garden, the kitchen garden where vegetables are grown, and the orchard.

The entire garden is fortified by a beautiful vermilion-colored brick wall of about eight or ten feet, and each of the three tiers is separated by a wall. Between each tier is a beautiful iron gate with a snake in the shape of an *S* at the top of each. Arthur pointed out the sweet peas in all their different colored flowers and told me they were an ancient variety of sweet pea and one of Victoria's favorite plants in the garden. There were great peonies and roses and innumerable flowers I had no idea what to call. Up in the orchard, beneath great gnarled and stout old fruit trees, were the remnants of thousands of daf-fodil flowers that had most likely passed their peak some weeks before. It must have been magnificent when all was in bloom in the orchard. Behind the orchard were three hives of bees and a small hut, which I imagined held tools and supplies for extracting the honey.

In the upper part of the kitchen garden beside the wall was a greenhouse filled with orchids. On the outside of the walls at intervals were great beech trees that Arthur said were likely planted when the house was first built.

I told Arthur I enjoyed the asymmetry of the house, the differently sized windows along the facade and the peculiar way that they were spaced. He told me that the house had likely been added onto at various times. On taking a closer look you could see the seams in the brick walls where past builders had tried to render things seamless. I thought this added great charm to the house. There were on one side of the house several false windows, or windows that looked like they had been walled up. I asked Arthur if these were built to be ornamental, and he told me that the walled-up windows were probably the victims of an old law that based taxes on country estates by the number of windows they had on the house. He said there were many such strange taxes throughout England's history. The bricks were a wonderful vermilion color, and at intervals were alternated with gray-blue ones. Arthur pointed out to me, as bricks are more expensive than mortar, that in modern houses there was often more mortar and less brick, but here the bricks were very tight.

I respected the gardener for his acute eye and sensitivity for detail. I made an ignorant comment based on my assumption that Victoria probably only watched the garden and didn't know much about it, but Arthur promptly corrected me. "Oh no," he said, "Mrs. Wakefield knows this garden better than anyone. She replanted the borders herself several years ago and has committed to memory the Latin names of every plant that grows within these walls."

This garden began to emerge as a passionate creation and I thought then that the best of gardens was like the best of books—unexpected beauty in every corner, nurtured from the very seed of design and enjoyed by the audience without sight of the labor, craft, and revision beneath. The best of gardens are supreme fictions.

Arthur said that Victoria helped as a volunteer in the planning and upkeep of numerous public gardens around Hampshire and London. Her own garden at Bramdean on occasion was opened to the public, and the money for admission given to charity. This Sunday was one of those public days, and Arthur told me they were preparing for the crowds. He picked some rhubarb and a head of lettuce from the kitchen garden and asked if I would take it in to Marguerite.

Dinner was bits of chicken in cream with butter and various herbs served over rice. It was quite good. My duty before going off to bed was to let Mr. Growler out for a pee. We got along quite well, and when it was dark, just before I went to sleep, we walked through the damp night freshness of the garden and smelled the violet masses of lavender flower, a scent that Walton speaks of so fondly through his character Coridon concerning the accommodations at the thatched house in Hoddesdon.

> Peter. Where shall we meet tomorrow night? for my friend Coridon and I will go up the water towards Ware.
>
> Piscator. And my Scholar and I will go down towards Waltham.
>
> Coridon. Then let's meet here, for here are fresh sheets that smell of Lavender, and I am sure we cannot expect better meat, or better usage in any place.

I woke at 7:30 A.M. and in the absence of a shower, took the first bath I'm sure I've taken since I was five years old. It was quite nice.

Clean now, with cotton clothes and wet hair that caught the coolness of the morning, I walked down the grand staircase to breakfast.

Breakfast was a homemade cereal of roasted oats and honey and Brazil nuts and hazelnuts and dried fruit. I had it with fresh whole milk, delivered in bottles by the milkman that morning, and Marguerite encouraged me to eat it with a spoonful or two of a rhubarb and honey concoction she makes especially for Hady Wakefield, Victoria's husband. I ate it in the kitchen, a wonderful kitchen with a huge stove that was kept hot all the time as Marguerite explained it would take more energy to get it up to speed every time she used it than to have it maintain its warmth in perpetuity. At about quarter past eight, just as I had finished eating, Victoria arrived from London in her Saab.

She buzzed into the kitchen like a hummingbird and as she did she greeted me and ran to the phone in the "morning room" which miraculously rang in anticipation of her arrival. "As soon as Mrs. Wakefield gets here the phone starts ringing," observed Marguerite.

After about five or ten minutes Victoria and I unloaded her car, put her things in place in the main part of the house, and, after she poured her coffee, sat in the morning room together. She was a very straightforward woman and quite beautiful in her white hair, and I loved her perfectly from the very start.

She got out her "diary," or daily appointment book, and we sat down to plan my day as well as my week at Bramdean.

She asked me whether I had any plans.

"A friend of mine at home arranged for me to fish the Test on the property of Lord Denning in Whitchurch, and I have plans to go there this afternoon," I told her.

"Well," she said, "I can get you very good fishing on the Test for this morning if you'd like, just upstream from Lord Denning's."

"Yes," I said humbly, almost cowering in reverence. As the Test is probably the most famous trout stream in the world, this was like asking a Catholic if he would like to go to heaven. From the moment she picked up the phone her alacrity and mastery as a communicator and planner became apparent. She left a brief message on someone's line.

"Well you'll be pleased to know," she said to me, "that I've arranged some fishing for you on the Itchen for Saturday at Ovington Mill."

"Yes," I said, "I met Roger Harrison at lunch at the Flyfishers in London just the other day."

"Oh did you, how splendid," and she smiled. "And how was Sir John's?"

"He is a wonderful man," I said, "and we caught many fish together."

Then the phone rang and I could remotely hear the sweet voice of a girl on the other end of the receiver, and then Victoria; "Oh, Nicola, how sweet that is of your father, how dreadfully sweet, and how jolly good for my American friend."

Mrs. Wakefield showed me on the map how to get to the home of Julian Sheffield just outside of Whitchurch in the small town of Freefolk. I was to fish the Laverstoke piece of the Test owned by Mr. Sheffield and have it all to myself. Victoria told me that I would likely be greeted by Nicola Sheffield, Julian Sheffield's lovely daughter, who was about my age.

I was indeed, and she was just as attractive and charming as Mrs. Wakefield had described. "I couldn't do much better for you, could I," she had said.

Nicola was very kind and called out for her father Julian, who was going to show me which part of the Test that I was allowed to fish. Nicola extended an invitation to call her if I got bored being all alone with Mrs. Wakefield. I later told Victoria, and she said, "You'd better get pretty bored," but I was not yet comfortable enough with English humor to know if I was being matched or mocked.

Julian Sheffield drove me down to the stream and showed me the spot I was to fish. The River Test here was a lovely small river with dark green ranunculus and starwort and watercress flowing in the current. Some bits of weed floated on the surface, and Julian explained that this was the weed-cutting season and the keepers on all the beats of the Test were trimming the ranunculus.

"There you are," he said, "you can fish up to the next bridge and a bit beyond. There is no one else fishing today. You may run across our river keeper, Mr. Owen. I told him to expect to see you on the water."

I began fishing a bit below the first bridge and worked back up to it. The banks of the river were trimmed and very well maintained, like a great green carpet. From almost anywhere you stood on the bank, there was ample casting room. I was wearing hip waders, though Wellington boots to your knees, or your best patent leather or living room slippers would have done it alright because there really was no need to wade. The river was very clear. I stared endlessly into the water, and a dozen trout materialized from the gravel before me. I had read in American books that the fishing on English chalk streams was very difficult and that most of the fish were raised in stew ponds and were stocked. Neither was the case on this stretch of the River Test. I had been told that small upstream nymphing was allowed on this section. Most areas of the famed Test and Itchen are dry fly only. I put on a small gray nymph and cast it on the nose of a nice brown trout that was feeding with great frequency, tossing its jaws from side to side, sipping small insects that drifted by. He turned slightly in the direction that my fly had landed and I saw the white of his mouth as it opened. I set the hook and had my first brown trout from the River Test. It was a beautiful fish, and if it had been stocked it had lived in the river for a time, because it had magnificent colors and its fins were lacy and intact. I admired it on the end of the line in the clear water and then landed it and let it go. I laid my fly rod down and sat on the bank, and then I lay down beside it and looked up at the sky and thanked whatever deity might be reclining up there responsible for all this.

All my fishing was by sight. I worked upstream and if I saw a rising fish I would pitch a dry fly to it, or if it were stubborn I would lay a small nymph on its nose. I hooked many nice fish this way, and by the time I'd stopped fishing at about noon I'd caught eleven trout and two grayling. Julian had instructed me to kill any grayling that I caught, to toss them on the bank, I suppose because they are seen by some as competition for the trout; but I let them go too. The grayling arched their great dorsal fins, displaying the red on the outer margin.

Shortly after being assaulted by two giant swans with young that hissed wildly at me as I passed, I came across Mr. Owen, the river keeper. He was very kind, and I told him I had caught several trout on dry flies and nymphs. He said that people usually fished with dry flies only but that it was alright that I was using nymphs. The fish I'd caught were up to seventeen inches.

By a little after noon I left the Laverstoke stretch, though there was much more water I had not touched. I was satisfied somehow, for one of the first times in my life, to know that the water was there and available and that I did not have to fish it, that I could let it alone. A good deal of the fishing I did in Connecticut was on small woodland trout streams where the adventure lies in exploration and discovery; in imagining what lies around the next bend. Here was a grand buffet set before me, and I was learning the art of temperance. This was perhaps the most prolific, fertile, and well-maintained stream I'd ever seen. Here I turn to a quote from Ted Hughes, a consummate trout angler and England's poet laureate.

> A trout certainly for me, always seems 'wilder' than any other fish. The falcon among fish. The wildness of empty hills, bleak and rocky lakes, frayed, wilderness rivers knotting into dark pools, worst weather, desolation. Those places where the great peace has an eerie sister—panic. Maybe that is why trout become, if that were possible, even more thrilling, more fascinating, in the most civilized and pampered waters.

I had a bit of time before my 1 P.M. meeting at Lord Denning's, so I bought a ham and cheese sandwich, a lemonade, and a big cookie in that loveliest of small English towns, called Whitchurch, and walked to the bridge near the small store under which the Test pushes. There off the bridge before my eyes were several massive trout in the four- to six-pound class. I was beginning to realize that this sort of thing was a common feature. These delightful streams always flow through equally delightful little towns, and often the trout become town pets. People bring bread and ball it up and toss it to the trout, and whatever the ducks don't get on the surface, the trout do. The trout grow quite fat on bread. One specimen off the bridge in Whitchurch must have gone seven pounds. What better news to a young angler than to hear that Lord Denning owned the fishing rights to this very water, downstream of the bridge in Whitchurch to his home, "The Lawn."

I returned to the store where I had bought my lemonade to ask the clerk if he knew where Lord Denning lived. The man pointed just down the street and said that it was the driveway on the left at the end of the great wall.

The introduction to Lord Denning had been made through a friend of mine at home named Dr. Coughlin, who had met Lord Denning's stepson John Stuart when John was visiting America. It may also be of interest to note that I met Dr. Coughlin through my sister, who met him at some medical convention, though my sister is not a doctor. Dr. Coughlin, being a Yalie, had recognized my sister's surname because of my trout boy notoriety, and they got talking about my trout travels and she had mentioned to him I was going to England, so here I was.

Dr. Coughlin had briefed me on who Lord Denning was, exactly. Alfred Thompson Denning, according to "Who's Who," is a life peer; Master of the Rolls 1962–82; honorable fellow of twenty-two universities, including Magdalen College, Oxford; born January 23, 1899; Judge of the High Court of Justice, 1944; a Lord Justice of Appeal, 1948–57; a Lord of Appeal in Ordinary,

1957–62; and innumerable other positions and honors. Suffice to say he is probably the most famous living judge in all England, and at ninety-nine years the oldest. He was recently appointed by the Queen to the Order of Merit, an exclusive order which is limited to twenty-four members. It is the sovereign's personal gift, and in this position he joins the ranks of such luminaries past and present as Florence Nightingale, Mother Teresa of Calcutta, the Duke of Edinburgh, Baroness Thatcher, and President Mandela.

Lord Denning lives in the town in which he was born, the son of a Hampshire draper. I was interested to see what Denning, former Master of the Rolls, might have to say about Walton in parallel to his situation, having risen in the ranks from a working-class family. He certainly was in good form, had held the position of Master of Rolls until he was eighty-three (before introduction of compulsory retirement at seventy-five), and was quoted as saying in an article in the *Times,* "You can do good work after 75. I think I gave some of my judgments of greatest value after 75." Readers of Walton may agree, as some contend, that his *Life of Sanderson,* published when he was eighty-five years old, was his best. As Walton had given to his hometown of Stafford, so Denning has contributed to saving an old village school in Whitchurch and to preserving public rights of way through the village.

Denning says the following of Izaak Walton in his anthology of English literature called *Leaves from My Library.*

> On Walton's retirement, during the last years of his life, he made his home in our county of Hampshire. He praises highly the fine waters of Hampshire "which I think exceeds all England for swift,

shallow, clear, pleasant brooks, and store of trouts." He often fished the upper reaches of the Itchen on his way to Winchester. He took a lease of "Norington farme" at Overton, three miles up from us, "near the headwaters of the finest trout stream in England." That is, of course our River Test which runs through our garden and where we delight to have our friends to fish.

At 1 P.M. I knocked on the door, and the woman who answered was Lord Denning's Australian nurse. I had contacted John Stuart and his wife Veronica, who live outside of London, to confirm my fishing date with Lord Denning, and they told me that they had invited another friend, Jane Bennet, who was also a "keen angler," to fish the river with me. They were scheduled to arrive shortly. In the meantime I was seated in front of Lord Denning, who was properly dressed in a three-piece suit and tie, reclining in a chair. He didn't look like he was ready to fish that day and quickly assured me that he was not an angler, which amazed me, considering he had such nice water. This communication was administered by the nurse who injected my words into Denning's ears in loud shouts. "JAMES ASKED IF YOU FISH!" The house is hooked up to a system by which you can speak into a microphone and the words go into his ear so he can have a conversation, as he is quite deaf, but at the moment I'd arrived he had not been hooked up.

It was a beautiful home, and the walls were plastered with law volumes, every one of which Denning had no doubt read. Jane Bennet arrived and was let in by the Australian nurse, and she introduced herself to Denning and sat

View of the River Test off the bridge in Whitchurch

down. Lord Denning apologized for not being able to hear us, Jane introduced herself to me and I her, and shortly after that John and Veronica Stuart arrived.

Denning took charge of the scene and gave Bennet and I the rules for fishing his water on the Test. He showed us his log of fishing visitors and told us we both had to sign it before we left. I don't think there were more than two dozen entries since 1967, which indicated to me that the fishing should be good. Denning told us that fishing was to be done from the bank and that only dry flies were allowed. An old man walked in through a back door from the garden, and Denning introduced him to us as his good friend Sir Peter Bristol. Bristol reported that he had not caught any fish and that he was resigning for the day. I would have guessed Sir Peter was in his early eighties. Glancing back in the visitor's book, I noticed that all the entries had been made, peculiarly enough, by a "Sir Peter Bristol." Before the fishing would begin we all circled around Lord Denning for a cup of tea as tribesmen have around chiefs.

After tea, Sir Peter volunteered to take us for a walk to examine the boundaries of the fishing. He suggested how he thought Miss Bennet and I should split the water, and then I let Miss Bennet decide which water she wanted. I, of course, knew which water I wanted to fish; I wanted to catch the big, bread-fed trout at the bridge. She chose correctly, I am satisfied to say.

I took my time getting up to the bridge; Sir Peter had suggested I drive to the bridge and fish below it. Before I did I chatted with John Stuart. Stuart told me that Richard Adams, the author of *Watership Down*, lived across the street, "if he is still alive." He proceeded to tell me a story of how, when Denning first went to the church across the street after moving into "The Lawn," he encountered Adams, who displayed a "do you know who I am?" attitude, and Denning said "Well, I've never seen you before." I said goodbye to the Stuarts and headed to the center of Whitchurch. Sir Peter had called the pool just below the bridge the "Silk Mill Pool" because it was by a silk mill. This is where I parked.

This very same pool was described by Plunket Greene one hundred years ago in his charming book about Hampshire trout fishing called *Where the Bright Waters Meet*.

> I took the Whitchurch mill fishing. I cannot remember much about it now except that it was a very small triangular beat, and that I got some very nice fish. We stayed at the White Hart and whenever the water wanted a rest we went off on walking expeditions.

The cookie I had bought at the store in town had tasted very good, so I went to buy another, and a lemonade, and I sat on a bench near the bridge. From the bench where I sat, I spotted Sir Peter, who had previously said he was leaving to go tend his garden or something. He was standing on the bridge watching the large trout. You could tell that he loved them. He switched from one side of the bridge to the other, taking the slow steps that his advanced age demanded. I would have said hello to him again, but chose to watch the old man with the trout and to eat my cookie.

Old Sir Peter finally tore himself away from the railing and left, and that is when I strolled up to the bridge to see the trout again. Denning's beat began below the bridge and most of the real monsters were above, where I was not allowed to fish. This of course is always the case. But I'd saved half my cookie and planned to use it to coax them under to my side. When that fun expired with my cookie, I walked to the car to rig up my fishing stuff.

I walked to the tail of the pool, maybe thirty-five feet below the bridge, and laid a big dry fly just under the bridge's shadow. My fly even grazed the brick of the bridge as it came to the water and held in an eddy there, in front of the nose of the biggest trout I could see. Naturally he took; he really had no alternative. He had been programmed to eat and he couldn't help himself. It was a very large brown trout, almost whalelike in his take, and played dead like lumber the moment he was hooked. "Maybe," I thought, "he's been through this before," or perhaps he thought this was some trick, the reward for which was a whole box of cookies, or maybe he just didn't know what to think—was fat on bread and not willing to fight, was sick from being well. I laid him on a bed of watercress, unhooked my fly, and measured him at twenty-four inches modestly. I was embarrassed that a lady on the bridge had seen me with the fish. "My word," she said, looking at my two-foot-long trout, "isn't that the most beautiful thing; what colors!" When I let him go, he returned to his coveted position next to half a dozen or so others of his size. I apologized to the fish, but I had to do that, every angler has a need to hold a monster trout in his hands every now and then. It's almost to remind oneself that they can even get that big. I walked down below the bridge nearer Denning's house and caught six more trout. After each trout I caught, I would take the fly in my hand and blow on it until its hackle bristled and was free of water again, check the thin monofilament tippet and the leader for nicks and knots, admire the limberness of the rod—simple rituals of the fly fisherman.

* * *

When I'd returned to "The Lawn," the nurse asked if I might like to meet Richard Adams. I confessed to not having read *Watership Down,* nor any other of his books, but that I would like to meet him anyway. She said she would run into town and get me a paperback of one of his books so that he could sign it for me. Denning called Adams and set up a meeting for 5:15 P.M.

There was still plenty of fishing to be done before then. I was happy to see Bennet reclining on a bench. She had caught two trout and was done for the day, as her feet were bothering her.

I took to Bennet's downstream beat until I was out of sight of her. There were many nice trout in this beat and ones not ever seen by the public or fed large quantities of bread. They were wild and smaller and more keen. As I stood hunched over by the stream, changing the fly on my tippet, the gardener came down the river to say hello.

"Hello," I said.

He told me that the pool I was fishing was called the tank trap pool, that it was a big hole dug during the war to keep tanks from crossing the stream. The story seemed flawed, as I did not see what would prevent the tank from crossing the shallow stream at any other point, but so be it. There were many large trout at the bottom of the trap. We chatted for a while.

Just upstream from the trap the stream was only maybe two-and-a-half to three feet deep, with lush locks of rich green ranunculus growing in it, sometimes indistinguishable from the dark backs of the trout. Four trout were rising for small dry flies in almost a perfect diamond shaped assemblage. They were holding in the current and feeding frequently. I told the gardener my strategy, that I would try to get the rear one first then the left one then the far one and then the one furthest upstream. It's not often that you get to call a trout stream like a pool table. I put on a small dry fly, a plump-bodied ball of hair and hackle we call a "humpy," and within two casts had the first fish. I eased him out of the diamond and released him, a beautiful wild brown trout. Then I tried for the second. The procedure and execution were the same. I landed the second, then hooked and lost the third and landed the fourth. The gardener was quite pleased, and to be honest, I was amazed myself.

In all, by 5 P.M. I had caught fifteen trout and a grayling. By then it was time to go to see Richard Adams.

Adams literally lived "across the street." I went to his house, which has a name, as many English homes do—Bemwells House. I was greeted at the door by Mrs. Adams, who told me that Richard was upstairs and was on his way down.

The small man, in his late seventies, came down the stairs on his cane and, reaching up when he had reached the bottom, put his hand on my shoulder. It seemed a congratulatory gesture, but at some point I realized he was using me for a support. I had his book in my hand and told him I hadn't read it but that my father was a great fan. From the report of John Stuart, who wasn't even sure that Adams was alive, I didn't know what to expect, but he was quite coherent. I followed him as he shuffled down a dark little hall, which opened up into a great library. He told me about some of his books and asked me to sit. His wife promptly arrived with tea and biscuits and cake. The first thing Adams gave me was advice on how to converse with Lord Denning. "Simply don't talk," he said, "let him talk."

I told Adams that I had come to England to travel in the footsteps of Izaak Walton. Adams quoted Walton from memory, "I envy not him that eats better meat than I do, nor him that is richer, or that wears better clothes than I do; I envy nobody but him, and him only that catches more fish than I do."

He asked me how many fish I'd caught, and I told him twenty-six. He said, "I am sure you are the best fisherman I have ever been in the company of."

He told me something of his best-known work.

"Watership Down," he said, "is a real place just near here, and part of the book takes place on Julian Sheffield's property at Laverstoke." I knew that the book was about rabbits, but he told me so, and that he has always loved rabbits. He told me he'd written *Watership Down* to entertain his children, and it was rejected by seven publishers before it was bought. I told him I had been working on a heaven-and-hell and God-and-devils story, and he said he'd like to read it and that he would in fact read the whole thing and give me his opinion on it. He was insistent, "when I tell you I'll read it," he said, "I'll read it."

I sat with him and talked and drank tea for a good hour and a half. I realized then that this man, with his blue eyes, small nose, and funny white whiskers looked very much like a rabbit himself. I hoped I didn't look like a fish. He exuded some kind of enthusiasm and reverence for books and writing that I just wanted to capture and hold in a jar to admire. You could tell he liked to be surrounded by books. I often like to sleep in rooms with books, I told him, because I think they sublime knowledge while I am under.

I gave him a copy of the book I'd done on trout. "Well, well," he said, "I must reciprocate," and gave me a copy of a book he'd done on his experiences in nature called "A Nature Diary." He signed it "To James, with every good wish—May 1966." I hadn't known I would ever receive a book nine years before I was born.

I headed back to Lord Denning's to say goodbye, as I had to be back for dinner at Bramdean. The Australian nurse sat me down in front of Lord Denning and a microphone so I could talk with him. He asked me to sign the visitors book, and I did, after the entry of Jane Bennet, who apparently had gone. The Stuarts had left too. Since I had given Denning a book, he extended one of his to me, a title he published at eighty-six years old called *Leaves from My Library*, an anthology of his favorite bits of English prose from the books he'd read. "I'd hoped," he said, "that this book would be read by schoolchildren as an introduction to the best of English prose." He encouraged me in particular to read his selections from Winston Churchill's 1940 speeches. "You should know them," he said. When I asked him about his thoughts on Walton he referred me to that chapter in his book. He did assure me that he thought Walton had fished this very same water. I kept in mind Adams's advice on Denning, to let him talk. He signed the book:

> For James Prosek—on his visit to our River Test in the confident
> expectation that he will rate it as the best of all the rivers with the
> best of our native brown trout—Tom Denning 99 1/3.

Denning talked favorably about America and said that during his university years at Magdalen College, Oxford, his favorite people were American Rhodes Scholars. "I have friends in high courts in your country," he said, "they are good people. Put in a good word for us back home and tell them we have the best rivers in the world." Looking into his still-alert, though wandering, eyes I wanted to cry for the world that would no longer have him.

From Denning's book I gleaned what was his favorite passage from Walton's book—the angler's encounter with the milkmaids. Denning writes a prelude to the scene to provide context, and then quotes Walton.

> As they were coming back from their fishing, they came up on a Milkmaid and her mother. The maid's name was Maudlin. Piscator had come upon them a few days before and they had sung songs for him. He decides to ask them to sing again: and in return to give them a chub they had just caught.
>
> The milkwoman thanks him, using good old-fashioned English words like Sillybub (a drink made of milk or cream, curdled with wine, cider or other acid), Verjuice (the acid juice of green crabapples) and a Hay-cock (heap of hay) for it.
>
> *Milkwoman. Marry God require you Sir, and we'll eat it cheerfully; and if you come this way a fishing two months hence, a grace of God I'll give you a Sillybub of new Verjuice in a new made Hay-cock for it, and my Maudlin shall sing you one of her best ballads; for she and I both love all Anglers, they be such honest, civil, quiet men; in the mean time you drink a draught of Red-Cows milk, you shall have it freely.*

If I had to describe my lifestyle during my stay at Bramdean in one word, it would be "seductive." I was not yet, as Walton had put it, "sick of being well," a phrase he used to describe the prosperous pre-civil war Londoners. I did find myself a bit uneasy at times or wanting to find faults in it. I wanted to slander this England, the families and people I traveled with, the government. It was probably my rebellious American genes; though I am descended in no way from early English dissenters, I was after all raised in "New" England. Could I sense an overall depression in this country, the cultural cringe that I was searching for? Were they suffocating under the weight of their own traditions? They all may think London is still the center of the world, but the England that houses it is just a small island in a cold ocean, right? I found strange reflexes resurging in me, the same kind that would tease the girl at school that I most admired. Imitation may be said to be the sincerest form of flattery, but slander at times is the deepest. I loved England.

It was a lovely cool and damp Saturday morning, and Victoria had arranged for my fishing with Roger Harrison at his water at Itchen Stoke. Hady had come in early that morning from London, where he is an executive for an American insurance company. By a bit before 10 A.M., the dampness had burned off and it turned out to be a glorious sunny day. They all thanked me for "bringing the good weather," which I figured they said to guests to make them feel good. I was to follow Victoria in my rental car to Roger Harrison's home, just about a fifteen-minute drive north. It was very sad, Victoria told me before we left, that one of Roger's daughters had died in a point-to-point riding accident just a few years back.

The narrow roads Victoria took me through were lined with trimmed hedges, and occasionally through a very small village, like Cheriton or

Ovington Mill House on the River Itchen

Tichbourne, you could glimpse tiny crystal spring creeks that I imagined fed the Itchen. On the way, we passed through the rare stand of trees, what they would call a "forest," and all at once we were there. Ovington Mill, where Roger and his family lived, was on the River Itchen. When I say *on* the River Itchen I mean on more in the sense of it being *over* the river, because the river went under the house. This was my dream house, as I have always been enchanted by the idea of living in a house under which a stream flowed. I told Victoria when I got out of the car that at this moment, on this late May day, there was no more beautiful place on the planet. She agreed. "Oddly enough," Victoria said to me as we walked through the open front door looking for Roger, "my mother almost bought this house when she was looking to buy a home in Hampshire." We walked through the dining room, under which rushes the River Itchen. There was a slight, unobtrusive murmur made by the water pushing through. It was a peculiar sensation to look at the great wood floorboards and hear music coming from them. It must be one of the greatest dining rooms in the world. We found Roger out behind the house in his hip boots watching wild trout rise to diminutive flies.

"Well, hell-lo Victoria," Roger said, and they hugged.

"James, it's wonderful to see you again; did you know, Victoria, I'd met James at the Flyfishers just a few days ago." Whereas normally I would have put a question mark here, the English, unlike myself, end their questions with a fall in voice, not a rise. The intonation is all different. Victoria said she would return about midday with the fixings for a grand lunch and wine. I could not wait for lunch on the river. You could see the water rush under the house and the trout over the light green starwort and water celery. The trout were rising within two yards of the house, all wild fish.

Victoria said goodbye. She said with the heat and heaviness of the day that the bees might swarm. I had promised to give her a hand in the afternoon tending her hives.

Once Victoria had gone, Roger helped me with my things and told me which flies to bring along. He looked at my nine-foot, five-piece fly rod like it was a telephone pole. "That's what we use in Tierra del Fuego for sea-run brown trout," he said. Before we set off fishing, Roger brought out of the house two old leather fly wallets and opening one up; he showed me what was written on the inside cover in beautiful calligraphy.

> *James Standerwick*
> *Ovington House*
> *near Alresford*
> *Hants*
> *1795*

On the next leaf were several flies with the gut leaders tied into them. These flies had likely been tied and used by a previous owner of the mill. "I can't imagine you'll find a fly much older than 1795 that's still intact," he told me. From the viewing of these flies I was possessed with a great sense of continuum.

Roger's wife laid out coffee for us by the river, and the keeper, who appeared across a bridge from the other side of the river, told me about his method of "tickling trout," or catching them with your hands by watching where they hide under the weeds and then easing your hand under their belly and grabbing them. He said he gave up tickling after a friend told him he'd had his hand bitten badly by a pike when he put it where he shouldn't have. After telling this story he looked at his hand and smiled a row of unhandsome teeth, but somehow he wore them well and they were particularly suited to his face.

After coffee we walked upstream, spooking lots of big fish along the way. Roger's black Labrador came with us up the stream. There was a nesting swan across the river, and Roger said that they were a great nuisance because they "absolutely scour the bottom of ranunculus." The Labrador ignored the swans' efforts to pick a fight, tossing his nose in the air as if to say, "well, Mr. Hissing Bird, I'm perfectly well suited to take you on, but the ruckus would spoil the calmness of this day and the civility I have worked to cultivate."

We came to a small weir and floodgate where, Roger told me, my fishing would begin. He explained to me that the farmers used to flood the meadows with the river by closing the gate on this weir and sending the water through various channels through the fields, covering them with fifty-two-degree Fahrenheit water. What this did, since the spring water coming out of the ground is constant all winter, was keep the ground from freezing and extend the growing season of the grass, keeping the cows fed through the winter. He said they flood the meadows in the winter every now and then for fun. It was one of the few places where the old equipment was still functional and it was possible to flood the fields. We stood and gave a moment of silence for farmer ingenuity.

Above the weir, where the river split, we saw a good fish rising only occasionally, feeding mostly on nymphs below the surface. Roger put me on the fish and guided my casts with spoken suggestions from the bank as I waded downstream of the fish so I could cast up over him. I could not see the fish from where I was casting, so Roger, hiding behind a tree, had to tell me whether my casts were good or not.

"No, not there," he would say. "He's just a little to the left . . . no, just four inches upstream from where your fly just landed . . . and to the right . . . oh, he's moved a bit, he's about a foot closer to the bank now."

After maybe two dozen casts the fish came up and took and there was applause from Roger and the keeper on shore. "Well done James, we induced him to take." If it weren't dry fly only, I could have caught that fish in one cast with a nymph. But I suppose the point was to create a challenge. We did indeed "induce" the fish that was not coming to the surface to take a fly there. Shortly after that fish, Roger and the keeper left me to my fishing, and Roger said he would come back to get me for lunch.

With a nymph now, I could have caught every fish in the river. I could see them all and didn't understand how it came to be that fishing a dry fly was a moral imperative. I really did consider putting on a nymph, but then a miniature David Scott came and perched himself on my shoulder.

"You can't break down James. I thought the whole point of it was to make it more challenging. That's the British way, you know, to make easy things as difficult as possible. First it's a nymph, next thing you know you'll be using dynamite. You have got to maintain standards. That's what the English, if anything, have taught the world."

So I contented myself with inducing small wild trout to take a dry fly and napping in the sun. I sat in the path by a large feeding trout and watched the white of his mouth as it opened to suck in nymphs. I pulled off my hip waders to dry my pant legs because I had taken in water. The sun was very kind, and generous with its rays. What could I do but accept such offerings with graciousness. After about thirty minutes, I put on my waders again and stood up. Shortly I heard voices. It was Roger, Hady, and Victoria coming along for a walk.

"How did you do?"

"Very well, three fish."

"Oh, splendid."

"What a wonderful day."

We walked upstream a bit, as Roger wanted to show Victoria and Hady a part of the stream they had not seen. Then Victoria said, "We must get Mr. James some lunch or he'll eat the trees." I laughed, as I had been wondering if I'd ever get any lunch. Walton well knew that eating was one of the best things about a day of fishing. We took a trail through the meadows on our way back, and Roger gave us a more complete explanation of the workings of flooding water meadows. We returned to the mill at Ovington, where a great spread awaited me, various salads and hard-boiled quail eggs, Stilton and brie and fresh rolls, a paté with pistachios in it, and a glass of good white wine chilled in the stream. A man who Hady said was the old Ambassador to Bermuda strolled onto the property. Hady explained that whenever he visited a country he would sign the ambassador's book and expect a call for drinks and the like. Shortly after, Hady and Victoria left for Bramdean, as they had company coming, and Roger detained me for a tour of the house and his paintings. He said he really liked the painting I'd done of Pike Pool on the Dove where Charles Cotton used to fish.

By early afternoon I was back at Bramdean and joined Victoria, Hady, and their guests for drinks in the garden. They invited me to do everything they did and treated me like a member of the family. Their son Teddy, who was just two years older than I, had arrived as well, and we all sat around drinking some ambrosial concoction from a glass pitcher. I later asked Victoria what it was. She said that it essentially was Pimm's, an English liquor which the bottle will tell you is a secret recipe, with champagne. Most people drank Pimm's with lemonade (lemon soda) but she explained that Hady liked it with champagne. These two ingredients go in the pitcher with ice and slices of orange, apple, lemon, and cucumber. She said that they also liked to put a blue flower, called cumphrey, from the garden in it. "Sometimes when we have company over," Victoria said, "and Hady is given the duty of touring guests around the garden he will stop at the cumphrey and pick some of the flowers and make his exit with the excuse that he has to go fix the drink." It is very drunk-making stuff.

So we drank the Pimm's and talked, and then Victoria suggested that we play some tennis. Their court was just outside the wall of the garden by a small grove of copper beech. I told Victoria that I needed sneakers, so I borrowed a pair of Hady's.

Teddy and I dressed for tennis and then walked up the garden together to the court. It was a glorious day, and we were dressed in white and tipsy on Pimm's. Teddy and I won a doubles match against his father and a guest. It was very satisfying to win on borrowed sneakers.

Fresh Sheets That Smell of Lavender

* * *

Later that evening I was employed to help Victoria tend her hives. We suited up in these white uniforms and wore wide-brimmed hats from which screens fell, which were to be tucked under your collar. My outfit looked second or fourth hand, and several holes in the screen had been patched. As far as I could tell, the mission of the hive invasion was to kill queen cells and collect trays of combs filled with honey. She said that hers wasn't orthodox beekeeping practice. I certainly had no idea. I asked her if she'd read book IV of Virgil's *Georgics* and whether that is orthodox beekeeping. She assured me that Hady had read Virgil in Latin at Eton. All she knew was that bees were not, as Virgil suggests, born from the carcasses of dead bulls.

From Virgil's *Georgics*, book IV, completed 29 B.C.:

> *A site must first be chosen for your bees,*
> *Fixed quarters, unexposed to winds (for wind*
> *Prohibits them from bringing home their food),*
> *Where there are neither sheep nor frisky kids*
> *To trample down the flowers, nor blundering heifer*
> *To dash the dew and bruise the springing grass.*
> *Let not the spangled lizard's scaly back*
> *Be seen in their rich dwelling, nor such birds*
> *As bee-eaters and the fabled swallow Procne,*
> *Her breast still reddened by her bloody hands;*
> *For these spread havoc, snatching on the wing*

263

The bees themselves to bear them in their beaks
As tit-bits for their cruelly gaping nestlings.
But let clear springs and moss-green pools be near
And hurrying through the grass a shallow stream,
A palm to shade their porch or a huge wild-olive.

If Victoria had chosen a good site for her bees, that is, according to Virgil's direction, the part about the "clear springs" and "shallow stream" being of particular interest, then these lines prophesied some certain good fishing for me.

We forged up to the garden in our outfits carrying a smoker used to subdue the bees, and Mr. Growler came happily along. We took the roofs off several hives and dove into the trays. Some of the combs were capped and filled with honey, which I would later help Victoria extract in a great centrifugal contraption. Hundreds of bees swarmed around my head, and in a twenty-minute period three had somehow got under my head net and stung me on the left side of my face. At one point Mr. Growler had come too near to the hives and got his share of stings, running off, rolling and rubbing the wounds in the grass and yelping. Victoria laughed sympathetically, "poor Mr. Growler," she said. Walton says of bees through his character Auceps in his defense of falconing and creatures of the air:

> There is also a little contemptible winged creature, namely, the
> laborious Bee, of whose, prudence, policy and regular government
> of their own Commonwealth I might say much, as also of their
> several kinds, and how useful their honey and wax is both for meat

and medicines to mankind; but I will leave them to their sweet labor, without the least disturbance, believing them to be all very busy at this very time amongst the herbs and flowers that we see nature puts forth this May morning.

Here at Bramdean I felt the subject of idylls. It was as Walton would have said "idle time not idly spent." And the beekeeping recalled book IV of Virgil's *Georgics* and all the wonderfully put practical matters and descriptions in *The Compleat Angler*. There was a music and a fragrance to everything. Take for instance Walton's description of an animal we may also find in the garden, something as common as a caterpillar.

> His lips and mouth sometimes yellow; his eyes black as jet; his forehead purple, his feet and hinder parts green, his tail two-forked and black; the whole body stained with a kind of red spots, which run along the neck and shoulder blade, not unlike the form of St. Andrew's cross, or the letter X made thus cross-wise, and a white line drawn down his back to his tail; all of which add much beauty to the body.

Victoria thought that before dinner she would take me up the hill across the road from the house to show me the bluebell woods.

Hady joined us, as well as Mr. Growler, who was happy to be invited into the back of the Land Rover. My swelling cheek felt as though it would soon occupy its own seat beside me. Mr. Growler found his way onto my lap in the back seat, but I didn't mind. Up and over several narrow roads lined with hedge we came upon a dirt road traversed by deep ruts made by vehicles when the ground was soft with rain. The road by now had mostly dried and led us up through fields of barley to a large expanse of wood. Victoria asked if I had ever seen a forest floor covered with bluebells.

"No," I said, and she told me regretfully that they were probably past their peak in bloom.

The sun was low in the sky and cast a yellow light on the early greens of the trees. Along the dirt road you could begin to see the bluebells, and though some were wilted, you could imagine the splendor that would have greeted us a week earlier. When we parked, Victoria assured me that the real spectacle was at the crest of the hill. The bluebells grew extraordinarily plentiful in the wood. It was mostly a beech tree wood, just as Gilbert White had described as typical Hampshire. There were several great beech trees in the wood which held themselves in the calm twilight with personalities that suggested higher intelligence. Walton experienced his most metaphysical and fantastical moments while reclining like Virgil's Tityrus under the shade of a "broad beech-tree." Hady, Victoria, and I walked along the edge of the field. The evening light was splintered by the tree trunks, exposing great parallel swaths of violet-blue flowers, so thick and expansive that they looked like the placid surface of a lake. Up close they were indeed bell shaped flowers drooping from a slender green stem. Coming over the fields then at a low altitude was a hot-air balloon, and Victoria recognized one of its passengers.

"Hello, Bruce," she yelled, but not too loudly.

Hady and Victoria apparently owned the wood and had cleared the underbrush. It was such a wonderful wood, one not willing to divulge that it had been wildly arranged.

By the time we returned to Bramdean, dinner was nearly ready. Hady fixed me a whiskey and soda and showed me their wine cellar. He asked me what year I was born in, and I said 1975. "Well we could have a '75 port, but I'm afraid it may be a bit young."

Their cellar had a low ceiling and in one corner a pile of coal, which I assumed was left over from some other time. It was pleasantly cool and dry, and there were cases and crates of wine on shelves.

"I often tease Victoria," he said smiling, "that I married her for her cellar. Not for what was in it, but it's absolutely the right temperature for wines." He chose a 1982 vintage, "'82 was an extraordinary year," he said. Hady expounded on wines, and I enjoyed his lecture, feeling an erudite breeze filling my sails. This life and its accouterments wrapped me in a blind contagion.

Dinner was excellent. By this time the company had mysteriously dematerialized, as well as their son Teddy. The dining room was composed of great wood columns and ornaments in a rich mahogany color. Two portraits of a lovely young Victoria hung at the far end of the room. Dinner was brought out on a rolling cart by Marguerite: roast beef, Yorkshire pudding, which is like popovers, roasted potatoes, and a great bowl of fresh asparagus. The beef was eaten with horseradish sauce. This is traditional English fare. The asparagus was from the garden and was very sweet, dribbled with butter and lightly salted. For dessert we had a wonderful pie made of black and red currants with whipped cream. We finished off the last of the wine with crackers and Stilton cheese.

"Tomorrow the garden is open to the public," said Victoria, which we already knew. She anticipated about a hundred and fifty visitors and might want some help with some last-minute weeding in the morning. "Or you could go to church with Hady," she said. I wanted to go to church not to get out of the duties of weeding but to experience another Anglican service. Walton most certainly would have attended services every Sunday morning. The garden was open from 1 P.M. to five or so. "Tomorrow we will go to lunch at my cousin Mark Baring's," she added, and made it clear that I was going with them.

"I have plenty to occupy me here," I said, not wanting them to feel as though they should be obligated to include me.

"Nonsense," she said, "while you are with us you are family, and we shall be delighted to have you along." She explained that Mark is the son of Lord Ashburton, who is sort of patriarch of their branch of the Baring family. "And Mark could provide some fishing for you," Victoria added. "They have a wonderful piece of the Itchen near Itchen Abbas. We can ask him. Would that be something you'd enjoy?"

"Yes," I said, "very much."

The next morning the left side of my face was swollen from the stings delivered by the bees the day before. My room was cool, but it felt as though the day would be warm. I looked out on the garden, and it was wet with dew. Somehow I dreaded a warm day, as my thinking was that a cool day would reduce my swelling. I took a bath around eight in the morning and wrapped myself in a fluffy white towel large enough to conceal a baby elephant. It was all so comfortable. I dressed in jacket and tie for church and, feeling dapper, walked down to breakfast. Anticipating comments about my swollen face, I offered to Victoria, who was seated reading the paper, and Marguerite that I had indeed observed this myself. It did not save me from Marguerite's slight chuckle and smile as well as her comment that I looked "like a dormouse." I asked Victoria if I should be concerned about the swelling, and she said there was nothing to worry about, that it would go down in several days. "James, you look quite smart," said Victoria about my church clothes. "And what a smart jacket." She was sipping her coffee and talking about the upcoming Chelsea flower show in London.

"How many people do you think we'll get today?" she asked me.

"Get today?" I repeated, as I do not function well in the morning.

"At Bramdean," she said, and I remembered the open garden.

"I'm not sure, how many do you usually get?"

"We've had as many as three hundred people. I think we'll see about half that today." She explained that they charge admission to the garden and that the money goes to the land trust or some gardening charity or something or other. I ate the oat and nut cereal with whole milk and that wonderful rhubarb and honey sauce. Victoria, as a kind of warning it seemed, said that Hady liked to sing very loudly in church. "Teddy used to get embarrassed by Hady's singing and deny that Hady was his father, particularly when we'd go visit Teddy at Eton and Hady would sing in front of all of Teddy's friends." Eventually Hady came down dressed in a suit and tie for church.

To say the least, it was somewhat strange to go to church alone with Hady, because I did not have an idea of what he thought of me. Was I just crowding his weekend out of London? Nevertheless he was very kind to me, and as we walked through one of the most glorious mornings I have ever lived, he explained that we were headed for a church that was built in the twelfth century. This was a totally alien concept to a Connecticut Yankee, as the very oldest home in my neighborhood was thought to have been built in the 1640s.

And somehow, greeting Hady and walking through the vestibule at Bramdean to the twelfth-century church up a small dirt road, I was engaging in something that Englishmen had done for centuries, that Walton would have done with Charles Cotton during a Sunday stay at Beresford Hall in Dovedale. Unlike the scene in which a modern Londoner performed, this was a picture of country life that I can't imagine had changed very much.

As we stepped into the diminutive nave, the bright morning was dimmed to absolute solemnity. You were forced to see natural light only through colored glass. Why man has chosen to worship God in the dark I can't understand. Perhaps it is because when you leave the church after an hour in obscurity, where the imagination can better have its way because it is closer to the mood under which dreams are cultivated, you are struck by a powerful gust of sunlight that smacks of nothing less than miracle, and you find yourself spiraling dizzily into divine rapture.

I was introduced to the vicar and recognized him as the man we had seen up in the hot-air balloon the day before. We sat in the front pew, and before us was a book of hymns and the King James Bible, the same version Walton would have known, from which came one of his favorite passages, which he frequently quoted "study to be quiet," or, in its context:

> And that ye study to be quiet, and to do your own business, and to work with your own hands, as we commanded you.
>
> That ye may walk honestly toward them that are without, and that ye may have lack of nothing.
>
> *(I Thessalonians 4:11–12)*

Hady expressed his opinions on the beauty of the King James Bible as compared with modern translations. I was briefing Hady on the importance of Walton's Anglican life, that his second wife Anne Ken was half-sister to Bishop Ken. Hady found one of Ken's hymns in the book before us and showed it to me. At the mention of the name George Morley, Walton's good friend with whom he lived in Winchester, Hady recognized the name, as Morley had been a provost at Eton.

Between readings we sang, and Hady sang loudly as Victoria had warned. He was not entirely in tune, but I admired him for his gusto, and thought him a peculiar case, as most commonly during services I had observed the practice of parishioners trying to sing very quietly or even just move their lips. Even though I did not know the tunes very well, I soon learned them and tried to harmonize with Hady. Singing as part of a harmony is the joy for me that comes closest to that instant when a trout takes a fly or, to bring it one step further by association, we can quote the English jazz singer George Melly, who said "catching a fish is the closest thing to an orgasm." I told Hady that Walton published in the *Angler* the words for a song with music written by Henry Lawes—music for both the tenor and bass in harmony, to be sung on the bank of the stream no doubt.

When the church warden came round to take the collection, Hady handed me a pound to put in the bag. I saw this as a completely thoughtful and gentlemanly gesture. With the tunes of hymns hanging like leeches on the turntable of the mind, we exited the church into the divine sun. Hady and I sat in the morning room reading the Sunday paper until Victoria had finished in the garden. While Victoria was washing up and changing for lunch, Hady gave me a tour of the paintings in the house, which seems to be something that hosts do. He briefed me on some of the better London galleries and had several stories of acquisitions made at auction. Christie's catalogues are requisite in such homes, piled on or near *Country Life,* and, if there are sportsmen in the family, *The Field.*

We went in the Land Rover and Mr. Growler came along. There was no telling him to stay in the back. Victoria told me it was a good day for "swarming."

"Yes," I thought, "but where can one get anything but a bath?"

But then she started talking about bees again, and the only dip she meant that we'd take was into the hive's coveted honey. She explained that such warm May days promoted swarming in the bees and that they could be captured in a basket called a "skep." I alluded that I considered my bee days over and that I would watch her capture a swarm of bees with a telescope if she'd oblige me.

Mark Baring lived on the property of his father, Lord Ashburton, with his wife and children in a modest mansion by the River Itchen. The property is over one thousand acres, and there are several homes and indiscernible stone ruins upon it. This immense estate is known as "the Grange." I would not see the centerpiece of the Grange until later in the day. When I did I was in utter awe, as I had not known houses ever to grow that large. It sat at the end of a great pond on the headwaters of this, one of the most famous trout streams in the world and somehow, though I had not yet seen it at the time, looked grander and more colossal than Versailles. Lord Ashburton had lived in the five-story mansion as a child, but it had since been abandoned and he lived in a rather more manageable home nearby.

For now, sitting over our lunch, I had to be satisfied with a black-and-white picture of the Grange's front porch, which Victoria and cousin Mark eyed affectionately, identifying uncles and grandfathers who stood beside columns as large around as venerable old redwood trees. It looked to be on a greater magnitude than the Parthenon.

The interior of Mark Baring's home was blessed by several huge paintings in gilded frames that looked like a strain on the walls. The house in general looked as though it showed the strain that several young children will put on a house. Lunch was just what we had had the night before, roast beef and horseradish sauce with more Yorkshire pudding and more glorious red wine. After lunch Hady and Mark stood before one of the grand paintings of a pheasant shoot at the end of a drive.

"That is my grandfather, there," Mark told me, "he was a remarkably good shot." Apparently the land depicted had once been owned by the Barings, but they'd sold it. The topic of conversation concerned the land, as it had been put up for sale for nine million pounds. The sentiment was that was way too much.

I could not tell then what it was I detected in the air. Was it the subtle smell of the death of tradition, like the burning of family albums? Was it possible to preserve in these times such vast country estates when temptations to sell them were powerful, and sometimes necessary? Were old gentlemen of Lord Ashburton's ilk an endangered breed?

After lunch, Mark, Hady, and I had mounted a walk along the Itchen. We were headed, in Mark's words, to "dad's" for coffee, and the ladies had taken the Rover there. We trudged through wet meadows in our Sunday clothes under talk of family investments and land and pheasant shooting. Mark's Lab followed at his side, while the freewheeling Mr. Growler was quite actively sniffing at field ends. His flushing of a pheasant ended his fun, as I suppose this was seen as mischievously and selfishly chasing game that was reserved for fall harvest. Mark called him in rather furiously, and his master, Hady, gave him some superfluous scorn, though Mark seemed much more disturbed by the dog's behavior and took off his leather belt to make a leash, handing the leash and dog to Hady as if to say "can't you keep your dog under control?" But the Grange. Around the corner from a small stone building it stood, at the end of a long pond, the most magnificent mansion I had ever seen; and it was, peculiarly, surrounded by snow.

I learned when we'd come at last to Lord Ashburton's home near the Grange that the abandoned five-story mansion reputed to have been designed by Inigo Jones had been leased by the producer Martha Fiennes for her brother Ralph's new movie. Martha had joined us for coffee and explained that the set was Russia in winter and that Ralph was coming home to the place he'd grown up and found it abandoned. I found it amusing that the acre of fake snow, a sodden pile of white paper shavings, was provided by a company called "snow business."

I had been offered that afternoon an invitation to fish the Baring's water on the Itchen.

"Tuesday? yes," I said graciously, "that would be great."

"Really," Mark's wife put in, "it doesn't get fished very often."

And so the day rolled on and fishing in the midst of all this became wildly appealing. But that was two days away.

Victoria, Hady, and I had come home to a garden full of visitors, 118 for the day, which Victoria saw as a modest turnout. She had expressed mixed feelings to me watching the hordes push through the rows of her secret garden, taking clippings of her prize antique peas. "I really hate it," she said. And though the feeling of invasion was probably like a very mild dose of the poison of coming home and seeing your house had been burgled, she held her head high and wrote it off as a glimpse into her charitable heart. I found it very peculiar that she could walk among the visitors not asserting any authority and watch them without them knowing that she owned the garden, had grown up here, had planted it. But at the same time a certain amount of pride in seeing her work enjoyed by others seemed to erase the initial shock of watching strangers tromp her territory. We shared some Lapsang Souchong tea, helped put away collapsible tables set up for the company, and retired. Toward evening, after dinner and after Hady had left for London, Victoria and I walked the garden with Mr. Growler. The rows were quiet now until in a far corner of the garden we heard a familiar and very high caw-cawing din. "I do love the rooks in the top of the beech tree," said Victoria. "They gather there every evening." It had every bit of that end-of-the-weekend feeling.

And now it was Victoria and me at the breakfast table on a Monday morning, and I was savoring that homemade cereal, fresh milk and rhubarb-honey condiment concoction. Victoria laid down the morning paper open on the table.

"I do live a privileged life don't I?" she said almost rhetorically.

"I admire you greatly," I told her, and I meant it.

"I mean, I have Mr. Growler and my bees and everything," she smiled and took Mr. Growler's head in her hands, "Well I'd like to go to London," she said as if speaking in the dog's voice, in the voice she imagined the dog to have, "but I do enjoy being with James and taking walks with him." It was very endearing.

I do admire Victoria. She is strong and a strong intellect and doesn't pretend. She is a pillar of the Winchester community, serves as the head of the parish council and all kinds of other committees. She is the antithesis of idleness. Hers is, in Walton's words, "idle time not idly spent." I told her I was going into Winchester today, and she answered that I should follow her to her first stop on her way to London, St. Cross, that she was helping with a garden there and I might like to see it, and it was on my way to Winchester. It was at St. Cross, a flint and pebble church complex that was very old that I said goodbye to

Victoria. I handed her a small watercolor I had painted of her garden as a gift. "Oh James," she said, "I shall cherish it."

I loved her, who she was and what she stood for and because for me, she was England.

The purpose of my journey to Winchester was to visit Walton's grave in the cathedral. It was easy to forget under the pleasant spell of Hampshire that it had been Walton who brought me to this country. Tony Bridgett had told me that many English people had been forgetting Walton. Ten years ago, the small chapel in Winchester Cathedral with its grand stained glass window dedicated to anglers was the Cathedral's broom and coat closet. Can you imagine! Over Walton's very grave! The room has since recovered, been restored and rededicated, a celebration at which both Tony Bridgett and Jonquil Bevan gave speeches on Walton's relevance and importance; it was a celebration I would have liked to have been a participant of so I could have met Bevan, though I was working to plan a meeting with her in Edinburgh in early June. The renovation included the commission of a great copper and wood altar carved with fish; it is really spectacular, and very fluvial looking, curvy benches on which to sit and admire the window. But actually the coat closet ideal is more in accord with Walton's humble nature. He stipulated in his will: "I desire my burial may be near the place of my death; and free from any ostentation or charge, but privately: this I make to be my last will this 16. day of August 1683." Though coming to know Walton as we have through our study and speculation, I think the man who desired to be seen as gentleman would have enjoyed knowing that he was now surrounded by articles of art and subtle ostentations that display a continuing admiration.

I had come into town and parked, with eyes to see the place where Walton rests. The spire of the cathedral or any height I might recognize as such was not yet visible to me. Because they are so massive, usually cathedrals are easy to find without asking anyone "where is the cathedral." I first bumped into a river, and no less a river than the Itchen herself, where I had fished upstream several days ago and would fish tomorrow on Mark Baring's water, also upstream of town. Whereas it had first been a surprise to see trout in rivers that flowed through towns, the sight of them now among the people and ducks and thrown bread did not startle me. I had walked many narrow streets in town, none of which afforded me a view of the cathedral, so I finally asked, followed the directions, and found it.

Winchester Cathedral was a mass of stone and glass erupting from a pleasant green lawn. It was a beautiful sunny day and lots of people were out to enjoy it, walking dogs, throwing frisbees, and lying on blankets, beguiling rays. I could have spent the day surveying the lawn engaged in all its pomp and color, but the doors and cool, dark cathedral interior seemed to request my attention. I paid the admission and asked where the Izaak Walton window was. They said it was in Prior Silkstead's chapel, down the nave to the right, and gave me a little map and circled it. You enter the chapel, simply a room on its own, through a little door.

I stood there before a maze of many-colored glass that on closer view materialized into a window with words and depictions of people. The window in its entirety, with all its angling images and spiritual messages, in all its stained-glass glory, began to look like a sparkling river bottom paved with brilliant, colored stones with black lines of shadow around them and gothic arches of river weed, the whole picture of it dimming and brightening as the sun's light was compromised by clouds. This is what I saw. An image of the Test at Whitchurch returned to me then, married with the one before me, and Walton walked again on the river's edge. And without even acknowledging it, I had drawn increasingly closer to this heavenly prospect, this window and light, and, looking down to my feet, found that I was standing on Walton's grave.

> *Here resteth the body of*
> *Mr Isaac Walton*
> *Who dyed the 15th of December*
> *1683*
> *Alas he's gone before,*
> *Gone to return no more:*
> *Our panting breasts aspire*
> *After their aged sire,*
> *Whose well spent life did last*
> *Full ninety years and past*
> *But now he hath begun*
> *That which will nere be done*
> *Crowned with eternal bliss*
> *We wish our soul with his.*

The words were engraved in a large black marble slab. The window was commissioned and erected by a group of devoted anglers in 1914. The cast of characters on the window with Walton were the men whose biographies he had written: Sanderson, Donne, Herbert, Wotton, and Hooker. Walton's brother-in-law Bishop Ken was also there and St. Peter, St. Andrew, St. Anthony, St. Wilfred, and the Lord Jesus Christ crowned over the words, "the lord sitteth above the water flood." Several other captions sat below other men and scenes—"I will make you fishers of men"— "They follow him"—"Bring of the fish which ye have now caught"— "In everything give thanks." In the lower left-hand corner of the window was a scene, by a river, of Walton standing in masterly stride instructing his pupil, a Charles Cotton-looking character, in the gentle art of angling. In the lower right was an aged and noble Walton, with St. Catherine's hill and the River Itchen behind him, reclining underneath a tree with an open book extended in his hand, giving life to Cotton's lines from his poem "Contentation":

> *Who, with his Angle, and his books,*
> *Can think the longest day well spent,*
> *And praises God when back he looks,*
> *And finds that all was innocent.*

It was probably one of the only full-size cathedral windows I understood, and whoever made or planned the design of this window was a master. If all such windows had so much in them to say and conveyed such beauty to those who know and understand them, then I might consider a life of learning to enjoy them. Such a thing as the construction of a cathedral window or a cathedral itself is the continued effort of generations, the cumulative passions of hundreds and even thousands of people walled into this mass of stone and glass. I suppose they can be enjoyed on many levels, but a greater depth of sympathy and appreciation can be achieved through a degree of learning. I sat there, just thinking about nothing in particular, but everything too, about the immediate repose of Walton near my feet and the immortality he had achieved and how that was doing him no apparent good at this moment. If I saw him, or met him, I thought I probably would not mention his works or ask him about them. I might talk some, but the man Walton, the living man, was not what he is now. Just as the cathedral is the cumulative effort of thousands of devotees, so is Walton with respect to his followers.

On a frosty December morning in 1683 Walton died in his daughter's home in Droxford by the River Meon. Droxford was only ten miles south of Bramdean, so I decided to go. I took one last look at Walton's window and his grave and said goodbye.

I passed by Victoria's house, now sad and grand because she and Hady were gone, and took the road south to the little hamlet where Walton died. It was a very warm day, and I bought an ice popsicle in a small store in town. The clerk called it a "lolly." Then I walked to the Meon to cast my reflection in yet another stream that Walton likely also had.

Trout that took the Rheingold fly

9

Fishing with Rheingold

Tuesday is finally here, and I called John Greene, the river keeper for Mark Baring and his family's water on the Itchen. "Just turn left onto a road past the church on your right in Itchen Stoke," he told me. I found the river nearly on the first try after getting slightly lost in Alresford and took the small road as Greene had instructed, past a small town sign that said "Easton" that stood just before a bridge over the river, which I found oddly comforting, as that is the name of my hometown in Connecticut.

John was standing, leaning on his old Rover, dressed in green as his name would suggest. His dress resembled a kind of warden character like my friend Joe Haines the old Yankee.

"You must be James," he said, "let's have a look at the river, shall we?" As we approached the water he said, "I think you'll find this to be one of the better stretches on the river." There are two beats on this stretch and neither are being fished and seldom are fished." Mr. Greene explained, "You can fish down to the weir and up to the next bridge. If you catch a rainbow trout kill it. You can keep two brace of trout. And grayling, we used to kill them all, but we've found there is no way to be rid of them, so do what you like. We used to try to cull them by electrofishing, but we found we could only get a small percentage." When I asked him why the grayling were undesirable, he told me they were not native to the Itchen and that they competed with trout for food. He turned from the river to me, "I'll leave you here, and I'm off for the day to get some supplies up north." He walked me to my car and said, "Right then—tight lines. You might want to wear chest waders if you have them because it's a bit deep in places."

"O.K." I said.

I walked downstream, mentally marking several nice fish I saw along the way. There was a small bridge before the weir, which Greene had told me was the boundary of the Baring water, and I walked out on it to watch a shoal of small grayling feeding up in very shallow water. I folded my arms on the railing of the bridge and rested my head on my arms and the sun worked on my neck. I had little desire to cast to them and was not sure why; I had one of the best stretches of trout stream in the world before me and I felt utterly complacent. But it was a dangerous complacence, the kind that breeds indifference, and that fine line to nothingness would nearly be crossed if I could not figure out a way to reinvent this day. I was at last, in Walton's words, "sick of being well"—had been duped by comfort. It was a feeling as Frost described on his long two-pointed ladder that stuck through an apple tree toward heaven: "I am done with apple picking now . . . I am overtired of the great harvest I myself desired." And I thought of the times when I was complacent toward relationships with women when they seemed to be going well, and complacence had bred neglect and slowly worked to destroy me. It was the length of time between moral and mental destruction and the complete complacence found in near perfection that I lived for; either extreme was difficult. I can't easily describe what these extremes are for me, something akin to screaming with your mouth open and realizing you are making no sounds at all. They are, to be sure, as difficult to describe as the ethereal call of the pheasant that mocked me in the nearby woods. But I have discovered one way to work myself out of them, and that is through writing. Another is through fishing, but those times when fishing is mixed with complacence, those are unsettling times for me.

I walked down from the bridge and to the weir. Below the weir through some trees, a man was fishing, and he didn't see me, so I spied for a bit through the trees. His casting was mediocre, and after several minutes he had not caught anything. At one point, through a hole in the trees I waved to him, but I suppose he wasn't looking my way.

At that point I started to work upstream, catching the occasional trout and grayling, catching any that I cared to. All along I had this profound wish to somehow return to a primitive—to cast a thread and bent safety pin with some bait, or use my hands to catch them.

I spent five hours on the river, from 11 A.M. to four in the afternoon. The downstream beat that I fished was not very long, but I nevertheless managed to spend five hours fishing it.

I made my way toward the head of the stretch at a small island in the stream that broke the current's flow. Below the island, as I approached it from the side, there were about a dozen fish taking flies on the surface. I kneeled down in the green grass of the bank to watch them; they were taking flies smaller than I could see, unless they were taking nymphs in the surface film. One of them was a very good-size wild brown, maybe twenty inches, and when he finished his rise his tail emerged—a graceful porpoising motion. I marked his position with a flower growing on shore, some marsh marigold I think, and a log on the island, deciding he was somewhere at the midpoint of the two, and then proceeded downstream to try an upstream cast on him. As I saw his tail come out previously and his flanks through the clear, cold water, he appeared to be bright red in color. I recalled at that point Charles Cotton's description of the trout being red in a small, gin-clear spring creek in Derbyshire called the Lathkill. There was considerable strategy involved in the taking of this fish, a cerebral march that reminded me of some of Vincent Marinaro's stories of fishing trout in difficult lies in his books on fishing the spring creeks of central Pennsylvania. He had factored in all the variables of current and backcurrent and had determined that the fish he was attempting to catch rose for a fly every two and a quarter minutes or some ridiculous observation like that. There was room in the halls of angling for Marinaros and Waltons alike. Marinaro's observations were not lost on me, they just helped destroy me, as technicalities often deeply mar romance, and at heart I am a romantic. It's not so much that Marinaro was solely a technical junkie but his writings helped breed them. Marinaro possessed a meek and quiet soul and respect and love for trout and cold water at a time when technical could still be art. There are no rules out here, there should be no moral exegeses for fly fishermen, in using a dry fly over a nymph—stupid idiosyncrasies started by a very immoral man in his private life, Frederic Halford, the chalk stream policeman. What really bothers me is how modern day "anglers" are critical of Izaak Walton's book because somehow they view his techniques for catching fish as obsolete or immoral because he indulged in the use of live bait to catch trout—heaven forbid. These are ignorant people, the kind that lend sour complexions to this gentle art— insecure people who hide behind that subtly destructive word "purist." Don't you see? The book's not about fishing, it's about life—or rather, it *is* about fishing, but fishing *is* life.

I cast to this glorious brown trout with a small nymph and a small grayling took it straight away. The big trout seemed little disturbed, but I let the water settle anyway, casting to a small fish just behind the island's eddy. It turned out to be a rainbow trout that ran across the stream where the big trout was feeding. I let it go, not remembering what John Greene had told me.

Uncertain where the big brown was now, I crossed the stream and returned to the bank to see if I could spot him from that vantage. I peered in and there he was, in the same place as before, feeding ravenously under the surface on little drifting bits of life.

I re-entered the cold flow of the stream and crossed to the left bank, where once again I could make an upstream cast to the fish. This time I could see the large fish from where I was. I cast to him, he moved for the fly, and I struck him. The Hardy reel singing to the Itchen, he ran up along the island. I steered him back and as soon as he was close to me he ran across the stream and up the island again. I used all nine feet of the rod to curb him and eventually his tired flanks eased alongside me, where I slid my hand under him, about twenty inches of wild brown trout. And my hand was cold from holding it in the frigid spring water.

"You are a grand fish," I said to him, and as his asphyxiating tragedy got under my skin, the blue sky grew bluer and the marigolds increased their yellowness to me. It was a beautiful red-sided and black-spotted brown trout, and I held him in the cold current until he was ready to swim on his own.

Trout continued to rise below the island, and I could not decide whether to take the left side of it or the right. I chose to stay against the left bank and continued to catch fish. Watching a pod of fish rising just beyond the island, I put on a dry fly to try and coax them—to no avail; they seemed to be taking something smaller than what I had proposed. I returned to a small nymph and moved one fish and then returned to a dry fly again—a small pattern that imitated a sedge emerger. One trout came up to inspect it but did not take it. I resolved to tie on a smaller tippet; as Cotton realized, recommending the use of a single horsehair, trout will more readily strike the finest lines. When I lifted my head all the trout had stopped rising but one, and I tied another small fly on a size twenty hook, a very small hook indeed, and cast it to this fish, presented it to him numerous times, right over him, but he would not take. He continued to feed, only not on what I offered him. This proved a challenge. He in fact refused most everything I offered him; the water moved around my legs, the dark weed swung like a giant eel in the clear water and that trout, not more than fourteen inches, kept feeding. "Of all the trout in England," I thought to myself, "this trout is the most finicky and fastidious." He did not even appear to be taking very carefully or swimming economically, he only darted about here and there, returning to his spot between two strands of ranunculus, taking minutiae. I had brought out ten years of experience with a fly rod on this, my Moby Dick, and was about ready to conclude he could not be conquered.

I dug deep in my vest pocket for the thinnest strand of tippet. I think it was transparent sewing thread, but it may as well have been a spider's gossamer; a strand I hoped was strong enough to both deceive and snare my prey. And taking out my box of very smallest flies, I found one I had remembered tying two years ago.

It was a pattern I tied after Marinaro's horsehair ant fly in his book *The Modern Dry Fly Code* of 1950. I tied it on an especially small hook, one of the smaller made, in fact—size twenty-four—it was a thin strand of horse's mane hair wrapped in the shape of an ant's abdomen with a bit of hackle from a grizzly rooster tied in the middle to help it float. This fly carried great sentiment for me, the most so of any in my box. I'll tell you why.

When I was a boy there was a horse named Rheingold that lived at the end of my dead-end street in my hometown of Easton. Rheingold was a golden-haired horse that could hear me coming when I was halfway down the street and came running to the fence along the paths that she had cut because she knew I brought her apples. Every day that I came to see her the white hairs about her nose increased, until, some years ago, she died of old age. About two years after Rheingold had passed away, my father found a small bird's nest in a bush of multiflora rose near where Rheingold used to graze, made from the woven hairs of her mane.

This nest sat on the mantle over the fireplace in our living room, and one day I decided I would tie a fly from her hair and try to catch a trout with my old friend. I selected one small hair and soaked it in warm water, so as to make it more supple, and used it as tying thread to make a little translucent gold ant fly. I made two of them from one hair.

The water still pushed and lunged in gentle nudges against and around my legs, the eddies that they made singing in a low gurgle. I had not noticed I was standing in water while I tied on the fly, but now I focused on the water and the whole scene I'd momentarily left came into view again.

The trout was still there, up a bit from where he'd been and near the over-hanging limb of a willow that grew on shore. The thinnest hangings of leaf and branch from the willow occasionally touched the water's surface and made a cast to the fish that was now feeding beneath them difficult. It took five casts before he hit, before I saw his dark nose come for the fly, a fine fish that sped downstream and under a bit of ranunculus and starwort. He freed himself from the weed and then sped upstream, and I was very tender with the line as I did not want it to break. Finally he came back down, spent and lying with his flanks to the English sun; a glory in this English afternoon. I let it go, carefully remov-ing the Rheingold fly, and returned to the bank.

This Itchen was so dense with feeding fish that in five hours I had only fished one of the two beats, maybe a hundred and fifty yards of stream. Somehow I was satisfied to end on this last fish, perhaps my last in England, and return to

Bramdean, leaving the rest of the Itchen for another day or another dream. The next morning I left Bramdean and drew a trout in the guest book.

Salisbury, not two hours from Bramdean, was my planned next stop. I had an appointment in the afternoon to see the books that Walton had willed upon his death to his son, Isaac junior, who eventually became the canon of Salisbury Cathedral and gave the books to that library at the end of his own life.

But in the morning I had arranged to meet, by Tony Bridgett's suggestion, perhaps the best-known living "fishing writer" in England, a man of ninety-one years, Bernard Venables.

With Bramdean behind, I headed north and west for "the bungalow," as Venables described it, his home in Upavon, four miles from Pewsey on the A345. I did not know what to expect in meeting Venables, this ninety-one-year-old man. I'd read a bit about him in the most recent issue of the London *Flyfishers Journal*, that he'd written and illustrated several books, his best known being *Mr. Crabtree Goes Fishing,* which purportedly sold two million copies. The cartoon-like strips that the book comprises, which he wrote and illustrated for the *Daily Mirror*, depicted a pipe-smoking gentleman, Mr. Crabtree, and his inquisitive son Peter recounting their adventures on the stream. And sadly, because the *Mirror* owned the rights to the drawings and produced the book themselves, Venables did not see a cent from one of those two million books. The other book he is known for, among dozens of others, is *Baleia! The Whalers of the Azores,* in which he tells the tale of the Portuguese whalemen after a two-year Melvillean adventure chasing the mighty mammal.

He told me later that it sold well but he never saw any royalties from it. But this did not seem to embitter him. Had we found at last Walton's meek and quiet angler who lives contentedly poor, thankful for what he has been given? Is the pleasure of creation enough for this talented man?

If you ever have the pleasure of meeting Bernard Venables, I think you will find there is no gentler man on the planet, a true "brother of the angle," who practices, as the other members of the Great Tew Circle did, the art of non-confrontationalism.

Anyway, I came to his very small "bungalow" after asking an old gentleman in town if he knew where Venables lived. "Yes," he said, standing under a shade tree by a bridge over a small, clear headwater trickle of the Avon, "Bernard lives just up the road here."

Venables greeted me at his door and welcomed me in. "I'm sorry that my wife is not here to meet you," he said, somewhat frail and shaking with a white beard and small frame. We came into a little sitting room and he offered me coffee. There were some oil portraits of his wife on the wall that he had done. "I fished a small upper tributary of the Avon yesterday," he said, describing it as the kind of small stream where you have to creep up and hide behind the nettles. He had caught a nineteen-inch wild brown trout and was very happy about it.

Excusing himself he went into the kitchen and carefully set sugar and milk on a tray with a small plate of butter cookies and two cups and saucers. He set the coffeepot on the small tray too, and brought it into the small room where we sat by a window with a view of the Salisbury plains. I had not read or even seen Venables's works and did not know how our meeting here would progress. I had simply come to talk to a fellow angler about Izaak Walton.

"My sight isn't very good these days," he said, "would you pour the coffee so I don't get half of it on the floor."

"Yes," I said, and poured it.

He lifted the plate of cookies, but only on one side, and they spilled onto the tray, so we picked them up. His dog came to greet us. "She's an old dog," he said, "my Lucy." She seemed uneasy on her feet but had the strength to walk over to beg for a cookie.

"No, Lucy," I said.

"No use telling her, she's deaf," he said, and gave her a tap on the rump. He leaned back in his chair. "So what is it you do," he said, "if you don't mind my asking."

I showed him the *Trout* book and some paintings I'd been doing for the Walton project and he said he liked them. Venables got up and went to the corner of the room to get his portfolio, and he showed me some originals of his, watercolors of British fish. "I have written the text for them as well, but I have not really looked for a publisher. There was a man at Penguin who said he might publish it, but he lost his job." There was a bit of silence.

"What's your favorite river?" I asked.

"The Avon near my home, but it's nothing like it used to be. There were salmon in it too," he said, "and it was air-clear. The Wylye was also a beautiful little stream. It is not as clear as it once was, but lately it has been improving. My circle of fishing friends have been looking farther south and west and have found beautiful little streams down there. We keep them quiet now."

"I love small streams with wild trout," I said.

And then somehow, as if someone had slipped a stimulant stronger than caffeine in his coffee, Venables's blue eyes shone bright and he smiled and it all started to come back to him.

"Yes," he said, "you have come here to talk about Walton haven't you; what did you say your name was again, I am terrible with names."

"James." The light grew brighter.

"Most of the people I fish with, my circle of friends, have read *The Compleat Angler*. Would you like more coffee? Please help yourself."

"But most people haven't."

"This is sadly true," he said in his quiet voice, "but he has been elevated to a saintly status, as God of fishing, and his work sits there untouched as the Bible is untouched. My friends and I once organized a little fishing club that met in unpretentious locations, in pubs, and there was one odd member who was always trying to introduce rules. We knew he didn't quite fit in. He wanted to make a patch for all of us to wear, and that didn't suit us." Venables was talking like a true Waltonian, disjointedly but in the same sense coherently, or perhaps on a higher level than I was hearing—in parables or something. He talked of the simplicity of angling, and as bitterly as a gentle man is capable, about the horrors of dry fly purists—the fledglings of Frederic Halford—the technical junkies: "military fishermen" is what he called them.

"I love fishing a nymph by sight," I said, "stalking a trout and plunking the nymph several feet in front of his nose and watching the white of his mouth open. I just know they'll take it, and just by their movement I know when they've taken, and . . ." Venables joined in by making a motion like he was setting the hook on a good trout.

"You can see it in their tail," he said with great quiet excitement, the most impactful kind, the kind of excitement that is read in the corner of mouths and in eyes. "It's funny," he lightly laughed, astonishedly, "sometimes you just know a fish took the fly."

"Or will take the fly."

"That was some of my favorite fishing before my eyes started to go bad."

"I think purists are unskilled and insecure, I mean, we could catch every fish in the river fishing a nymph well."

"Don't you pity those people who can't catch fish. You know it's just those same military fishermen who criticize Walton for using bait, who sometimes complain about his quaint natural history and his violent opposition to the otter. We know that's not the point."

"Yes," I said.

He bemoaned the general poor quality of books and magazines on angling and their profusion mostly because they were "military fishermen," whose object was only to "catch, catch, catch." Venables would have agreed with American novelist Tom McGuane, who said of *The Compleat Angler*: "the technocracy of modern angling has not been conducive to the actual reading of Walton."

"They are obsessed with the technical," lamented Venables. "They have wronged the art—taken the art out of it. They try to correct Walton when he says a pike lived four hundred years or that grayling fed on gold, but that's just what makes the piece so brilliant and its pages so fragrant. He was a man of his period—would we have him otherwise? It's a part of Waltonism as rightly there as the milkmaid's song."

I poured more coffee for both of us. Venables's wife Eileen had come in and I introduced myself. The old man asked his wife if there might be something he was forgetting to tell me about Walton.

"I'm not religious or a Christian or anything," he said, "but I've come to read the King James Bible. There is an art to the way it was written, a rhythm that is lost in modern translations." Eileen, who had seated herself nearby in the kitchen, helped reveal to me that Bernard wished to draw a parallel between the art of Walton's writing style and that of the King James Bible, which is losing favor because of the claim that it is difficult to read with all the thous and thees. Modern translations of the Bible sat in Bernard's mind on the same shelf with modern, completely artless technical fishing books.

When I returned home to Connecticut later that summer, a letter from Venables was waiting for me which put into his own words what he was trying to articulate that day in his living room in Upavon at the edge of the downland valley not far from the low stone bridge underneath which trout were still rising.

Regarding my reference to the King James Bible; it and Walton were of the 17th century, when the glorious English of Shakespeare's era was still the common usage, and no more gloriously exemplified than in the King James Bible. In our time the established Church in its dreary heavyfooted way, has sought to "bring it up to date," putting it into limp modern English. That is comparable to "bringing Izaak Walton up to date." Only the dead of soul would do either.

I hope all goes very well with your Walton book.

When we had finished our coffee and butter cookies, Venables and his wife walked me out into the very warm day. I asked him if he had any advice for me concerning the book on Walton I wished to do. And on the steps of his bungalow he left me with these words. "Keep in mind that your audience is not just anglers. And of course, the *good* book on Walton, the one which you are going to write, is not an academic book, and it is not a book just on fishing."

They warmly said goodbye and I headed off for Salisbury. I stopped at a pub on the way down to eat mushroom soup and ham on a baguette with tomato. Then I pushed on south for my 3 P.M. meeting with the librarian at the cathedral.

STUDY TO BE QUIET

Walton window in Winchester Cathedral

10

Mind the Butterfly

ver since I had first heard from Jonquil Bevan by E-mail in Oxford that some books from Walton's personal collection existed in Salisbury Cathedral Library, I had put a considerable amount of energy into planning a visit to see them. I had obtained the rules for viewing and visitation from the library and requested letters of reference from both Steve Parks and Michael Suarez, which they speedily sent to the library, assuring the librarian and keeper of muniments that I was indeed a "serious scholar." I had discovered that her name was Susan Eward, had sent her the address and phone at Bramdean House for correspondence, and when I first arrived at Bramdean, now several days past, a letter was awaiting my attention, which said in essence that my plans had met a dead end. Suzanne Eward had been ill, and was officially off work on doctor's orders. Although she was planning to return to work at the library, she was also planning to work short days, and was single-handed, which would make my working in the library inconvenient. Then she added a question which I found disquieting—she asked what I could hope to discover from the books that Dr. Jonquil Bevan ("the foremost scholar on Izaak Walton") had not already made public in her writings and lectures!

I was not used to librarians making editorial statements about a proposed researcher. If I knew what I would discover from these books I would not need to see them.

When I called the cathedral and found a receptionist who was willing to give me Ms. Eward's home number, she told me that last she heard Ms. Eward was recovering quite fantastically. I was saddened to get Ms. Eward's mother on the phone, who told me her daughter had been very ill. Then Ms. Eward picked up the phone. I made the plea to her that I was in England only this once and that I was studying Walton and may do a book on Walton and that I felt it essential that I see these books, less for research purposes than for spiritual reasons—to hold a book that Izaak Walton held and to read words from pages he once read.

"But I'm afraid," said Ms. Eward, "I really don't think I can accommodate you, as my doctor would be against my climbing the thirty-seven steps to the library and lifting heavy books."

I pleaded for her to provide me with just one hour of her time and that I did not need to see more than two of the thirty-three odd books with Walton's name signed by him on the flyleaf. And finally when she realized I would not let her off the phone, and finding herself too proper to hang up, she gave in and agreed to give me one hour with the books.

"Well," she said, "I can show you one or two of the books, and we will meet at 3 P.M. on Thursday in the cathedral, in the south transept by the door into the cloister."

The Avon flows less than a hundred yards or so from the door to Salisbury Cathedral, and the feeling I got when I stood in the midst of all this was akin to what I think Norman Maclean meant in a line from his book on life and angling: "eventually all things merge into one, and a river runs through it."

I considered trout, as those swimming in the Avon, here on whose banks I stood—creatures saturated with class and genteelness while also well-known as cannibals—to be the root of civilization, and that everything in the end was related in some way to trout fishing. This is an ethereal concept, but one example is that I have experienced a similar joy when holding a trout as I have when holding a beautifully bound or well-loved book. Steve Parks, my curator friend at the Beinecke rare book library at Yale, once showed me a copy of assorted French poems from his Osborn Collection which had once been owned by Charles Cotton. It had been signed by Cotton on the inside cover and had obviously sustained a dunking at one point because it was severely warped and watermarked. "He may have dropped it in the River Dove himself while out fishing," said Steve, appealing to my fluvial and piscatorial imagination. Part of what this book we are reading here is about, my travels in the wake of Izaak Walton, is the love of books. Walton clearly loved books, he refers to them frequently and took good care of the ones he owned. Anyone who lives by the passage "study to be quiet," loves books. I wanted to see his books as I have always loved books, not necessarily reading them, but simply holding them and looking at them, enjoying their aesthetic and tactile qualities. When I was six years old, I sewed blank pages together and copied the text of Peter Rabbit so I could illustrate it. There are so many other aspects of books and what we gain from them than simply the text value. One would hope any librarian to be among the group of people who might sympathize with these feelings.

I was now waiting in the south transept by the door to the cloister wondering if she would even show, and within ten minutes of my sitting down, a burly man in uniform came around the corner pushing a woman—my stomach sank—in a wheelchair. At last, Ms. Eward had come to give me my hour with the books, but the sinking feeling in my stomach was preparing me to apologize and let her recuperate in peace. She did not give me time to sympathize with her state. Instead, she leaped from the chair to her feet and barely greeted me. Taking out a large mortice key, she jammed it in the keyhole of a giant oaken door which led to a series of dark spiral steps. She spared no drama in ascending the thirty-seven steps with her cane in the dark gothic spiral stairway to the library. I followed in silence. On ascending the twenty-second of the thirty-seven steps, we came to a small window that shed some light on our situation. If I had closed my eyes then to her square black shoes on the dark stone steps, I would have told you I was in Notre Dame trailing a limping hunchback to a belltower, but she displayed some distant glimpse of beauty when, on spotting a butterfly on the very step by the window she exclaimed to herself: "Oh dear, I wonder how that got in here!" as if an open window weren't clue enough. And then she stopped to say to me, "Mind the butterfly."

She de-alarmed the library and sat me down at a big round table facing her at her desk. "I still don't see what you will learn from these books," she said—

I sighed deeply, audibly. I felt very much like I was in after-school detention. The whole scene reminded me of schooldays and a teacher the kids used to fear named Ms. Killcoin, the prefix of her name being reason enough to raise anxiety. But these were the type of teachers I used to most enjoy, those whose praises were hard won. Their scolding had to be justified, but if you could make them crack a smile, that was worth a thousand praises from any other.

I have already issued my complaint that I had but one hour to skim the thirty-three books from Walton's personal collection now in custody of Salisbury Cathedral Library and its reluctant librarian. My strategy for getting anything out of them involved a bit of sympathetic assimilation. I looked at my paperback copy of *The Compleat Angler*, one of my most read books, and noticed that there were probably more words of mine written in the margins than Walton's in the text. I decided that if personal notations and underlining were any judge of an individual's favorite book, in particular an individual with whom I felt a spiritual tie, then I would find Walton's this way. So it was that after gently flipping through a half-dozen or so beautiful leather-bound piles, I came to *The Christian Obligations to Peace and Charity*, delivered in an advent sermon at Carisbrook Castle, by H. Hammond D.D., London 1649. This book of Walton's was very heavily underlined, and it appeared to me the general gist of it coincided with Walton's philosophy of possessing a meek and thankful soul and accepting what God has given you as best, a basic part of Jesus's teachings: "what our savior says in St. Matthew's Gospel—Blessed be the merciful for they shall obtain mercy—Blessed be the pure in heart; for they shall see God—Blessed be the poor in Spirit; for theirs is the Kingdom of Heaven.

And—Blessed be the meek; for they shall possess the earth." As commentary to this passage in *The Compleat Angler,* Walton adds:

> —not that the meek shall not also obtain mercy, and see God, and be comforted, and at last come to the Kingdom of Heaven; but in the mean time he possesses the earth as he goes towards that Kingdom of Heaven, by being humble and cheerful, and content with what his good God has allotted him: he has no turbulent, repining, vexatious thoughts that he deserves better: nor is vexed when he sees others possessed of more honour or more riches than his wise God has allotted for his share; but he possesses what he has with a meek and contented quietness: such a quietness as makes his very dreams pleasing both to God and himself.

These are powerful words to live by. Basically, if I haven't already called it enough things, *The Compleat Angler* is Walton's interpretation of the teachings of Jesus—it just happens that these interpretive words are mixed with a little practical fishing knowledge along the way. Ultimately, my interpretation of Walton's work is too prodigious an undertaking, as interpreting Walton's word also means taking on Jesus's and, some would argue, the word of God, which too many people have already had a crack at. I can only buzz along the periphery of all these sublime ideas, diving in once in a while to take some pollenic wisdom from this awesome flower. Angling as a metaphor for life is indeed common and overused as literary trope and device, I being a humble contributor, but it cannot be denied that this is what Walton is doing, and since he was one of the first to do it, it's O.K. I do have a point, and I suppose it involves getting back to the book in Salisbury Cathedral Library.

Of the many passages underlined by Walton in his personal copy of *Christian Obligations*, the following seems most appropriate to our discussion here.

> I beseech you observe, there is a double submission to God, to his will, and to his wisdom, that to his will revealed, as well as secret, revealed for the duties, secret for the sufferings of this life; the first is active, the second is a passive obedience to heaven.
>
> This the higher philosophy of submitting to his wisdom the acknowledging God the best chooser for us, the stripes which he sends far fitter for our turns then all the boons we pray for, for his denying of our demands, the divinest way of granting them, and in a word, the resolving that whatever is, is best, whatsoever he hath done, best to be done, whatsoever permitted, best to be permitted, whatsoever is revealed to be his will by its coming to pass among us, yet better and more desirable and eligible for us, then all friends and patron guardians in heaven and earth, yea and our own souls could have contrived and chosen for us.

Walton wrote in the margin "suffering and submission," and drew a hand in the margin with the index finger pointing at the underlined passage, not unlike the little hand icon on a computer used to highlight something. Fascinating really, but what does it all mean?

The key line in Walton's passage from *The Angler,* above, is that man should be "content with what his good God has allotted him." This goes very much hand in hand with Hammond's passage, the essence of which says that "God is the best chooser for us," and that "whatsoever is, is best." This seems a very passive way to live life, that one should just accept what God has given him and live with it, but it is more that man should accept what God has given him and do his best with it, knowing that all is for the best. The line I really loved and thought most thought-provoking from Hammond's book, which is the line to which the hand was pointing, was "for God's denying of our demands, (is) the divinest way of granting them." The way I interpret this is that by denying our demands God increases our desires and brings us into action. We are in passive submission to God in terms of what he has given to us, but we are to be active in doing what we can with what we have passively received. My demand may be to catch every fish in the river or to harvest every apple, but really, innately what is best for my enjoyment is that my desire to catch them be increased by my not catching them. By denying my wish to catch a fish, my enjoyment is increased. And though Ms. Eward hadn't known it, she had increased my enjoyment with these books by chaining challenge and drama to this now expeditious journey. This passage was read out of context, so my interpretations may be off, but at least, even through a misreading of Hammond, we have been made to think. My demand to know all, by being denied to know all, increases my zeal to learn. We are given what we are given and then denied the rest.

Bright May light showed lazily through the window, dancing, dappled by clouds, on the floor, as I watched the clock on the wall wring its devious hands until they conspired to end my hour. By even the titles of Walton's books I had been fascinated and instructed—a churchly score of bound wisdoms; W. Pindar's *A Sermon*; Donne's *Eighty Sermons*; Sibbes's *Bowels Opened* and *The Saints Cordials*; Bishop Cowper's *Heaven Opened*; W. Perkins's *Cases of Conscience*; Charron's *Of*

Wisdom; Shute's *Divine Cordials*; Eusebius's *Ecclesiastical History*. A whole lot of divinity here and not exactly beach reading; what do the titles in a man's library tell us about the man? For one, these titles alone communicate that Walton was deeply concerned with his obligations as a Christian. Were there any fishing books among them? Well, there really weren't many fishing books around back then, relative to how many there are now, and this of course is not Walton's complete library. But we have to think that our great forefather of angling as recreation would have at least kept a couple around for reference, as we know he culled much from other books on the subject. Fishing, it seems, was Walton's vehicle through which to innocently divulge his own theories on how to live life as a good Christian and generally a good person. Therefore, angling was in a sense a religion for him, or at the very least, anglers were the people who received God's word, who somehow knew something the rest of the world had left behind. England was rivers to Walton and anglers were the wise men who stopped to contemplate them.

I picked up Walton's copy of *Christian Obligations* and walked over to Ms. Eward hunched at her desk. "This is why I wanted to see the books," I said, holding it open to the passage that Walton had underlined, a passage that had been of great importance to him. "Look what I have seen, what I have felt by knowing Walton had hunched over a table too with his pen in hand and had underlined these very words himself," I wanted to say. I held the book and said, "look at the little hand he drew in the margin, isn't it playful—it tells me Walton had a sense of humor. That is why I wanted to see the books." She lit a half-smile and said: "I see." She didn't.

I put the book down on the table, gathered my things, and she opened the door which led down the spiral stairs. On leaving the cathedral I was blasted by sunshine and started walking toward the River Avon.

There was a particular view of Salisbury Cathedral I wanted to see; that view as Constable had painted it, with the River Avon in the foreground. I had etched in my mind the general composition of Constable's 1826 painting "From the Bishop's Garden" as I had remembered it in the Frick Collection, my favorite museum in New York City. The cathedral is framed by two large, nondescript sort of trees which could be oaks or could be elms, and, to the left of the tree which divides the canvas, is a man dressed elegantly in black with black hat, holding the hand of a woman, standing on a bridge over the river, and pointing to the cathedral's spire with his cane. It is now other buildings and not the odd large tree that frame the cathedral, and though the bridge is at or near the same place, it is no longer a dirt path but a paved arc. It happened that quite near to this bridge was a delightful antiquarian sporting book shop which I walked into in the hopes of buying a copy of Bernard Venables's most famous book, *Mr. Crabtree Goes Fishing*. With more copies in print than any other fishing book, save *The Compleat Angler*, you would think it not difficult to find a secondhand copy. But the bookstore owner, Judith Head, assured me it was one of the more difficult books to get a copy of, mostly because people who owned it kept their copies. It so happened, she said, that a copy had just come into stock and she was willing to sell it to me for thirty-five pounds. I was glad to have it. It was a tattered old copy I figured I would rebind on returning home. Mrs. Head and I got to talking; she and her husband had just returned from New York, where they closed the deal on the purchase of the largest and most complete collection of *Compleat Angler* editions extant, including translations from Swedish to Japanese. It was owned by a gentleman named Rudolph Coigney and had already been purchased by some wealthy Englishman who planned to stow the collection away in his castle. It was the largest transaction they had been involved with. What would Walton have thought of all this?

The days following my visit to the cathedral library were spent on the River Avon just north of Salisbury in the refreshing company of an American friend, Jim Murphy, who founded and was president of an American rod company. We were both attending a fishing show of sorts, an exposition and assemblage of tackle and lecture on the riverbank, and partook of all the panoply and revelry that comes when "quiet" anglers convene. Murphy brought a bottle of fifteen-year-old port he'd got for his birthday out on the river one day with two proper Englishmen. We disposed of it in the hot sun, and then had casting contests with the fly rods and even caught some trout. Jim's theory about being around Englishmen or any foreigners is to act like a stereotypical American, that is, boisterous, loud, and flailing. And for him it works, as he is well loved and does a good business in the United Kingdom and Japan. Three hundred or so people showed up on the Saturday of the exposition, three hundred anglers of all kinds in a seeming Shangri-la, from fish bums who live out of their 1972 Land Rovers to proud and proper estate owners. We had great barbecues with great food and drank ourselves silly. Would Walton have approved of such excess? I think so, even though in theory it was all moderation, always middle road.

And these days of respite were good because it was my intention now to traverse the entire country of England, a good ten-hour drive, to visit Dr. Jonquil Bevan, the foremost modern authority on Izaak Walton, at her seat in Edinburgh University, Scotland.

Brown trout with fishing rod

11

I Wanted to Edit

y communications with Dr. Jonquil Bevan, senior lecturer in English at Edinburgh University, had been attempted by telephone for the last two weeks of the trip. Tony Bridgett had told her of me and my interests, as had Michael Suarez. Tony had provided her office phone number, and after a hundred or so attempts I managed to reach her. This was early on, and we'd set a date and time to meet for lunch. I called to confirm on the road to Edinburgh, and she told me she could only meet on the day after we had planned; that was fine. But when I called the next morning from Edinburgh, she said she was not certain if she could even meet at all—I did not tell her that I had driven ten hours just to see her, to this city near the North Sea on the Firth of Forth in southeast Scotland which is not on the way to anywhere. In the end she said to come to her office the next day at 11 A.M. and that she felt reasonably certain that she would show up.

And so, Dr. Bevan had wrapped me into a challenging puzzle which required my juggling flights and fares, as I would no longer have time to drive from Edinburgh to London but now would have to fly.

At that point I was torn as to how I should approach my visit to meet the foremost living scholar on Walton. My esteem for her, you may understand, which had been building greatly over the past few weeks, had since somewhat deflated—but I took the issue sensitively. I resolved that we cannot, or perhaps should not, value the scholarly by their private lives and ways, for more often than not, in my experience, scholars are withdrawn and peculiar people. I had explained that I greatly admired her work and was writing my essay and maybe a book on Walton, which I envisioned as a popular, not entirely scholarly piece, with hopes that Walton's works may enjoy more readers. I had hopes that a prominent scholar who had devoted a good part of her life to the study of one book would be receptive and joyed to meet another person who shared a love for it too. But Dr. Jonquil Bevan, for all the reverence I had for her and her works, remained a very difficult fish.

She had edited Walton's *Compleat Angler* and written an excellent book of criticism on it, entitled *The Compleat Angler: The Art of Recreation*. Somehow I had concocted in my imagination this delightful tale that I would catch a brace of trout and bring it to Jonquil, I even liked her name, and that we would cook them using one of Walton's recipes, and talk about the beauty of his prose over a glass or two of white wine. But I had developed a kinship with this woman through her books that seemed to belie the actual. My beautiful concluding episode with the foremost Walton scholar, a dream that was to mature and fructify, was beginning to get sick and to die a slow death.

I had not been without warning. Tony Bridgett, who had extended his kind-ness to me on no one's recommendation, said that she could be somewhat hard to communicate with; whether it was arrogance, insecurity or timidity he had found in her I could not be entirely certain, because he was not the sort that would speak ill of the devil. He talked of her always with respect and rever-ence, as if she was the first to find the key to Walton's great chest of mystery and wisdom. "She is not an angler," he said concluding. Michael Suarez had met her, but he offered a charitable, mostly objective description and said only that she seemed somewhat awkward around people.

Though she had explained that, being exam period, it was a very busy time for her and her students, I had the feeling I was being overtly dodged, and began as I sometimes do, to take it personally. But in a strange way, I almost enjoyed those solemn feelings of uncertainty in dark and gray Edinburgh the night before my meeting with Dr. Bevan. I started the day somewhat infuriated. Then to calm myself, I read Walton. Of course, that only reminded me of why I had come to Scotland and left me wondering whether it had been a mistake to come at all. Some gross transmutation of Ms. Eward's words kept fluttering before me like a butterfly coated in creosote, "and what, Mr. Prosek, may I ask, do you hope to discover during a meeting with Dr. Bevan," as if she herself guarded and growled at the gates to Dr. Bevan's datebook. But anglers being persistent, even against the sublime forces that nudge us down the paths toward least resistance, I continued to naively draft a list of questions I wished to ask her about Izaak Walton.

When I awoke to another dim morning in Edinburgh, the insight arrived in me that my paramount inquiry to Dr. Bevan was how she had become interested in Walton in the first place. I was to meet her at her office on George Square at 11 A.M. on the seventh floor of David Hume Tower, room 706. I was there fifteen minutes early.

An hour and a half later I was still sitting outside her locked door. But after three years of university life, I had grown accustomed to waiting for professors at their office hours.

The elevator bell rang on my floor several times within the next hour, but no one came to the door of Dr. Bevan's office. Finally, at 1 P.M., an oldish woman with an unclear complexion, long neck, and square stance, inched down the hall, came to her door, and looked at me only so much as to avoid tripping over me. She was spookily wide-eyed with definingly thin eyebrows, and she tilted her head as some animals do when we anthropomorphize that they are inquisitive, and looked somewhat peculiar. She did not say sorry for being late, and may not have said anything to me and locked the door behind her had I not lifted up my head and uttered, "I'm James, I called you about Walton," as politely as I could under the circumstances. And she humphed and walked into her office and I followed and I said calmly, "Do you have a moment?" She didn't say anything. "If you don't that's O.K., I know you are busy."

"No," she said, "do sit."

So I sat, and there was light in her room—there had not been any in the hallway—and I looked out of a long horizontal window, somewhat dirty, and perused the Edinburgh silhouette beyond the uninspiring view of the university buildings. I expected her to say, "what can I do for you," but she only sat and looked at me blankly.

"I've come to see you," I said, "because you really are one of the only people living who has read and written on Walton's *Angler* with a critical eye. I'm fond of your book," I said, and produced it for her to sign, and she displayed a mere shadow of a smile across her face, small hairs backlit by the light from the window, whiskers almost, and a ruddy complexion. There was something warm and strange about her, almost cartoonish, and I thought she resembled a Dr. Seuss character. The grinch wasn't who I had in mind, but you may have thought of that. "My name is James," I said, "if you might personalize it." And she wrote simply;

To James

Jonquil Bevan.

And with nothing left to do and oxygen in the room running low, I simply jumped into my questions, which I had written in small handwriting on a three-by-five index card. I wanted to promote a conversation with her on the meanings of the three more essential words in *The Compleat Angler*: *content*, *simple*, and *quiet*. She seemed to suggest that they signified much of the same things that they did today, though I said, and she agreed, that *simple* for Walton also alluded to a return to primitive Christianity, and that *quiet* may have also connoted "moderation."

I introduced some of my own opinions on the *Angler*, admittedly philosophies I had implanted in Walton's narrative, inseminating his text, if you will, in order to produce a hybrid one.

One theory I opined was that by 1650 or so, Walton and Cotton had considered fishing as a religion. Dr. Bevan at first disagreed, but then sort of gave in. And too I suggested that through angling a kind of immortality could be achieved, a transcendence of incidents of time and decay. I quoted the lines of Ralegh in *The Compleat Angler,* "I was then lifted above the earth/And experienced pleasures not promised at my birth," talking about them as metaphysical and otherworldly. We discussed Donne as a metaphysical poet. I introduced my contrast theory through Walton's quote about the people of London as "sick of being well," and inquired whether Walton could have written such a calming and quiet, generally soothing book if he had not experienced some measure of tragedy. I also asked if she thought Walton might have possibly read and been influenced by Lucian's dialogue *Piscator*. She said Walton could not read Latin, and she did not know if there had been a translation.

And then I asked her the question I had somehow stowed in my shirt pocket, the one sewed nearest my heart. I asked her how she first came to study Walton, as I knew from Tony Bridgett that she was not an angler.

"I wanted to edit," she said.

Jonquil Bevan was a student at Oxford and she went to the head of her department and she said, "I want to edit," and handed in an essay she'd written on T. S. Eliot.

"'This is good,' my supervisor said, and she displayed a list of the texts that needed editing for Oxford editions." Bevan pursed her lips and looked upwards a bit; "Cowley, Walton . . . and I said, I say—how wonderful . . . Walton's *Compleat Angler,*" which Bevan pronounced *angla*, "and I went home and thought about it and the more I thought, the more I liked the idea of it. I began to draft a letter to the head of the department with my choice. But she had already contacted Oxford press and told them, 'I have a pupil to edit

The Compleat Angler,' and I was a bit miffed that she had not consulted me. It just happened to be the text I'd chosen."

Bevan talked about the process Walton likely went through in writing *The Compleat Angler*—that he had probably kept a commonplace book throughout his life, now lost, in which he wrote down passages from texts he'd read that he liked or practical techniques on fishing, and that he probably kept a second one for poems too. Bevan emphasized the peculiarity that all the twenty-six or so poems that appear in *The Compleat Angler*, from all the ones he could have quoted, were composed either by himself or friends of his.

I had brought some paintings of the English countryside and trout to show her. She was very inquisitive about my watercolors. "Oh I say, aren't these lovely," and she held them at a distance which appeared to enhance her enjoyment of them. She liked the trout under water considerably, and she also liked the one I had painted of Cotton's fishing house on the Dove and pike pool.

"You know," she said, "Cotton tells us that Walton's son had drawn a black-and-white landscape of pike pool."

She offered without my asking that she had been born in central Wales and that she loved Hay on Wye and told me of the beauty of the River Wye and how it has changed since she was a child. This soliloquy of hers was quite endearing. Then she returned to talking about the "angla." Several students stormed into the office to claim papers and left with hanging heads when Dr. Bevan, after considerable shuffling of papers, was not able to produce them.

"Yes," she said, recovering from the interruption and fixing her eyes on her thoughts again, "I am very sad that *The Compleat Angler* has been in neglect.

It is a wonderful book, and I hoped," she added, "that my little book would bring it attention, but alas it has not."

My anger for all her tardiness, and frustration at her elusive and aloof properties had fled some time ago. I had to come down to such a humble, peaceable, and quiet tone to communicate with her that it would have been nearly impossible to hold on to any hostility. My anger had been beguiled by solemnity and Dr. Bevan—Jonquil—blossomed like the fragrant southern European flower of her namesake.

I showed her how I'd broken the text of Walton's description of the chub into iambic pentameter lines. She read, tapping her foot to the meter and said, "marvelous."

And we mused together on the beauty and subtlety of Walton.

It was nearing 2:30 P.M. and I had to go to the airport to catch my flight to London. And that dream emerged again, the one in which Jonquil Bevan and I subject a trout to one of Walton's recipes, so clearly now that I could almost smell the aroma of a trout baking in its own juices.

Directions for Dressing and Cooking a Pike

First open your pike at the gills, and if need be, cut also a little slit towards the belly; out of these take his guts, and keep his liver, which you are to shred very small with Thyme, Sweet-marjoram, and a little Winter-savory; to these put some pickled Oysters, and some Anchovies, two or three, both these last whole (for the Anchovies will melt, and the Oysters should not); to these you must add also a pound of sweet butter, which you are to mix with the herbs that are shred, and let them all be well salted: these being thus mixed with a blade or two of Mace, must be put into the Pike's belly, and then his belly so sewed up, as to keep all the Butter in his belly if it be possible, if not, then as much as you possibly can, but take not off the scales; then you are to thrust the spit through his mouth out at his tail, and then take four, or five, or six split sticks, or very thin lathes, and a convenient quantity of Tape or Filleting, these lathes are to be tied round about the Pike's body from his head to his tail, and the Tape tied somewhat thick to prevent his breaking or falling off from the spit; let him be roasted very leisurely, and often basted with Claret wine, and Anchovies, and Butter mixed together, and also with what moisture falls from him into the pan: when you have roasted him sufficiently you are to hold under him (when you unwind or cut the Tape that ties him) such a dish as you purpose to eat him out of; and let him fall into it with the sauce that is roasted in his belly, and by this means the Pike will be kept unbroken and complete: then, to the sauce which was within, and also that sauce in the pan, you are to add a fit quantity of the best Butter, and to squeeze the juice of three or four Oysters, two cloves of Garlic, and take it whole out, when the Pike is cut off the spit, or to give the sauce a haut gout, let the dish (into which you let the Pike fall) be rubbed with it: the using or not using of this Garlic is left to your discretion.

This dish of meat is too good for any but Anglers or very honest men; and I trust, you will prove both, and therefore I have trusted you with this secret.

EPILOGUE

During the time since I returned home from England and graduated, the time that the words that are this book have been put down and relived, I've been planning a trip to fish the forty-first latitude; that parallel which begins—and ends—at my home in Connecticut. I will travel around the world with a fishing rod, following Walton's tenets, which perhaps have always been my own as well—to live with these three concepts as paramount: content, simple, quiet.

ACKNOWLEDGMENTS

I thank Yale University for contributing to four years of my life, the students and various departments and the individuals in them I had a chance to know, in particular Harold Bloom, Sterling professor of Humanities and advisor for my senior essay. I thank Stephen Parks for many good dinners, wines, and conversations at his home in New Haven. To the Branford Class of '60 committee and fellowship who gave me money for my first trip to England I am grateful. I thank all the people who are a part of this book, those in England, civil war historian David Scott to Victoria Wakefield, as well as those in America who provided introductions, Reece Howard and Dr. Francis Coughlin among them. To those people who have loved and worked with Walton, alive and no longer alive, within and without the academic world I am thankful: Arthur Munson Coon and Tony Bridgett, Sir John Swire and Jonquil Bevan. More immediately I thank my sister Jennifer Prosek and agent Elaine Markson, Allison McCabe at HarperCollins and Larry Ashmead, executive editor at HarperCollins for his support and his "inquiring, searching and observing wit."

RECOMMENDED READING

Aylmer, G.E. *Rebellion or Revolution; England from Civil War to Restoration.* Oxford: Oxford University Press, 1986.

Arte of Angling. Facsimile of book of 1577. Edited by Gerald Eades Bentley, with an introduction by Carl Otto Kienbusch. Princeton, N.J.: Princeton University Press, 1958.

Bevan, Jonquil. *Izaak Walton's* The Compleat Angler; *The Art of Recreation.* New York: St. Martin's Press, 1988.

Boswell, James. *The Life of Samuel Johnson.* New York: The Modern Library.

Bottrall, Margaret. *Izaak Walton.* Published for the British Council by Longmans, Green & Co., 1955.

Cotton, Charles. *Poems of Charles Cotton.* Edited by John Buxton. Cambridge, Mass.: Harvard University Press, 1958.

Recommended Reading

Coon, Arthur Munson. "The Life of Izaak Walton." (Graduate thesis, Cornell University, 1938.) Cornell University Library, call # Thesis PR 15 1938 C777+.

Craven, Arthur Scott. *The Compleat Angler, A Play.* New York: Samuel French, 1915.

Ellmann, Richard. *The Artist as Critic, Critical Writings of Oscar Wilde.* New York: Random House, 1968.

Hall, Henry Marion. *Idylls of Fishermen; A History of the Literary Species.* New York: Columbia University Press, 1912.

Landor, Walter Savage. *Imaginary Conversations and Poems.* New York: J.M. Dent & Sons Ltd., 1933.

Lindley, Keith. *Popular Politics and Religion in Civil War London.* Aldershot: Scolar Press, 1997.

Liu, Tai. *Puritan London; A Study of Religion and Society in the City Parishes.* Newark, Del.: University of Delaware Press 1986, pp. 41–42, 175–6.

Macleod, M.D. *Lucian: A Selection.* Warminster: Aris & Phillips, 1991.

Marston, E. *Thomas Ken and Izaak Walton.* London: Longmans, Green, and Co., 1908.

Martin, Stapleton. *Izaak Walton and his Friends.* New York: E.P. Dutton & Co., 1903.

McDonald, John. *The Origins of Angling; An Inquiry into the Early History of*

Recommended Reading

Fly Fishing with a new printing of The Treatise of Fishing with an Angle. New York: Lyons and Burford, 1997.

Novarr, David. *The Making of Walton's* Lives. Cornell University Press, 1958.

Pepys, Samuel. *Passages from the Diary of Samuel Pepys.* Edited with an introduction by Richard Le Gallienne. New York: The Modern Library, 1921.

Plato *Symposium.* Translated by Benjamin Jowett. Indianapolis, Ind.: Library of Liberal Arts, 1948.

Porter, Stephen. *London and the Civil War.* London: St. Martin's Press, 1996. For impact of the civil war on London, especially chs. 6 and 7.

Shakespeare, William. *As You Like It.* New York: Penguin, 1996.

Shepherd, Richard Herne. *Waltoniana, Inedited Remains in Verse and Prose of Izaak Walton.* London: Pickering and Co., 1878.

Walton, Izaak. *The Compleat Angler.* Edited by Jonquil Bevan. London: Everyman, 1993.

Walton, Izaak. *Walton's Lives.* London: George Bell and Sons, York Street, 1884.

Walton, Izaak and Charles Cotton. *The Compleat Angler.* (Any reprint of the 1676 edition with Cotton's addendum, esp. edited with an introduction by Richard Le Gallienne.)